This is the story of a you
Austria. Because of the h
war and immigrated to the United States in 1952 as a displaced person. Though David Bugno became a Christian through the influence of the girl he married, he describes his mental, emotional and spiritual journey of confronting his past and his lengthy struggle in developing his own personal identity. But you get more. His story will introduce you to a period in German history and culture that is hard to duplicate. Having grown up in a religious German community myself here in America, my heart is deeply moved by his amazing story. I've often thought that young men my age were a part of the Nazi regime! By God's grace, I was far removed from this evil influence. However, David Bugno's story will give you an even greater appreciation for the great truth in Romans 8:28.

Dr. Gene A. Getz
Professor, Pastor, Author

Fascinating, compelling and eye-opening, Reich Child tells the incredible personal story of a woman and her son trapped in Hitler's monstrous ambitions. Late in life, David Bugno discovered a shocking truth about himself, one his mother, suffering from her own emotional scars, threw in his face. While I thought I knew about the Nazis and the Lebensborn program, Bugno and Garrity helped me see historical realities I had not understood, from not that long ago.

Reich Child is a story that needs to be told and read widely. Not only does it shine a light on a dark time through the window of one mother and her son, it also gives hope to those with difficult childhoods. Redemption is possible.

Bruce B. Miller
Senior Pastor, Christ Fellowship
Author, *Big God in a Chaotic World* and *Sexuality*

Reich Child powerfully reveals the sovereignty of God. Nothing would stop His plan, His purpose and His destiny for David Bugno's life.

Each chapter drives you to find out how this story will end. Simply amazing!

Greg Vaughn
Founder, the Video Biography Company
Founder, Letters from Dad

REICH CHILD

A Lebensborn Life

The True Story of a Mother and Son Caught in Himmler's Legacy

By David Bugno
with Jennifer Garrity

Entrust Source Publishers

For more information, please go to: www.entrustsource.com.

ISBN-10: 1-942308-10-8
ISBN-13: 978-1-942308-10-2

Cover created by Entrust Source LLC, Judy Buckert

Printed in the United States of America

Entrust Source Publishers
281 Camino la Pasida
Rio Rico, AZ 85648

www.entrustsourcepublishers.com

I dedicate this book to my dear wife Jaclyn, who has stood faithfully by my side throughout my journey, and above all to my Lord and Savior Jesus Christ.

CONTENTS

Chapter 1 1
Chapter 2 19
Chapter 3 31
Chapter 4 45
Chapter 5 59
Chapter 6 75
Chapter 7 91
Chapter 8 105
Chapter 9 121
Chapter 10 135
Chapter 11 149
Chapter 12 165
Chapter 13 181
Chapter 14 197
Chapter 15 211
Chapter 16 225
Chapter 17 241
Chapter 18 253

Epilogue 265
List of Lebensborn Homes 268
Acknowledgments 269
Sources 271
Sources for Chapter Heading Quotes 273
Notes 276
About the Author 284

"Only that nation which has drying diapers flapping in the wind next to its flag has a secure future."

Joseph Goebbels

The German people must now demonstrate
that it can fulfill its historical mission
by placing themselves at its great leader,
Adolf Hitler's disposal for his gigantic achievement—
German people—strong, healthy and in mighty numbers...
Germany must again become a nation of children!

—SS propaganda brochure

CHAPTER 1

One summer evening, my true identity joined our family dinner as an uninvited guest. Stark naked, it stumbled into the room and brought what had been a glorious vacation to a crashing halt.

My mother, Elfriede, had served up one of her famous old-world German meals. On gold-rimmed Dresden china plates, pork Schnitzel and Silesian dumplings nestled cozily together beneath a blanket of gravy. What a delightful two weeks it had been! Even though Mom, as usual, requested that I mow her grass, trim her shrubs and repair various broken things around her house, my wife Jaclyn and son Andrew and I had managed to seize an opportunity to steal away from Colorado Springs to hike and picnic in the Santa de Cristo Mountains and Phantom Canyon at Cripple Creek. We reveled in the cool, dry atmosphere, so refreshingly different from humid northeast Texas, where we made our home.

With its six bedrooms and spacious living and dining rooms, my parents' house accommodated us easily. It felt good to return home from a rugged hike, jump in the shower, and plop down on soft beds and plush carpet. Andrew, our youngest son and last child left at home, devoured his grandmother's cooking with teenage gusto, while Jaclyn, my adoptive father Clem and I savored it until pleasantly satisfied.

What, exactly, were we discussing? I don't remember. Perhaps some question of injustice in the world, or an inexplicable tragedy in a friend's life, or the evening news. Whatever it was, it prompted me to utter the comment that would change my life forever. Pushing my empty plate away, I said something to the effect, "Well, life sure doesn't make sense. I'm just glad that when I'm in heaven one day, I'll finally understand all its mysteries." Those words, so innocuous to my ears, poured gasoline on a smoldering fire concealed deep in my mother's core.

She glared at me over hands clenched in a tight ball, her bejeweled fingers exchanging sparkles with the crystal chandelier suspended above us. "Everyone, out!" she ordered. Gold bracelets jangled as she swept her arm dramatically to clear the room. "Everyone except David."

Accustomed to obeying her imperious commands, Clem, Jaclyn and Andrew exchanged brief, confused glances as they scooted their chairs back and rose from the table. I watched them file out of the mezzanine dining room and down the steps to the far end of the living room. Someone turned on the television. Clem and Andrew sat down to watch. Jaclyn, curious, hovered close by and out of sight trying to listen in, but the television obscured the words my mother now shot at me like bullets.

"You think you're so good," she said, "acting all holy, talking about how you're going to heaven. Well, it's about time you knew the truth about yourself. You're not as lily white as you think you are."

I thought, *Here we go again*. Did I really have to explain for the umpteenth time something my mother stubbornly refused to understand—that by identifying as a Christian, I wasn't claiming to be perfect? In fact, I was claiming the opposite. I was a flawed person who needed God's forgiveness. Why couldn't she grasp this? Never once had I claimed to my mother or anybody, to be holy, perfect, or even good enough to earn divine favor. My choice to become a Christian in young adulthood had always rankled my mother for reasons I never fully understood. Why couldn't she simply let me be happy in my faith instead of unjustly accusing me of being sanctimonious and thinking I was superior?

"Actually, Mom...."

"Listen to me. You are not what you think you are. You're illegitimate, *ein uneheliches Kind!"*

I blinked as if slapped in the face. "Excuse me?"

Seated across from me, she straightened her petite frame in the high-backed mahogany chair. It struck me as ironic, such messy words coming from this woman to whom an impeccable appearance meant everything. Her cropped, permed hair hugged her head in perfect uniformity; her busy, strong hands, so often stained with garden soil, were prettied up with the diamond rings Clem had lavished on her. Mom had known little luxury in her young life; now she reveled in her husband's gifts of expensive jewelry, clothing from high-end shops and the latest model television or kitchen appliance. From lifelong habit, her own spending remained frugal. Yet she cared deeply that people admire her; she craved status and respect.

"A *bastard*," she repeated. "You were born as a result of something shameful, just terrible. During the war, I was raped by a general but I managed to give birth to you in a very special, elite hospital where we had the best of care. Getting there was difficult, but I managed it for your sake. You were intended to be a member of the pure Aryan race, a Nazi child. *Now* what do you think of yourself? I guess you can't brag about being such a goody-goody anymore."

Utterly speechless, I gaped at her with open mouth. A smug, satisfied expression settled on her face. She had always resented me taking joy in my Christian faith. Now she was sure she had wiped what she perceived to be the self-righteous smile right off my face.

"But…but I don't understand," I faltered. "You always said Dad died when I was three. He was killed fighting the Russians."

"Rudi was Heidi's father, not yours. Your father was the man who raped me."

Feeling my lungs deflate, I struggled to breathe. "But my grandparents!"

"They were *Heidi's* grandparents," she corrected. "They adored Heidi and they only put up with you for her sake."

As I reeled inwardly, a parade of images from childhood danced before my eyes: my grandfather's features screwed up into a hard knot as he glared at me; a photograph of my bassinette lined up with others in perfect uniformity; my mother, snatching the pencil from my hand, flipping it around to erase the last name I had just scrawled in childish letters, saying, "Kobsch isn't your last name, Wolf. It's Kober. Always remember to write Kober."

So many scraps, floating across the surface of my life like flotsam, now seemed to pull together to form a larger entity. Yet huge gaps kept it from taking shape into something recognizable.

"But why?"

"That's all!" she snapped, rising to clear the table. "I've told you all you need to know."

At the sound of dishes rattling, Jaclyn hurried back into the dining room. "You're white as a sheet!" she gasped.

In hushed tones I confided to her what my mother had just revealed. She felt me shaking as she held onto me protectively.

"David, don't forget that God can use for good what people mean for evil," she whispered. "It says so in the book of Genesis; remember the story of Joseph and his brothers? I feel certain that something good can come out of this."

I spent the rest of the evening in shocked silence. Clem and Andrew, absorbed in the game show *Jeopardy*, hardly noticed my uncharacteristic lack of chattiness. The evening dragged on. Would bedtime never come, when I could disappear into the dark oblivion of sleep? Jaclyn cast me occasional sympathetic glances or squeezed my hand while Elfriede Kober Kobsch Bugno merely smiled to herself, obviously pleased with her revelation's effect on me.

Finally, bed. Jaclyn allowed me to reflect in silence as I lay back on my pillow, a 57-year-old man who had lost his identity as suddenly as a car might lose a tire to a blowout on a freeway. The limping vehicle of my life now came to rest in my wife's tender arms as I cried silently into the darkness, *Who and what am I?*

Majestic Colorado had never looked so good in the rearview mirror. I couldn't wait to blend back into my daily routine in homely northeast Texas, where I'd retired early from a long career with Texas Instruments and started a small construction business to keep me occupied. Once back home, I plunged immediately into putting up walls, tiling floors, installing plumbing and electrical wiring. In my spare time, I fixed my friends' computer problems, served as an elder at my church, volunteered on various committees and helped members of the congregation with household repairs. All our children lived nearby, so Jaclyn and I basked in the close proximity of our growing brood of grandchildren. The constant activity kept dark thoughts at bay.

Still, my mother's words dogged me. To my friends, neighbors and fellow church goers, I was still the same old David—a helpful, gregarious guy who loved a cold ice tea or a smooth glass of wine and a long conversation. Only Jaclyn knew that something inside me had crumbled. Alone with my wife, I brooded silently.

"Shouldn't we talk about this, David?" she gently probed.

I shut her down with a terse "No."

She didn't give up. Time after time she coaxed me to deal with my feelings. "Is it the illegitimacy that's bothering you?"

"Of course not," I snapped. "We hardly live in a day and age where society considers that scandalous."

"Then why won't you talk to me about it?"

"Because I don't want to acknowledge it. I don't want to know where I come from. I'm afraid of what I'll find out."

"David," she said, "you *need* to know. Deep down, everyone has a need to know about his or her origin. Your mother lied to you all these years and your parentage isn't what you thought it was. That doesn't make you less of a person; you're just as valuable as anyone else."

Jaclyn's persistence gradually wore me down. Admittedly, I had been difficult to live with of late and a change was in order. I began to confide in a few trusted friends, fellow elders at our church, Christ Fellowship in McKinney. They listened compassionately as I poured out the pain of learning my mother had concealed the truth from me throughout my adult life, that I was the spawn of a cruel rape, that the man I'd always imagined to be my father had no connection to me whatsoever. "Why couldn't she have trusted me with this knowledge earlier?" I wailed. "She could have sat down with me when I was in my twenties and explained it all gently. Why did she take such joy in flinging these facts so viciously at me, so late in life? What kind of mother does that?"

These dear friends prayed with me and for me. With characteristic grace and compassion, they pointed out that Elfriede must suffer from deep pain and brokenness, for how else could she enjoy inflicting such emotional wounds on her own flesh and blood?

"You were blindsided by this," they reminded me, "but none of it has taken God by surprise. Seek him, ask him, trust him, and he'll show you what to do."

When I finally felt ready to tell the children, I learned that Jaclyn had beat me to it. They'd approached her privately with questions, worried about how strangely reserved and brooding I'd become. The children had seen all too clearly what I thought I was hiding so well—my dark confusion and sense of isolation. Jaclyn asked them not to speak of it until I was ready. When that time came, they reassured me of their love and support.

"Dad, we want to know all about your heritage. Tell us the details when you find them out. Remember, it's our heritage too."

Their compassionate interest touched me deeply. How desperately I needed their encouragement! Each day I had tried to put on a mask of competence and strength, but behind it cowered a frightened, lonely child.

A child in filthy *Lederhosen* and thin, ragged shirt.

My right arm bears a scar that wraps completely around the wrist; it's wide, like a watchband, and white against the rest of my Texas-tanned skin. Like a science fiction time machine, it has the power to transport me back to the mid-1940s anytime my eyes happen to fall upon it. That scar testifies to my fondness for a small garden plot just outside Görlitz on Germany's far eastern border. My earliest memories are of that garden. Just as they do today, urban Germans owned or rented gardening space on the circumference of the city, and Grandma and Grandpa Kobsch, whom I called "Kobsch Opa and Oma," took particular pride in their little patch of green.

So dearly did I love that garden with its leafy solitude and abundance of sweet fruits that when I was five and six, I stole away to it in secret over and over again. A small child alone, slipping furtively through the city, darting down alleys, crossing busy boulevards and racing down dirt lanes hardly attracted attention in those days. People were too preoccupied with getting enough to eat and trying not to attract the notice of their Russian conquerors to bother about a skinny, unsupervised boy absconding to what he perceived as his only safe haven.

The first several times I went there, no fence enclosed the vast patchwork of green space. I knew exactly which plot was ours and through which particular gardens to tramp in order to reach it. Suddenly one day, a metal mesh barrier stood there, high and menacing, laced with barbs. It had sprung up overnight to keep out pilfering Russian soldiers and our own starving countrymen. A barb sliced my flesh as I climbed over. The sting around my wrist and the dripping blood seemed a small price to pay for the pleasures that awaited me there: tart currants, succulent, low-hanging pears, blackberries, gooseberries. From its place in one corner of the garden, a rickety wooden wagon kept silent company with me. It felt like a special friend. Mother and Oma told me it had carried me to Görlitz from far away. That was a long time ago, they explained, when I was very small.

Mostly I went to the garden in search of the feeling I got while sitting there, alone, arms wrapped around my knees, back pressed against the furrowed bark of the old plum tree. That small green space contained the only tender memories I could recall at that point in my life.

In the autumn, Oma made *Pflaumkuchen* from the plums that grew there, slicing them in half lengthwise and layering them over a simple white cake batter, sprinkling crunchy streusel on top. She would pack a picnic basket with what little food was available: sour rye bread, a dab of butter, almost never any meat or cheese. Mostly she conjured up baked goods from the fruits and vegetables harvested on that very spot and we would carry it back to eat in triumph. A sturdy wooden hut stood in the center of the plot. This was our garden *Laube*. Inside it Opa stored a chaise longue and beach chairs, the folding kind with a strip of cloth down the middle. A wooden table and chairs, a few cushions for comfort and gardening tools made up the bulk of the *Laube's* contents. If weather permitted, we pulled these out into the sunshine and feasted on meager fare made rich by the garden's generosity. This little plot of earth lifted us a notch above the refugees encamped in Görlitz's parks—the flea and lice-bitten ones, many of who died daily from what we called hunger-typhus.

Mother spoke sweetly to me in the garden. Her voice softened to a gentle purr as she asked me things like, "Are you having a nice time, Bub? Do you like it here? How does that cake taste; are you enjoying it?" She sang and hummed as she knelt in the dirt harvesting beans and rhubarb. She smiled as she watched me play my silly spinning or hopping games. Outside the garden, she had no time to indulge such tender sentiments. There she devoted all her energy to looking for work, begging and bartering for more substantial foods like eggs and cheese, and scouring farmers' fields in search of potatoes or squash left behind by harvesters.

Food was scarce in those postwar years but the garden ensured, at least in summer and fall, that we would taste a little sweetness in the cakes baked by Kobsch Oma. Tenderness and affection were likewise scarce. And like each precious bite of Oma's cake, Mother's sweet words were doled out sparingly and only in the garden. No wonder I ran there whenever I could. Fleeing to its serenity, sheltering beneath the rustling leaves of the fruit trees was my only way of recapturing those warm feelings of being wanted and cherished.

On the few occasions my mother caught me sneaking off, she smacked my behind. It didn't stop me from returning to the garden again and again. To my relief, she didn't tell Opa. Though he had never actually hit me, I feared that if Kobsch Opa knew about my secret wanderings, about the way I toyed with the padlock on the door of the *Laube* in hopes he might have absentmindedly forgotten to secure it, that while there I devoured sour currants and gooseberries and blackberries to try to sate my constant, growling hunger, he would lash out at me with a violent fury. I sensed hatred emanating from him, a white-hot anger bubbling just beneath the surface of his stoic exterior that, confusingly, was directed only at me. Yet during our picnics in the garden, beneath the trembling pear and plum leaves, a gentler side of Opa emerged. Sitting in a folding chair in dappled sunlight and enjoying a slice of cake, his rigid expression softened and he appeared to forget his cares and enjoy his blessings. My baby sister, Heidi, was clearly his greatest blessing. Both he and Oma would smile and coo at her as she lay in her basket in the sun, or beneath a string of candle-lit lanterns on dusky summer evenings. Tenderly Opa stroked her soft hair, caressed her tiny face. Watching this, I soaked in his affection vicariously. Was it because Heidi was a baby, so sweet and immobile, unable to cause any mischief, that he loved her so? I was a four-year-old boy who darted about, splashed in puddles, asked too many questions and touched things with sticky hands. Surely that must be why he loved her more than me.

Kobsch Opa had a shiny bald head. His sharp, beaked nose led down to thin lips, giving him a hawk-like appearance. Reserved and controlled, he never flew into rages or raised his voice. But whenever I happened to be left alone in a room with him he would turn to me, his cobalt eyes fixing me with a piercing intensity.

"I hate you!" he hissed.

Quickly I would stop to assess with childlike reasoning what I'd done to provoke him. No, I hadn't broken anything. Neither had I made a loud noise. Confused, I inevitably gave up.

"I can't stand you!" he often added for good measure.

There was no mistake; he was talking to me. These intense, private declarations of loathing stung and baffled me, coming as they did out of nowhere. If I had knocked over a crystal dish or accidentally trod on his toes, it might have made sense to my childish mind. Yet these words often spilled forth when I was doing nothing more than playing quietly at his feet or sitting obediently beside him on a sofa.

It's because I'm a boy, I remember concluding once with juvenile logic. *He loves Heidi, and she's a girl. I make noise and I make messes. Opa must like girls better than boys.*

I never told Mother about Opa's hateful words. A deep sense of shame convinced me I deserved them and to call them to the attention of my sad and weary single parent would have been asking for more trouble. Likewise, I kept the secret from Kobsch Oma. While Opa mostly looked through me, seldom making eye contact and barely acknowledging my existence, his wife acted more kindly towards me, sometimes wrapping soft, wrinkly arms around me and whispering, "You're a good boy, Wolfi." Her displays of affection toward Heidi were far more frequent and demonstrative, but that made perfect sense to me and I never questioned it. Heidi was the preferred child in the Kobsch household. It didn't occur to me to think this unfair; it was merely the reality of my little world in Görlitz, Germany in 1946.

Now, over 50 years later in McKinney, Texas, I thought I was finally beginning to understand why Kobsch Opa had hated me so. Hazy memories long buried began to surface, keeping me awake at night and distracting me by day. Within me it felt as if doors were unlocking, yet frustratingly, I couldn't get them open. I was David Bugno now, but Wolfgang Rüdiger Kober haunted me, following me everywhere, whispering in my ear that I was an imposter. I'd been kept in the dark for over half a century. Now if I wanted the truth, however unpalatable, I would have to go and search for it across the Atlantic Ocean on the continent of my birth. Mom had made it perfectly clear that she was unwilling to reveal any more details.

"Do it, David," urged Jaclyn. "It's the only way for you to find peace. We'll go together. I'll be by your side the whole way."

Bolstered by my wife's encouragement, I picked up the phone with trembling hands and dialed a few long distance numbers scrawled in my address book. Exercising my rusty German, I spoke with voices familiar yet long silenced by the busy years of pursuing a career and childrearing. We discussed options and an itinerary began to take shape. Jaclyn and I bought tickets, packed suitcases, asked our kids and a few trusted friends to pray that I would have the emotional strength to face my ghosts. I would meet Wolfgang Rüdiger Kober where I thought I had left him behind forever, and where he still waited expectantly for me.

As Germany's lush, verdant landscape flew past the train window, I could feel my heart racing. Butterflies cavorted in my stomach. Jaclyn and I had just spent two weeks near Karlsruhe with friends from Texas, participating in a two-week mission project in which we helped turn an empty tobacco factory into a church building for a lively and growing congregation made up of young families. Together we had gotten our hands dirty, laughed a lot, and enjoyed the feeling of deep satisfaction that comes with working hard for a good cause. Now it was time to get serious and confront the past. Even as I recoiled mentally from the task ahead, the train seemed to speed up as it approached our destination.

In Münich, we rented a car and made our way northeast to the town of Landshut. Peter's house was easy to find, his instructions precise and impeccable. My cousin and his wife met us at the door with a hearty handshake and proudly gave us a tour of their domain—an exquisite, well-tended garden of fragrant roses, neat rows of vegetables and a wooden *Laube* like the one from our shared childhood. Their modern home was equipped with floor heating but contained an old-fashioned tile oven just for atmosphere. Jaclyn and I devoured slices of delectable homemade apple cake with our afternoon coffee, then followed Peter into the living room while Gerda graciously insisted on cleaning up alone. We settled ourselves on one sofa while he sat opposite us on another. From the kitchen came the clatter of china punctuated with the opening and closing of cupboard doors. Afternoon sun streamed through lace-curtained windows and would have made me drowsy had my entire body not been buzzing with nerves.

"Bub, it's so good to have you in my home," said Peter, using my childhood nickname, which simply means "boy" in German.

I assured him of how happy I was to be there and thanked him for his hospitality before cutting to the chase. "I wanted to see Germany again, but I'm here for another reason too. Mom recently confessed that Rudi Kobsch wasn't my father. She claims she was raped by a general, but she won't tell me anything more. I'm trying to discover the truth. I just want to know who I really am and where I come from."

Far from the shocked scowl I expected, Peter's smile disarmed me. I felt myself relax as he settled more comfortably in his seat, crossing his legs, dangling the ubiquitous German house shoe from one foot.

"What a relief!" he exclaimed with a sigh. "I wasn't looking forward to having to keep the secret from you again."

"Secret? What secret? What do you know?"

Running his fingers through his graying beard, he looked me squarely in the eyes. "Not just me, but everyone—my mother, Uncle Werner, all the cousins. We all know that you were a Lebensborn child, born in one of the Nazi homes for pure Aryan children. But Bub, your mother wasn't raped. She told that tall tale for years, trying to throw everyone off the scent of the truth. Why she embellished the lie with a general, of all things, none of us could ever figure out. Maybe she thought it would raise our opinion of her to think she consorted with a high ranking officer, however unwillingly. Better yet, she might have figured no one would question her not reporting the crime since her 'rapist' had so much clout. No, the simple truth is that your mother had an affair with a married policeman in Prague. And like all policemen at the time, he was connected with the SS."

As if intuiting my sudden sense of dizziness, Jaclyn gripped my arm firmly and asked, "What does 'Lebensborn' mean? Is that the special hospital Elfriede told us about?"

"Lebensborn was rumored to be a Nazi breeding program," Peter explained. "It wasn't true, but that didn't matter; lots of Germans *believed* it was true. After the war, there was so much shame in anything connected with Nazism that no woman would ever openly admit to having given birth in one of those places. No wonder our family closed ranks and agreed to keep Elfriede's secret. I'm just so glad I don't have to keep it anymore. It's well past time you knew the truth, David."

The geographical location of my birth hardly interested me at that moment. "Peter, who is my father? Do you know his name?"

Peter shrugged. "I only know that he was a policeman. I never heard any more details about him. Ask my mother, or Aunt Helene or Uncle Werner. Maybe they know."

And so I did. Jaclyn and I visited and queried my aunts and uncles, one by one, both elsewhere in Bavaria and in a small town near Dresden in the former East Germany. Peter's mother, Lisbeth, so good-natured and grandmotherly, smiled compassionately and said, "*Ja, Ja!* What my son has told you is true. I kept Friedel's secret for years, but now that she has told you the truth, I confirm it. David, we just didn't want you to experience the pain of knowing."

So I was the result of an affair. The rapacious general was nothing but a ruse, a story Elfriede had concocted to protect her reputation. Her tale of carrying bravely on after a traumatic rape was perhaps also a way of bringing dignity to a sordid situation. Fortunately, details my mother stubbornly refused to divulge to me, she had confided in her sister decades ago and because so many years had passed, taking with them some of the stigma, Aunt Lisbeth didn't hesitate to share those details with me now.

Sadly, however, these relatives, who for the sake of their own reputations as well as hers had kept my mother's secret for so long, could tell me nothing of my father except that my mother had willingly engaged in a sexual dalliance with him. But they eagerly filled me in on many other details of Elfriede's life. Hairline fractures in the family structure had grown into broad fissures over the years. Of the Kober siblings, only my mother and Lisbeth and Helene had maintained close relationships. Bitterness and backbiting flourished between many of them, between them and their children, and between cousins. Dishing the dirt on my mother seemed second nature to some of them, and they dished it likewise on each other. Jaclyn and I sifted through the muck to glean whatever we could that might help me solve the mystery of my existence.

The next summer when our yearly Colorado vacation rolled around, we resolved to confront Elfriede about the German relatives' version of her story. Thinking neutral ground would be the best environment for such a discussion, Jaclyn and I invited Mom and Clem out to a local Chinese restaurant. A dimly lit corner table seemed appropriate.

Not until the plates were cleared did I launch the first salvo. "Mom, I need to ask you something. You told me my father was a general who raped you. But your sisters and brother, as well as cousin Peter, all say my father was an SS policeman in Prague, and that it was a consensual relationship."

"That's a downright lie!" she snapped.

"Really? Every single one of them is a liar?" I couldn't help raising my eyebrows skeptically.

Clem rose immediately to her defense. "Yes, David, they're all liars. They're just jealous of all that Elfriede has and of the life she's built for herself here in America."

"You know that lot," she groused. "Most of them are money-grubbers and backstabbers. Back in Silesia, my father stole the farm from his own elder brothers. Werner did the same; he stole 150,000 *Deutschmark* that should have been distributed amongst all of us siblings. He told Lisbeth I didn't need my share, that I was a rich American, and that it should go to him instead. He ended up with all of it, didn't even share it with the ones left in Germany. And your cousin, Rosel! She pressured her mother to sign over all the inheritance to her, so Peter got nothing and had to take her to court. That's the kind of people they are. You can't believe anything they tell you."

She had a point. Resentful, vindictive comments had flowed freely amongst my relatives, each about the other. My cousins Peter and Rosel, who were no longer on speaking terms, were carrying on a well-entrenched Kober family tradition of strife and fractured relationship. Money seemed to drive these conflicts, but what would any of them stand to gain by passing along salacious information about the circumstances of my birth? Peter had shown no spiteful glee in revealing the story of my mother's affair. Rather he had expressed immense relief at finally being able to let down his guard and tell the truth. It was, after all, inconsistent for a family so splintered by infighting to continue to close ranks and guard their honor by concealing an embarrassing secret.

Guarding that secret had made sense in an occupied post-war Germany where even the thinnest thread of connection to the disgraced and despised Nazi Party was snipped and severed in order to save face. But over half a century had passed. These things were little more than a fading memory, hardly at the forefront of anyone's consciousness anymore.

Except mine.

"Mom, they were not lying," I persisted, trying unsuccessfully to keep the irritation out of my voice. "They had no reason to lie, and even if they had, I would have sensed it. I'm begging you to tell me the truth."

Oblivious and smiling, our waiter interrupted with the bill and fortune cookies. Tight-lipped, we waited while he processed my credit card.

"I *have* told you the truth," Mom insisted when he had gone.

"Are you calling your mother a liar?" challenged Clem. He slipped his arm protectively around her shoulders. "Elfriede was raped. She did the best she could to cope with that and to bring you into the world in a decent hospital and take care of you during terrible times. Can't you see how you're upsetting her?"

I looked down, feeling helpless. Clem had always been a kind and generous adoptive father to me, and as a child I had loved him all the more for how he protected my vulnerable and overburdened mother. Could I now fault him for continuing to protect her?

Jaclyn squeezed my hand under the table. Unsure as to whether it was a signal to charge or retreat, I did the only thing thinkable at the time—I dropped the subject, feeling defeated. Indeed, Mom had kept me and Heidi alive and kept our little family afloat against overwhelming odds. The critical, materialistic woman of today was not the same young mother who had spoken so sweetly to me in the garden at Görlitz, who risked her life to guide my sister and me to safety in the West, who'd begged and scrounged for food to feed us, thrown all her energy into finding a way to take us to the country that to her represented plenty and safety—America. The woman who sat before me now was the complicated result of an abusive childhood and years of unresolved and hidden shame, guilt and secret keeping. Was she even capable of telling the truth?

I was not to learn the answer to this until she became a widow for the second time.

Clem died on a cold January day in 2009. A lifelong smoker, he succumbed to emphysema. For a woman who had lost the man who for over 50 years had devoted himself to her and indulged her every whim, Elfriede held up admirably. Though devastated, she masked her emotions as always, refusing to cry in front of others.

Thinking she might need our company at Christmas, we drove to Colorado and spent the holidays with her. On Christmas Eve, we took her to a local candlelight service, a favorite tradition of hers and the one time a year she attended church. She wore a white mink shoulder cape that announced to the world that she was the proud relic of a bygone era. Back home again, we played scratchy German Christmas records on a turntable. Mom and I sang along, she in a shaky, warbling voice. Tears formed in her eyes and slid down her wrinkled face as if she were melting from the warmth of the season, the burning candles, the tenderness shown her by family and the fact that her beloved Clem was no longer there to play Christmas carols on his Wurlitzer organ.

Days later, I sat down to help Mom go through some paperwork. Clem had neatly filed old insurance claim forms, property deeds, ownership papers for the three motor homes he and Mom had purchased. As I inspected the fine print and dates, trying to decide which of them should be tossed and which kept, Mom slipped quietly from the room, rummaged through a closet and returned with a tattered cardboard box. Dust flew upward as she tossed it onto the table in front of me.

"Here you go, David. It's all in there for you to find."

"Find what?" I chuckled. "More tax forms from 30 years ago?"

"Information about your father. His name was Kurt Novak."

My stomach plunged as if on a roller coaster dive.

With a deep sigh she conceded, "Oh, it can't hurt to give it to you now that Clem is gone. I only wanted to protect my husband's honor. You can't blame me for that. Even now, I don't like talking about it." She turned abruptly away as if to say, *Find the truth if you can. I'm done talking.*

I packed the box in our car and drove it to Texas, feeling as if I carried an explosive device in the trunk. A thick fog settled over my brain each time I contemplated approaching the box and lifting its lid. Yet if I wanted to discover the truth, I had to peruse those documents. Finally, with Jaclyn's gentle encouragement, my fear gave way to determination. I plunged in. Inside I found 60-year-old mimeographed papers documenting the births, baptisms and marriages of ancestors I had heretofore not even known existed. Some of the information dated back to the mid-1700s. The place names of their residences and life events sounded strangely foreign, unlike the German towns I'd come to associate with my ancestry.

Elfriede had tossed me a challenge. Could the child who had never quite been smart or successful enough for her manage to unlock the secrets of her past? I now had permission to try. She had been slippery over the years, telling my brother Bruce one thing, my sister Heidi another, and me still another. Now she seemed weary of all the subterfuge, ready at last to come clean, at least partially. These dusty documents, the recollections of German family members and extensive historical research, would be my main tools along with the specific memories and details Mom gradually consented to offer up.

How little I understood, as the story emerged in bits and pieces, that my experience was shared by anywhere from seven to twelve thousand other souls, a whole brother and sisterhood of Lebensborn children who in middle age have clawed and scratched their way toward an elusive truth, uncovering it in small increments, as shame-addled mothers gathered the courage to reveal it.

Clem and Elfriede Bugno

Geburts- und Taufschein

Zahl 342.

Auszug aus der Geburtsmatrik

Band VI Blatt 35

Familienname: Brunn

Taufname: Maria

Geburtsort: Pawlowitz Nr. 49

Amtsgericht: Plan b-M

Mädchen

Vater: Brunn Michael

Beruf: Maurergehilfe

Pfarramt Damnau am 19. Jan. 1939

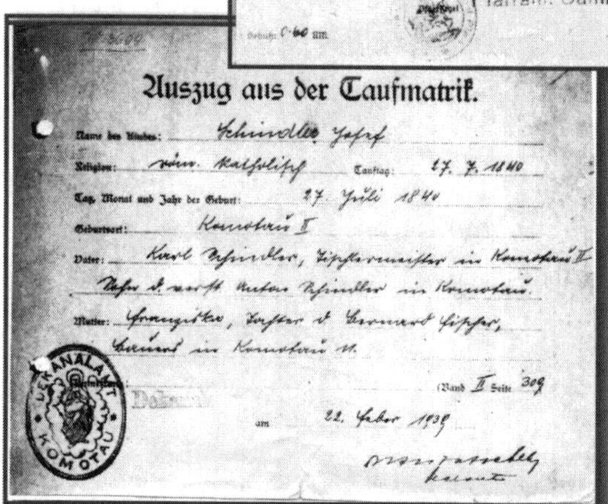

Auszug aus der Taufmatrik.

Name des Kindes: Schindler Josef

Religion: röm. katholisch Tauftag: 27. 7. 1840

Tag, Monat und Jahr der Geburt: 27. Juli 1840

Geburtsort: Komotau II

Vater:

Mutter:

Band II Seite 309

am 22. Febr. 1939

Dekanalamt Komotau

Documents proving Kurt Novak's German ancestry

The future of the people rests in the lap of the German female, because the dying out of our race will be our unavoidable destiny if she refuses to be fruitful... National Socialism has taught us that women are the guardians of our pure blood and as such, carry a great responsibility... She must heed her call of destiny and fulfill her duty to her people.

—Franz Kade

CHAPTER 2

When I look at pre-World War II maps today, I'm astonished at how much territory Germany ultimately lost by igniting that conflict. In its violent quest for *Lebensraum,* or living space, vast swaths of territory such as Pomerania, East Prussia, and Silesia were forfeited. Now part of Poland, the Silesia of my mother's birth was once thoroughly German and her ancestors had dwelt on its rolling farmland for generations.

Elfriede Kober was born in February, 1921 on a farm that has now gone to ruin in a community that has all but disappeared. Neulöben, its German name, is a cluster of houses and barns just outside the town of Sulików, which used to be called Schönberg. She lived there a mere three years before her father acquired a larger farm in Aschitzau near Bunzlau. All these place names are now Polish: Aschitzau has become Osieczow and Bunzlau is Bolesławiec. The neighboring village of Thommendorf, where she went to school, is now called Tomisław. But remnants of the original German inhabitants still linger; stone walls surrounding collapsed roof tiles and massive barns built in the half-timbered style. The city of Bolesławiec still produces the coveted hand-stamped pottery originated by Germans back in the eighteenth century. Artistic Poles have taken the ceramic industry to new heights, creating their own stunning patterns and shipping it all over the world.

Elfriede's was far from a happy childhood. Paul Kober was a harsh, exacting man whose wives lasted little longer than the birds on his 5,000-chicken farm. With his first wife, Martha, he fathered five children, of whom Elfriede was the third. She and her sister Lisbeth, so close in age, clung together for warmth in bed when Paul clomped in before dawn to rouse their eldest sister

Gertrude and order her outside to muck out chicken coops. As his eldest daughter, whose out-of-wedlock conception had trapped him into an early marriage, Gertrude bore the brunt of Paul's cruelty, though there was plenty left to go around. The younger girls pretended to sleep deeply, hoping he wouldn't yank them out of bed too. "My children must work to earn their keep!" was Kober's oft-repeated mantra. Every day Elfriede, her mother and sisters collected thousands of eggs, hauling them away in heavy buckets to wipe them clean and pack them in boxes to be sold.

Paul Kober was as mercurial as the weather. The same man who could hand his daughter a sweet, ripe pear to eat could also be cold and cruel as the harsh winter winds blowing over the Silesian fields. During fits of temper his fists rained blows on Elfriede and her sisters, leaving swollen lips and ugly bruises. He'd already built a new house, and when he decided a bigger barn was in order, he demanded his wife help with the construction of it. Wearily she obliged. One day, in the courtyard, she strained at a rope to raise a concrete bucket up to where Paul waited on the barn's second story. Somehow she lost her grip. The bucket plunged to earth, crashing into her skull. Her shrieking daughters ran to her side but she lay prone and unresponsive. Together they managed to get her into bed. There she languished for nearly a year—a 38-year-old woman, incapacitated, suffering from debilitating headaches. With anxious eyes, her children watched her steady decline until at last she slipped from their grasps. They felt comforted only by the knowledge that she no longer suffered.

It was whispered about in the village that Martha's death had been no accident. Everyone knew Paul was having an affair with a woman named Grete Schönfelder. Wasn't it just like him to tamper with the rope or let it slip from his hands at an opportune moment, in order to relieve himself of the burden of his wife? No one ever publicly accused him, but the rumors made their way to his children's ears and haunted them for the rest of their lives.

With Martha's passing, the Kober children lost the last shred of tenderness in their environment. Only she had cared for their daily needs. Paul Kober was at best neglectful and disinterested, at worst physically brutal. Elfriede and her sisters, now completely at the mercy of their father, sneaked out to their mother's fresh grave at night. There they sobbed and confided to her through the newly packed earth about the abuse they suffered at their father's hands. Certain he would ignore the little ones, they did their best to help care for young Helene and five-year-old Werner.

Kober built up his farm into a state-of-the-art enterprise, for he was a pioneer of sorts in factory farming. Equipped with the most modern technology, his chicken farm drew the attention of the local university. Agriculture students made regular tours of its premises. The students, enamored with the cutting-edge facilities, hardly noticed the haggard-looking children whose labor was exploited by their own father.

Paul was heartily disliked by his fellow villagers. Regarded as self-absorbed and spiteful, he was known about the neighborhood as a braggart, rambling on and on about his accomplishments, ad nauseum. One woman found him appealing, however. His paramour, Grete Schönfelder, happily married him shortly after Martha's death. "Die Schönfelder Grete," as she was called, accepted Paul's two youngest children but had no use for his three older daughters. She quickly persuaded him to move their beds out of the new house and into the empty shell of the old one which also served as a storage place for hay, straw and equipment. The old house was freezing, frightening and cavernous. Gertrude, Lisbeth and Elfriede shivered their way through winter nights, persuading themselves that the eerie sounds they heard were only foxes prowling the perimeters of the chicken coops and the wind in the attic. Eventually their night terrors yielded to exhaustion and, huddled together for warmth, they fell into a deep sleep.

Still, they were young teens bursting with an energy that neither Grete's intrusion into their family nor the heavy regime of farm labor could squelch. At school in nearby Thommendorf, Lisbeth and Elfriede were beginning to notice boys and to hone the art of flirting. When Elfriede flashed her brown eyes and dimpled smile at a boy only to have him respond with a blush and nervous smile, she felt a new kind of power surge through her, a novel thrill for a girl who had only ever been treated as a drudge. Her best escape from a bleak regimen of chores and schoolwork were these innocent flirtations and a few stolen hours at night.

Paul Kober kept a motorbike in one of his sheds, an old Zündapp with a two-speed gearbox. Sometimes when Elfriede and Lisbeth saw the last light extinguished in the new house across the courtyard, they quietly dressed and crept out of their sleeping quarters. Stealthily they opened the creaking door of the shed. Wheeling the cycle down the road, glancing nervously behind them, they kick-started the motor and drove along dark country lanes, through neighboring villages, as far as a rise from which they could see the city of Bunzlau glowing in the distance, its street lamps illuminating the night sky. They had no destination. It just felt good to ride, to get away from home, to fly through the countryside with the wind in their hair. In the wee hours they returned, cutting off the bike's motor well in advance before placing it back exactly where they found it. The real trick would be to stifle their yawns the next morning at the breakfast table where Grete so grudgingly fed them. To their astonishment, they always managed to fool their father, who, in any case, paid little attention to their whereabouts.

They envied their elder sister Gertrude, who had tired of Grete's maltreatment and left home to become a live-in employee at a bakery. Still, there were distractions from their misery. Something bigger was afoot. Massive changes originating with the new German government in Berlin were beginning to touch even the lives of obscure, Silesian farm girls.

The rise to power of Adolf Hitler and his National Socialist Party in 1933 ushered in a new era in German family policy. Its ideas about women and their role in society contrasted sharply with that of the preceding government, the Weimar Republic. World War I left a battered and demoralized Germany reeling. More than one and a half million men had fallen in battle, leaving families torn apart and destitute. During that war, the German birthrate fell drastically and remained low during the 1920s. Increasingly, people were choosing to have small families and even married women aborted unplanned or unwanted pregnancies. At the same time, a spike in the illegitimate birth rate along with a soaring divorce rate, convinced many Germans that their country's morality had collapsed. The Weimar government tried to shore up the crumbling foundations of the German family, but seemed to be fighting a losing battle since, in Parliament, its many political parties found it difficult to come to a firm consensus about anything.[1]

Weimar-Era women desired independence, education and employment. Like the American flappers of the 1920s, they shortened their skirts and bobbed their hair, danced and drank and pushed boundaries in unprecedented ways. More traditional Germans believed these modern women were putting off marriage and childbearing just when their country needed them most, when it teetered on the brink of demographic crisis and the German people were hurtling towards extinction.[2]

Now, in the mid-1930s, Hitler's National Socialist German Workers' Party announced that it would finally do what the impotent and incompetent Weimar lawmakers had failed so miserably to do—increase the German population and clean up the lax morality of the 1920s. Nazi leaders spoke out against women's selfishness in refusing to start families and focusing on their own pleasure and fulfillment. They pledged to support the traditional family, for it was through the family that a stronger Germany would emerge.[3] The Nazis despised democracy, the system which had made the Weimar leaders so pathetically ineffective.

According to the Nazis, another major cause of the degeneration of the German people, besides modernism, feminism and the influence of communist ideology, was intermarriage with those of inferior race. In 1935, the Nuremberg Laws banned marriage between Jews and non-Jews. A nation poised at the edge of extinction needed strong leadership. Hitler was a man among men, one who would make the tough decisions and get the job done. Society's ills had gotten out of hand and now, thankfully, someone was at the helm of the ship and steering a clear course for survival.

The Nazis wasted no time in ushering in a racially-based population policy and this had clear implications for women's roles in society. Soon the National Socialist philosophy regarding marriage and childbirth began to trickle down to young people in Hitler Youth organizations. Although cabaret-frequenting career women were more in evidence in Berlin and Hamburg than in Silesian farm villages, Elfriede and Lisbeth enjoyed their own brand of liberation by joining the *Bund Deutscher Mädel* (League of German Girls), known as the "BDM." The two sisters felt so grown up wearing the crisp white blouse and blue wool skirt that made up the uniform of the BDM. The skirt enhanced their slender waists and hips while the black neckerchief, so like a man's necktie, and black lace-up shoes lent a boyish cheekiness to the ensemble. They proudly wore these uniforms to school as well as the BDM meetings and outings. Membership in the female branch of the Hitler Youth couldn't have come at a better time for Elfriede and Lisbeth. All the organized activities, including Saturday classes in gymnastics and swimming, were a godsend, a welcome relief from their dismal home life.

So enthralled were the girls with this exciting social outlet that they barely noticed they were gradually being thoroughly indoctrinated in Nazi philosophy. At school they had already learned the motto, "You are nothing; your nation is everything." Now, in the name of National Socialism, they took part in admirable community service projects and various political activities. Seated around crackling evening fires, they thrilled to tales of ancient Germanic heroes and heroines. While bending and stretching and doing flips during weekend gymnastics sessions, they were told that maintaining their health was vital to the future of the German race. They must put their bodies at the disposal of the nation—Germany's future depended upon their self-sacrifice and fulfillment of duty.

But what, exactly, were those duties?

Paramount among them was to give birth to and raise a new generation of pure Aryan children who would become the future leaders of the Third Reich. Early marriage was encouraged and in 1938, the legal age of marriage for women was lowered to 16. The Nazi government offered young couples marriage loans to be repaid by producing children. In order to qualify, the bride had to agree to stay out of the work force, thus freeing up jobs for men and keeping her in position to raise a family. Upon the birth of a fourth child, the loan was considered paid in full.[4]

Although National Socialism, like its Weimar predecessor, recognized that society's ills rested in large part on the disintegration of the family and could be at least partially cured by supporting and strengthening families, Adolf Hitler's party added a new twist, a flavor distinctly its own to the mix: racial ideology.

The BDM girls, as well as the Hitler Youth boys, were admonished to consider the good of the nation above themselves, even in highly personal matters. At all costs, they must avoid marriage with those of inferior non-Aryan blood. They also had a duty to

Germany to marry only genetically healthy partners so as not to burden the Reich with inferior offspring, those with birth defects or inherited mental and physical illnesses. A young person must thoroughly investigate the family health history of the person he or she hoped to marry. To be lax in this matter was to betray one's nation. It also meant breaking the law. In October of 1935, the laws banning marriage between Jews and non-Jews were stretched to include a ban on marriage between the healthy and the unhealthy. And according to Nazi doctrine, racial inferiority didn't just include questions of ethnicity or physical characteristics but moral ones as well. Women with lax morality who repeatedly bore children out of wedlock by different fathers, men who couldn't seem to hold down a job, those who couldn't get their act together and finish the most basic educational requirements, were considered to suffer from genetic "mental weakness."[5] For the Nazis, it was completely undesirable that such people marry, reproduce and pass down their character flaws.

A strong Germany would stand on the proud shoulders of robust National Socialist women who took their honored place in society as mothers. During the decadent Weimar years, motherhood had slipped off its pedestal and been shunted aside by women's selfish ambitions. Now stay-at-home mothers would enjoy respect. Floozies with bobbed hair, showing all kinds of leg and painted with garish make-up, were becoming a thing of the past. The National Socialist woman was to be all natural, a non-smoker, glowing with health and vitality. Her pure Aryan beauty would shine through, unobscured by cheapening make-up. Earrings, necklaces and bracelets were unnecessary baubles and to wear them was in poor taste. Bravery, sacrifice and heroism were the new marks of beauty for the true Nazi woman.

The BDM girls learned a song:

Mothers, you are all fires,
You are all shining stars.
Mothers, deep in our hearts,
Beat the hearts of the whole world...[6]

At long last, mothers of large families would be given the honor they deserved—not because every child was precious and valuable, but because in bearing many children, they were increasing the Aryan population. Beginning in 1939, town mayors and local Nazi party leaders nominated women in their districts to receive the award of the Mother Cross. A woman who had borne four or five children qualified for bronze, with silver awarded to mothers of six or seven, and gold to mothers of eight or more. To receive the blue and white enameled piece of metal with the swastika in its center, bearing the inscription, "To the German Mother," both the woman and her husband had to be judged racially and genetically fit. Should the woman show any signs of inferior intelligence, genetic weakness, flawed character or "political unreliability," she was judged unworthy of the award. Some towns made very public presentations of Mother Crosses, with formal ceremonies and receptions including coffee and cake served in a decorated hall. Adolf Hitler himself had instigated the awarding of Mother Crosses, for he believed mothers of large families were doing a great service to Germany.[7]

With these incentives, the ruling Nazis hoped to raise the birthrate of racially pure children. Respect for motherhood had to be cultivated early among the ranks of the nation's youth, and these youth were willingly seated at the feet of National Socialist teachers.

Teenage girls of the mid-1930s had been born into the Weimar Republic and in their young years had most probably absorbed the decadent mindset of 1920s women through wayward aunts, mothers or older sisters who put off marriage and limited family size to one or two children. Elfriede and Lisbeth, however, were not cosmopolitan girls from Berlin or Hamburg. They were farm girls made to do backbreaking labor and submit to the authority of a tyrannical father. Their mother, Martha, had given Paul Kober five children and met a crushing end, dying without his ever having expressed appreciation for all her hard work and sacrifice. The marriages they'd most closely witnessed—their father's—had played out against a backdrop of mud and manure, of beatings and rejection by a stepmother in a cheerless home from which they couldn't wait to escape. What were Elfriede and Lisbeth to make of the Nazi assertion that their greatest service to their country would be early marriage and a life of domesticity, raising large Aryan families as stay-at-home mothers?

A paradox entered here. The same Nazi ideology that encouraged a return to old-fashioned values, albeit with the twist of racial purity, was also preaching something else, something edgy and new: The important thing was that babies be born. Whether those babies were born in or out of wedlock was irrelevant. National Socialism, while cheered on by many Germans for holding up traditional family values, simultaneously contained elements of a radical new sexual morality. This new morality was necessary in order to raise the birth rate. A baby is a baby. Germany needed more babies and the most honorable thing a girl could do for her Führer was to present him with the gift of a racially pure child—whether or not she had a husband. Such children would help secure Germany's future.[8] "Give the Führer a child," became the popular new motto.

It sounded strange to a young girl's ears. A "loose woman" was considered of inferior stock and discouraged from marrying, even forcibly sterilized, while at the same time young girls were encouraged to bear illegitimate children. To Nazi minds, however, there was a big difference between the industrious, healthy young woman who made a conscious choice to bear children with a racially valuable man, and a lazy, immoral woman who bore children indiscriminately, fathered by just anybody, simply for lack of self-control.

Attempts to usher in this new morality were tenuous at best. Even prominent Nazi leaders found themselves divided on these issues. Some felt offended by the new ideas; others pushed for change. Ever attentive to the nuances of his people's culture and solicitous of their deepest sensibilities, Hitler refrained from publicly supporting the new morality, but in private conversation he said he believed change was necessary if the German *Volk* (people) were to survive.[9]

Many German women of my mother's generation have claimed these teachings trickled down through the League of German Girls and were discussed during the League "Home Evenings."[10] It was all so shocking and titillating. Many traditional Germans were too old fashioned to accept the new ideas, but the fact that their father would likely disapprove made them all the more enticing to Elfriede and Lisbeth. Young people weren't shackled by antiquated ways of thinking. They were blank pages upon which National Socialist doctrine could be eloquently written.

Perhaps this was why, after one co-ed camp of Hitler Youth and BDM girls in 1936, around 900 girls returned home pregnant. Parents complained and a larger German society was horrified. In response, the decision was made the following year to no longer allow BDM girls to camp alongside their male Hitler Youth counterparts.[11]

Elfriede relished BDM social activities such as dances and hikes with local Hitler Youth boys. She loved having an excuse to leave the farm for activities her father and stepmother could hardly object to for fear of running afoul of the Nazi authorities. Before long, however, like a wicked stepmother in one of the Grimm brothers' fairy tales, Schönfelder Grete found a way to rid herself of the excess baggage that had come with her new husband.

Tactlessly, Paul and Grete announced to the girls one day that they had made arrangements for them to leave Aschitzau and work as servants in other households. Lisbeth would go first. Now 16, she had been hanging around home for the better part of a year after graduating basic high school at age 15. While her labor on the farm had been helpful, Paul and the now-pregnant Grete felt it was ultimately in everybody's best interest for Lisbeth to go out in the world and earn her keep somewhere else. They had already found a position for her in Görlitz, where she would function as live-in housekeeper for a prosperous family.

For 15-year-old Elfriede, there was a family named Friedrich in Bad Freienwalde who needed a live-in helper. As soon as she completed the minimum nine years of required education, she would depart. The Kobers had done some checking around and found that this coming nine months of servitude could count as a BDM *Landjahr,* or voluntary year of service to the nation. This "land year" was meant to teach girls like Lisbeth and Elfriede the useful skills of housekeeping and farming—skills vital for the roles they would play in the coming German Reich.

Lisbeth packed up and was shipped off at dizzying speed. Elfriede missed her sister terribly. Now she slept alone inside the pitch-black, empty shell of a house to which she was banished. She tried to settle herself down each night by anticipating the next Wednesday night "home party," where she and her friends, guided by their BDM leader, would hold discussions on such grown-up topics as art and culture, all with a Nazi slant of course. When the day finally came for school to end and Elfriede to pack her suitcase, she harbored few regrets about leaving. Her time as a BDM girl had been all too brief. She would miss her school friends and her young siblings. She would miss the cool, constant Kwisa River which gurgled along just behind her father's property, and the secret night rides on the motorbike with her beloved sister. But she would not miss the pervasive stink of the chicken coops or the tedious task of wiping chicken droppings off eggshells and lifting heavy buckets and crates. And she would not miss the Grete-witch that had taken her beloved mother's place and made her feel unwelcome, even despised, in her own home.

Elfriede Kober

Paul Kober and his first wife, Martha Heide

Paul Kober and his second wife, Grete

The assured victory with weapons must be followed by victory with children... Therefore, early marriage and large families stand at the very foundation of National Socialism.

—SS propaganda brochure

CHAPTER 3

Nine months passed during which Elfriede rose early each morning to light the Friedrich family's fire and boil water for their coffee. She helped Frau Friedrich throughout the day with laundry, cooking and gardening. In the afternoons while the woman of the house rested, she occupied the younger children. Although she did not relish being at Frau Friedrich's beck and call, the atmosphere was far more welcoming than her father's home and she wasn't so foolish as to wish herself back in Aschitzau. At least in Bad Freienwalde her labor was appreciated. As her *Landjahr* approached its end, Elfreide's father showed up unexpectedly one day to discuss her future.

"*Ach*, there is so much work to be done on the farm these days! Now Grete has baby Manfred to look after, and Helene and Werner have to go to school. We could use an extra pair of hands."

Bluntly, Elfriede informed him that as long as Schönfelder Grete was living with him, she would never return home.

He shook his head in frustration as he confessed, "Your sister Lisbeth just told me the same thing! Where will you go, Friedel? Do you want to stay here, with the Friedrichs?"

"No. I don't want to do someone else's household chores for the rest of my life. Find me another placement," she replied, disliking the thought of continuing in servitude but seeing no other option, "a place where I can learn skills other than housekeeping and gardening."

Paul Kober found her a place in a town called Spremberg with a family named Brocke. Elfriede made the switch with hardly a backward glance. True to her wishes, she performed only light household chores there, spending most of her time in the office of Herr Brocke's small business learning typing and bookkeeping, answering the phone and filing. She enjoyed sitting at the big desk, organizing papers, making figures add up, sounding so professional each time she picked up the phone off its cradle and said, *"Brocke, hier Fräulein Kober, Guten Tag!"* with clipped, precise diction.

In late summer of 1937, Elfriede's father showed up again and presented her with a letter that had arrived in Aschitzau, addressed to her. Elfriede tore it open and read the official looking document inside:

> *You are called to complete your six month service to the German people. You must report...to the Reichsarbeitsdienst for duty in October...*

An address jumped out at her—that of a Labor Service camp near a town called Demmin in Pomerania.

The *Reichsarbeitsdienst*, or Reich Labor Service, had existed in one form or another since the 1920s as a way of providing employment for ex-World War I soldiers and other unemployed Germans. In 1934, the Nazi government declared that service in the Labor Service was no longer voluntary, but compulsory. Technically non-military, it functioned as an auxiliary to the military with separate departments for males and females.

Elfriede felt a twinge of apprehension as she continued reading:

> *Life in the Reich Labor Service is ruled by the laws of loyalty, obedience and comradeship. These laws are required by a true National Socialist life. Every Labor Service worker must promise on solemn oath to fulfill these requirements. Every deed and failure come under submission to these laws. Heil Hitler!*

During her brief membership in the League of German Girls, she had learned about the Reich Labor Service in which high school graduates were required to donate a year's labor for the good of the Reich. Lisbeth had received her conscription letter the previous summer. Her letters home detailed days spent doing farm chores, factory work, and childcare for large families, only to return home to the Labor Service camp each evening and perform more chores such as cleaning and cooking. Elfriede sighed. Now that she had found an office position, albeit in the lowly capacity of a live-in servant, was she to abandon it to toil in muddy fields and sooty factories? Baulk though she may, it was non-negotiable. After showing the letter to Herr and Frau Brocke, she gathered her few belongings and returned to Aschitzau with her father.

September couldn't pass quickly enough for Elfriede. As far as packing was concerned, the letter instructed her to bring only the clothes on her back and the shoes on her feet. As the October date of her departure drew near, she pulled together the few miscellaneous items she was allowed to bring: note paper, pen and pencils, and a few basic toiletries. "Soon it will be your turn," she told Werner and Helene as they watched her every move. "I'll write and tell you all about it, so you'll know just what to expect."

Lying sleepless on her pillow that last night at home, listening to the scurrying of mice in the hay and the wind in the attic, she hoped with all her heart that after her time in the Reich Labor Service was finished, she might find a way to never return home again. For the first time, it occurred to her that this new adventure might hold great things in store. Whatever lay ahead was a mystery. It might not suit her perfectly, but then again, it just might be a stepping stone to a much-desired independent life.

As it turned out, the Reich Labor Service suited Elfriede very well. The camp had a neatly raked assembly yard with a flagpole from which the organization's standard cheerfully flapped. Its red field with white circle and black swastika bore the added symbol of two heads of wheat, symbolic of the farm work in which the girls engaged. The wooden barracks were Spartan, but sparkling clean. The camp leader welcomed Elfriede with a hearty handshake and a "*Heil Hitler!*" Elfriede found her bunk and settled onto the straw-filled mattress, watching her new camp mates arrive and listening to their nervous introductions and high-pitched giggles. Each girl was issued sheets, blankets, straw pillows and a small cupboard in which to store clothes and other belongings.

After a simple but satisfying meal, the girls gathered around their camp leader who explained that they would be assigned to various work locations during the day, then divide up between them camp chores such as cooking, cleaning, gardening and laundry.

"Whenever you greet someone for the first time each day," the leader instructed, "you are to say, '*Heil Hitler*!'"

The girls learned that they would be doing gymnastics together as well as going on hikes and getting together for occasional parties with the boys from a nearby Labor Service camp. After the time of instruction, when they trooped outside together and gathered around the flagpole, Elfriede felt a welcome sense of relief. Yes, the work would be hard but she was no stranger to that. The camp leader, if a bit austere, seemed fair and trustworthy. Any twinges of homesickness she felt were for her young siblings and the tasks she had so enjoyed in Herr Brocke's office. She sensed that these would soon fade.

As she lowered the flag, the camp leader sang a song. A few girls warbled along with her:

We lower the flag
It comes to rest with us,
And tomorrow it will rise to fight again....[12]

Back inside, clothing was distributed. Sports suits and shoes for gymnastics, two pair of thick woolen socks, two pair of thin white socks, along with underwear and bras. A blue dress, aprons, red kerchief and robust black shoes for farm and factory work. Brown shoes for indoor wear and free-time outings. Elfride's heart sank a bit. These shapeless, unbecoming garments were almost painful to look at for a girl who eagerly followed the world of fashion and daydreamed about owning stylish clothing.

Then she saw the suit. Cut from brownish gray wool, it had a narrow, tight skirt and a tailored jacket that would accentuate her figure. A smile formed on Elfriede's lips. The brown felt hat could be worn at a jaunty angle on her wavy chestnut hair. The matching purse was actually cute. At least in her free time, she would look like the attractive, worldly young woman she felt herself becoming.

That first night, as the girls put away their things and sewed nametags into their new clothing, the camp resonated with bubbly, non-stop chatter. To corkboards on the wall they proudly pinned photographs of fathers, brothers and boyfriends in uniform and began to share confidences and hopes for the future. Elfriede had brought no photograph of her father. The only uniform Paul Kober wore was that of a *Blockwärter*, or Block Assistant, for the Nazi Party. In that simple brown jacket and red armband emblazoned with the swastika, Kober strutted around the villages of Aschitzau and Thommendorf in the role of thuggish enforcer, making sure his neighbors conducted themselves in a manner that conformed to Nazi doctrine. If he spied inappropriate behavior, he reported it to local party authorities. Paul also collected donations for the party. His attempts to ingratiate himself with the Nazis by bullying his fellow villagers and pressuring them to give up their hard-earned money caused them to dislike him even more than they already did. Elfriede would sooner gag than display a photograph of him. Still, she reveled in the giddy camp atmosphere and quizzed her new friends about their photographs. *This is almost as good as being with my sisters,* she thought. She liked it already.

At 9:30 PM, the camp leader sang a goodnight song to the girls, all tucked in their bunks:

> *Good night comrades, cherish this day.*
> *The stars rise out of the fir trees,*
> *Into the blue heavens,*
> *And shine on the world to banish darkness.*[13]

At the sound of her leader's high, clear voice, Elfriede felt her heart stir with a longing she had learned to suppress. Oh, how she missed her mother! Martha used to sing to her children at bedtime before her voice was silenced forever by a falling bucket of concrete.

Life in the camp was highly regulated, but there was comfort in routine. The girls awakened at 5:45 AM and slipped on their sport clothes for early morning calisthenics. Afterward, sweaty and famished, they washed, dressed for the day, devoured breakfast and raised the flag. As the flapping standard ascended, the leader shouted, "You, German youth, follow our flag!"

Then together they sang one of the many flag raising songs, such as:

> *Greet the flag, greet the times, greet the Führer who has made them.*

Greet all who die for you, faithfully following the call.
Whether we are victorious or we die, our flag stays pure.[14]

And they raised their right arms in salute.

Soon came the formal ceremony, synchronized with other ones all around Germany, in which the Labor Service girls took an oath. In unison they recited, "Work done for Germany is never forced, rather it is an honorable, voluntary service…Through this oath we *Arbeitsmaiden* vow to unconditionally follow the Führer and to pursue the goals of National Socialism throughout our whole lives long."[15] Afterward, each one received a silver-plated brooch to be worn at the neck to hold blouse or dress collar together.

Every day the girls marched to and from their various work sites, giving the Hitler salute to camp leaders upon arriving home again. I am convinced this is where my mother learned to be so zealous and exacting in her cleanliness, critical of anyone who fell short of her standards. The girls were scolded severely if their shoes weren't properly shined, if their freshly made beds had so much as one wrinkle, if the kitchen pots and pans didn't shine brilliantly after a thorough scrubbing.

While other girls struggled with homesickness, my mother took to the regimented life like a trout to a cool stream. Letters arrived from Helene and Werner, scrawled in large, childish hand, but Elfriede found herself reading about the goings on back home with diminishing interest. There was more than enough to occupy her in her new surroundings. Gregarious and friendly, she, along with the other working girls, eagerly anticipated the compulsory, chaperoned "visiting evenings" with their male Labor Service counterparts. Both sexes packed into the main dining hall of the girls' barracks, singing marching songs to accordion music beneath the watchful gaze of the Führer's portrait. On sunny days, they picnicked together in meadows and forest clearings, getting acquainted while munching on farm bread generously spread with liverwurst.

The days passed quickly. Dispersed to surrounding factories or farms, blue work dresses flapping in the wind, the girls performed light chores in fields, gardens and assembly lines. They acted as nannies and took on menial chores around the houses of overburdened housewives, fulfilling the National Socialist promise to aid mothers of large families. They helped in local kindergartens. Sometimes they cared for the sick and elderly. For all this they received no salary, just pocket money with which to buy little necessities like soap and toothpaste.

That February, Elfriede's birthday was acknowledged with a little holly wreath placed at her breakfast plate, a rousing song from her fellow workers and a congratulatory handshake from the camp leader. The personal attention made her feel warm inside; she couldn't remember a time, at least since her mother's death, when her birthday had been celebrated with such enthusiasm.

When they weren't working or enjoying the boys' company, the girls learned folk dancing and gymnastics. Competitive sports were off limits lest they encourage rivalry and diminish the sense of equality the organization sought to foster. Instead they attended political class where they absorbed Nazi ideology, and sat in a circle in the evenings singing folk songs.

Even after the novelty wore off, Elfriede remained an enthusiastic *Arbeitsmaiden*. Her character fit seamlessly into the Labor Service way of life. Her supervisors took notice of how she performed her work and household chores conscientiously, with an eye to perfection. Her six months' service assignment was coming to an end. Unwilling to lose such a dedicated and valuable asset, the camp leader approached her.

"Would you like to become a camp leader yourself, Elfriede? If so, we're prepared to send you to a training school near Stettin."

The pay wasn't great and there was no predicting to where she might ultimately be assigned, but wherever Elfriede landed, she would be guaranteed room and board and security in uncertain times. And indeed, the times were increasingly uncertain. National radio broadcasts warned about an approaching war, one that Germany didn't want but that other nations were provoking. When would it come? What would it all mean?

The camp leader's offer was timely for Elfriede had no intention of returning home. The chicken farm of her youth was now Schönfelder Grete's domain. Never again would she darken the door of that farmhouse, where her selfish father had worked her mother to death then allowed her to languish in a dark bedroom without securing the ongoing medical attention she so desperately needed. Grete could have Paul Kober and his smelly chicken coops; as far as Elfriede was concerned, she deserved them.

Elfriede enjoyed the punctilious atmosphere of the Reich Labor Service, where one knew exactly what to expect at all times and all she had to do was perform her duties faithfully and competently in order to be accepted and treated with respect. It took little soul-searching to arrive at an answer. Besides, she saw no viable alternative. She would stay with the Reich Labor Service and become a leader. Where that might ultimately take her was a mystery, but anywhere was better than home.

Even as Elfriede considered the exciting possibility of becoming a camp leader, hundreds of miles away a young husband and father received a heady offer, one that boosted not only his self-esteem but his bank account.

Josef "Kurt" Novak was a policeman. An ethnic German, he was born and raised in Komotau in the Sudetenland, the far western German-speaking part of Czechoslovakia. Although Novak is a Slavic name, Kurt and his forebears had for the most part kept their German bloodline pure with surnames like Schindler, Jackl, Hanke and Brunn in the family tree. These ethnic Germans found themselves, after the dismantling of the Austro-Hungarian Empire at the end of World War I, lumped in with the newly formed country of Czechoslovakia despite their separate ethnicity and language.

In the autumn of 1938, through crafty political maneuvering, Adolf Hitler managed to unite the Sudetenland with Germany as well as lay the groundwork for the occupation of the rest of Czechoslovakia. The Sudeten Germans rejoiced, having long hoped to be connected to the Reich. In Komotau, they poured into the streets and cheered as German tanks rolled in, greeting their "liberators" with the Hitler salute and embracing the red, black and white Nazi flag as their own. The following March, German troops rolled into the magnificent city of Prague. Czech citizens raged inwardly or wept openly. Prague's minority of ethnic Germans tossed flowers at the occupiers and rejoiced. Bohemia and Moravia now belonged to the territories of the German Reich and would henceforth be called "The Protectorate." The Sudetens felt proud that one of their own, *SS Gruppenführer* Karl Hermann Frank, was appointed Minister of State.

On March 16, 1939, Adolf Hitler himself, who had entered Prague during the night before, appeared on a balcony to greet the cheering Germans in the city. He felt as gleeful as they.[16] Bloodshed had been avoided, and it had all been done so smoothly, so skillfully.

But how to go about policing this great city of Prague? The dominant Czech population, seething with resentment, wasn't a reliable source for loyal policemen to keep the city under control. Better to bring in Sudeten Germans for the job. Their devotion and trustworthiness would be unassailable. So Kurt Novak, in his mid-thirties, moved his little family from Komotau to Prague and continued his career as policeman. As if moving to the glittering, magical city weren't promotion enough, he found himself no longer just a beat-walking cop, but part of a powerful, elite organization under the leadership of the *Reichsführer SS*, Heinrich Himmler.

Himmler, who had in 1936 combined the SS and police under his leadership, was granting policemen easy entry into the ranks of the SS. All Kurt had to do in order to join was meet the requirement of standing at least 5'6" tall, pass physical and hereditary health exams and provide proof of his German ancestry by submitting mimeographed copies of family marriage and birth certificates dating back to 1750. Though I possess no paperwork proving Kurt joined the SS, it is hard for me to imagine he would have turned down the opportunity for advancement, prestige and a pay raise. His ancestral documents were obtained from Komotau in 1939, the year he would have joined Himmler's "elite" force, not in 1942, when they were needed for other purposes yet to be revealed in this book.

Among my German family, Aunt Helene stands alone in believing Kurt was never a member of the SS. She insists my father eschewed the opportunity to join Himmler's special corps, but she also claims that Elfriede, despite my mother's eventual admission to the contrary, did not give birth in a Lebensborn home. Factoring in the deep shame associated with the SS and Lebensborn, especially for Helene's generation of Germans, I can only conclude that Helene has never wanted to acknowledge the embarrassing fact of her sister's involvement with an SS member and the Lebensborn program. Neither was she privy to my mother's secrets during the war, as was her sister Lisbeth. I am quite convinced that my father joined the SS, but even if, by some chance, he didn't, the fact remains that Himmler fused the SS and police together into one entity. As a policeman, he would have been inextricably linked with the SS.

During the war, even policemen who did not officially join the SS were granted the privilege of wearing the black SS uniform. They took their orders from the SS, received SS indoctrination, and as policemen, performed the work of the SS. This meant that Kurt Novak was now enlisted not only to keep order in Prague but to join in the larger National Socialist war against enemies of the Reich such as Jews, criminals and various other "sub-humans."[17]

Kurt settled his wife, Emma, and two young sons into their new and unfamiliar surroundings. As a chief squad leader, or *Hauptscharführer,* his annual pay of between 2,100 and 2,800 *Reichsmark* wasn't exorbitant, but it was certainly adequate, and as an SS member, he would be eligible for extra allowances. His new rank meant he would be assigned as enlisted staff personnel either to Prague SS headquarters or work with the security police and the Gestapo. Proudly he donned his new gray-green uniform with its insignia of two silver pips and black collar patch with silver stripe. His jacket was further adorned with the double *sig* runes that resembled lightning bolts but actually stood as a symbol for victory, and a swastika emblem on its patch pocket. Thus suitably attired, from now on Kurt would receive regular indoctrination in the ways and philosophies of the SS, which were really those of Heinrich Himmler.

The Reich Labor Service stressed absolute equality among its workers and by design, its daily routine and structure made it possible for a farm girl like Elfriede to rub shoulders with and even assume leadership over girls from wealthy, even noble families. This was no small achievement in a society that had always been class-conscious. Here was a world in which loyalty to National Socialist doctrine and dedication to rules and hard work won out over claims of blue-blooded or educational superiority. In this milieu, Elfriede thrived.

She, like other young women chosen to become camp leaders, underwent intensive training in how to run a large household as well as care for the physical and emotional needs of the girls in her charge. She would be assuming responsibility for 50 young workers, overseeing their labor and leisure activities, their ideological training and daily house chores. To aid in this daunting task, the Labor Service laid out a system of punishments for misbehavior. And lest her authority go to her head, it also provided opportunities for the girls to air their grievances and make complaints to Elfriede's superiors. She would have to watch her step at every turn, be diligent to wield her authority wisely if she was to make a success of herself.

Fortunately, through her experience both at home and as a servant in another family, Elfriede was used to helping care for those younger than herself. Organizing their activities and chores and making sure their physical needs were met would be no problem. Now it fell to her to welcome the new girls with a handshake just firm and distant enough to convey that she meant business, while her engaging smile sent the message that she had their best interests at heart.

On the first night of her new responsibilities, after she finished singing the goodnight song to her charges, Elfriede crawled into bed exhausted. It was like being mother to 50 children! She felt she lacked the patience for it, but determined to develop whatever skills necessary to excel at the task.

Wistfully she recalled the days when she had no more responsibility than the silly-headed working girls she now supervised. She'd been free to enjoy the company of the Labor Service boys at get-togethers, flirting to her heart's content and enjoying their attentions. Many of those boys had been funneled into the military, bustled off directly from their camp to basic training with the Army, Air Force or Navy, and if war came, they would, in turn, go off to battle. Only yesterday, it seemed, they had been sitting beside her singing folk songs and sharing bread and liverwurst. How she missed them!

Fortunately the Reich Labor Service's regimented daily schedule left her little time for contemplation. Up by 5:45 AM, she had the task of waking the girls and leading them in early morning calisthenics. After the flag had been raised and breakfast eaten, they arranged their chairs in a circle for group singing, an activity that never failed to build community spirit. From 8:00 AM to 3:00

PM they worked hard. With clipboard in hand, Elfriede directed some girls toward factory jobs and local farms or the homes of "child-rich" mothers. When they returned, she distributed their mail and ordered them to lie down and rest until coffee was served at 4:30 PM. After that, it was time for political class or outdoor activities, followed by a punctual 6:30 PM dinner. The two hours of free time following dinner were spent by the girls either curled up with books or giggling and gossiping in small cliques.

Elfriede had little time for herself. She needed to be there for the girls, especially those who were homesick or needed advice and direction. Any impertinence had to be dealt with swiftly and decisively. She had to review the materials for National Socialist instruction, learning it backwards and forwards so she could present it to the girls. Thus, her days passed in rapid succession. Weeks became months and turned into years. Paul Kober and Schönfelder Grete were busy with the farm and raising their son, Manfred. Helene and Werner, still barely tolerated by their stepmother, were growing up fast. In 1939 Germany had invaded Poland, kicking off the war Elfriede so feared. But the Führer seemed a wise, effective leader. Victory after victory was reported as the Wehrmacht mowed down everything in its path. The war was expanding to the North and West now, with the German invasion of Norway and Denmark then France, Belgium and the Netherlands. The Fatherland seemed destined to conquer and rule all of Europe.

As camp leader, Elfriede shone brightly. So trustworthy and hardworking was she that in October of 1941, her group leader approached her with an order that seemed more like a gift.

"You're being transferred to Prague," she informed Elfriede perfunctorily. "The Reich Labor Service has established a new War Help Service department. Now all *Arbeitsmaiden* are required to give a second six months to the war effort, so you'll be supervising the workers in a quartermaster depot. It's a big responsibility, keeping track of silly young girls in such a large city. But we believe you're up to the task."

Elfriede had to stop and catch her breath. Prague! She'd seen pictures of it on postcards of course, but had never dreamed of seeing with her own eyes that city whose lights glittered in the Vltava River and made Bunzlau look as insignificant as Aschitzau. How far National Socialism was taking her from her humble origins!

October was the scheduled break in the Labor Service's cycle of six-month work assignments, so Elfriede packed her own suitcase right alongside her departing workers and joined them in a tearful round of good-byes before boarding a Prague-bound train. As its cars clacked rhythmically along, the German countryside gave way to the wooded hills and valleys of Bohemia. Prague was a city of theaters, cafés, poetry and intellectuals. It boasted elegant Art Nouveau architecture and exuded romance. Now she would live in the heart of all that excitement. From the train window, she could see her past life slipping farther and farther behind her, receding into the background like the steam from the engine until it dissolved completely. Never again would she return to Aschitzau. This new assignment, she sensed, would lead to better things which would in turn lead to even better.

Elfriede in the Reich Labor Service

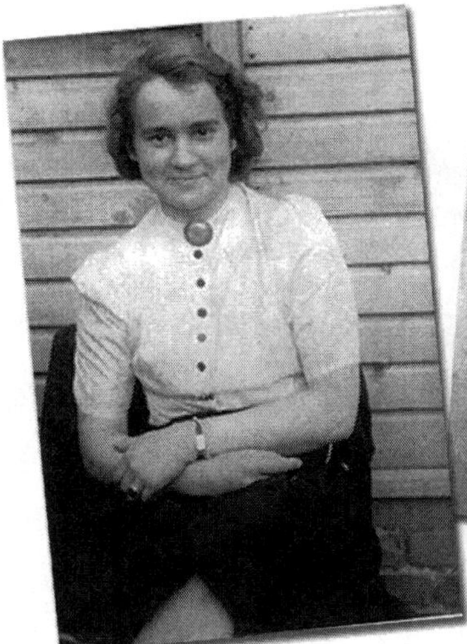

Elfriede in the Reich Labor Service uniform

The SS is a National Socialist order of soldiers of Nordic race and a community of their clans bound together by oath…what we want for Germany is a ruling class destined to last for centuries and the product of repeated selection…The SS is a nation, tribe, clan community, an order of knights that no one who, by virtue of his blood has been accepted into, can ever leave; he belongs to it body and soul as long as his earthly life shall last…wives and children of SS men enjoy all the protection and care that we offer our clan.

—Heinrich Himmler

CHAPTER 4

The fearsome SS of the war years was founded in the early days of National Socialism, more specifically in 1925 when Adolf Hitler began to feel he required a bodyguard. SS stands for *Schutzstaffel*, or "protection squads," small groups of men providing security during public meetings and rallies at which prominent Party members were speaking.

When Heinrich Himmler took charge of it in 1927, the SS was still in its infancy. Eager to please and aware that Hitler desired the organization become a vital force within the National Socialist movement, Himmler set about molding it into an elite corps, the living embodiment of his racial ideology and the advance troops of his ambition toward a pure Aryan utopia.

Said Himmler in a speech to SS leaders in June 1931: "The SS must become a force that includes the best human material that we possess in Germany; it must be held together by the shared community of blood. We have been given the greatest and most magnificent task that a nation can be faced with. As far as the value of our blood and the numbers of our population are concerned, we are dying out. We are called upon to establish foundations so that the next generation can make history, and if we create the right foundations, it will be a great one."[18]

Every member of the SS had to meet strict racial standards, and Himmler scrutinized each application personally. The *Reichsführer SS* thoroughly inspected photographs submitted by applicants, hoping to find evidence of Nordic appearance: above average height, long head, straight nose. Blond hair and blue eyes were a big plus, but not mandatory. Carefully he scoured applicants' photos for the prominent cheekbones, slanted eyes or round face that could indicate dreaded Slavic blood.[19] He couldn't be too careful. For it was through SS men and their offspring that Himmler would build the future leaders of the Greater Germanic Reich.

By the time Kurt Novak as a policeman was absorbed into the SS, it had grown to nearly 250,000 strong and was known for its fierce loyalty to Nazi party leadership. Mercilessly it crushed and oppressed those who dared to oppose Nazism. But it was more than a powerful machine employed to stamp out Hitler's enemies, both real and imagined; it was a community and a culture unto itself presided over by an ever-doting Himmler. This SS culture was of his making, with each ingredient calculatingly and painstakingly added as if he were a master baker concocting a cake. The *Reichsführer SS* decided how an SS man's family life should look and by which principles he should live. Himmler had always been somewhat of a meddler in other people's affairs, a quality that drove people away from him in his youth. Now he oversaw a legion of elite men whose lives he could happily shape and control. Besides sharing his specially-constructed neo-pagan religion with them, he imparted advice on healthy eating and drinking habits and interfered with their most intimate decisions.[20]

Once Kurt submitted his genealogical records, passed his physical exam and met the racial criteria for membership in the SS, he became an official member of a clan of Germanic blood complete with cult rituals and symbols, infused with the racial ideology of National Socialism. He swore allegiance to his Führer by publicly proclaiming, "I swear to you, Adolf Hitler, as Führer, Chancellor of the German Reich, that I will be loyal and brave. I pledge obedience unto death to you and to those you appoint to lead. So help me God." Over the next 21 months, Kurt underwent a program of SS indoctrination. During weekly meetings, he read and discussed portions of *Mein Kampf* as well as essays on the subject of racial theory. He learned about the inherent inferiority of the non-Germanic races by reading pamphlets issued by SS Headquarters: *(The Slav is) a frightful creature...just an approximation to a human being...but intellectually and spiritually inferior to any animal.* He sat through lessons identifying the enemies of National Socialism, particularly Jews and communists, and learned about SS culture and custom—the Teutonic rituals and celebrations so dear to Himmler's heart such as the eschewing of Christmas in favor of keeping the pre-Christian Yule on the day of the winter solstice.[21]

Had Kurt been unmarried he would have received instruction in how to choose a racially appropriate wife, preferably one young enough to bear many children. Advice on choosing good Germanic names for these children was also forthcoming. Kurt and other SS recruits were given gifts as rewards for loyal service, among them porcelain figurines of historic Germanic heroes and busts of Adolf Hitler, yule lights, vases and dishes with Germanic emblems. Earlier SS members had been presented with death's head rings, with "swords of honor" going to those who rose to leadership positions.[22]

Another somewhat shocking message came to Kurt through these indoctrination sessions and through articles in the official SS journal, *Das Schwarze Korps*. The Reich encouraged SS and policemen to father as many children as possible, even outside of marriage. Said Himmler in an order to this group issued on October 28, 1939: "Stepping outside the bounds of otherwise important social laws and conventions to bear children outside of marriage can be a lofty duty for German women and girls of pure blood—not out of imprudence or recklessness, but rather in the deepest moral sense...the men and women whose place, decreed by the state, is here at home, have the sacred obligation of becoming the mothers and fathers of children."[23]

Should providing for these illegitimate children prove problematic because of one's marriage and family obligations, Heinrich Himmler himself would do his best to insure that the fathers be spared from child support suits, and see to it that the SS organization provided for their offspring, insuring they were well cared for.[24] Through persistent SS rhetoric, Kurt heard that for too long the Christian church had imposed its antiquated morality on society. This was a new era. The time was ripe for a new morality, of which the SS would be the vanguard.[25]

Germany's need for babies superseded old fashioned notions about right and wrong. What mattered now was that the birthrate rise by whatever means possible.[26] So many soldiers were falling in battle. Who would replace them? Germany was conquering more and more territory, spreading itself over all of Europe, especially the East. Once the Slavs and Jews were eradicated, who would populate these vast swaths of fertile land if German men and women did not rise to the occasion and produce more Aryan offspring? And who better to produce this offspring than the men who had already been chosen for their physical superiority and racial purity—men of the SS.

Even as far back as 1937, Heinrich Himmler had spoken of these things to SS leaders. On February 18 of that year, he stated: "All matters involving sex are not private matters of the individual, but rather they affect the life and death of the nation...the nation that has a lot of children can expect to become a world power and achieve world domination."[27]

The *Reichsführer SS* had kept these ideas private for the most part, because in his opinion a prudish, traditional German society had not been ready to accept them. Now the increasingly unfortunate realities of war rendered the people's approval moot. It was necessary to go public. Thus, in 1940, Himmler officially and explicitly commanded SS men and police officers to father children with pure-blooded German women, within or outside of marriage.[28]

To her surprise, the Prague in which Elfriede arrived in 1941 felt strangely like home. As she crossed Wenceslas Square after leaving the train station, she heard German spoken all around her. The conquerors had settled in. Their Nazi flag flew atop government buildings. German soldiers, both Wehrmacht and SS, patrolled the streets in a relaxed manner as if out for a pleasant stroll among the splendid buildings and verdant parks. They eagerly patronized the Czech bakeries, buying cakes piled high with whipped cream. All appeared calm and peaceful as if the Czechs had accepted, if grudgingly, the inevitability of German rule.

Not apparent on the surface of things was how many of Prague's Jewish lawyers and doctors had been quietly forced to abandon their practices, how many Jewish professors and university students were forced out of classrooms. Jews had, by this point, been removed from all public and government positions. Jewish children were barred from attending public schools and their parents severely restricted in obtaining food rations. As far as they were able, Jewish people had been streaming out of the country in hopes of reaching Palestine, England or France, or anywhere else they perceived as safe. Those who remained in the city tried to blend in and become invisible, even as their rights and privileges as Czech citizens were systematically stripped away.

Elfriede wouldn't have noticed these things, but she did notice immediately that Prague had a dazzling night life. The city boasted a vibrant cinema and café culture. There were also plenty of good-looking young men about. Czech girls were no competition; as a rule, they didn't date the German soldiers in town, who would in any case have been strongly discouraged from becoming romantically involved with Slavs. But plenty of Sudeten German girls had come to the big city to expand their horizons. As if wanting to act more German than even the Germans, they wore braids and *Dirndl* skirts, which Elfriede thought made them look ridiculous against the backdrop of their sophisticated surroundings.

In the evenings, both Czech and German couples walked arm and arm through the medieval streets of the city center. They strolled along the banks of the Vltava River where Jews were no longer allowed to set foot. Each group frequented its own set of theaters, cabarets and cafés, but in the most popular haunts they sometimes mingled, keeping to separate tables of course. So many filled the streets at night one would never suspect there was a war on. Yes, Prague was deceptively giddy. Elfriede could hardly believe her good fortune.

Once her Labor Service supervisor had shown her around the barracks and the quartermaster's depot, Elfriede used any free time she had to wander Prague's quaint, narrow lanes. She stood on the Charles Bridge, gazing down at the gray-blue Vltava River and up at Hradĉany castle as the city lights began to twinkle star-like beneath the dusky sky. In a city like this, work was a necessary evil even to a conscientious, responsible German girl. Oh, to be strolling on the arm of a handsome soldier through the charming medieval streets! Elfriede eyed with envy the Sudeten girls who saw her watching and clung possessively to their boyfriends. Deep down, she sensed that some kind of adventure was in the offing. Elfriede dreamed of a sweeping romance. Surely it lay just around the corner, waiting for her somewhere in that magical city. In the meantime, she had work to do. As always, she would do it diligently.

Every day she supervised her cohort of working girls as they served Wehrmacht and SS soldiers and policemen in the quartermaster's depot. The men entered in a steady stream to be issued mess kits, shoes, boots, belts and uniforms. Naturally they lingered a little longer than necessary, for the bolder girls shamelessly flirted. A few naughty girls furtively applied lipstick during their breaks. Elfriede, only two years older than they, scolded them by repeating the Führer's oft-used slogan, *"Die Deutsche Frau schminkt sich nicht!"* (A German woman does not use make-up!), but secretly she understood their weakness in the face of temptation. She herself longed to dress up in a flared skirt and high heels, to put on rouge and lipstick and go dancing.

It was at a dance that my father and mother first laid eyes on each other. From his on-stage perch as a member of the police orchestra, Kurt spied the agile and petite Elfriede whirling in the arms of her dance partners. When he came to the quartermaster's depot in search of a new uniform jacket, new insignia or leather belt, he was delighted to run into her again. They felt an instant attraction.

It's a story as old as time. The older man felt flattered by the flirtations of the fresh-faced, petite young woman who looked as if she were playing at being a grown-up in her no-nonsense shoes and uniform jacket that just happened to show off her slender waist to full advantage. She moved with such confidence! She spoke with such authority as she directed younger workers. Performing her duties efficiently, she still took time to smile and converse with *Hauptscharführer* Novak as if genuinely interested in him as a human being rather than regarding him as a faceless, nameless customer passing through.

She blushed when he gazed appreciatively at her, unconsciously dropping his eyes from her face to her feet then back up again. Obviously he admired her silky brown hair and lithe figure. Did he really need to come back for an item he had forgotten the previous day, or had he merely used it as an excuse to see her again?

Yes, he was 15 years her senior, but she liked that. For a girl whose father had mostly belittled and beaten her, this attention from an older man felt good, like a warm blanket wrapped around shivering shoulders. When Kurt asked her to accompany him to the cinema, she accepted without hesitation even though she had noticed the gold wedding band on his right fourth finger. Somehow his marital status made him all the more mysterious and enticing. That night, Elfriede defied Adolf Hitler's wishes and rouged her cheeks. She popped the lid off a tube of cherry red lipstick and slid it artfully over her lips before pulling on a pair of silk stockings that she had been saving for just such an occasion. Rationed only four pair per year, she had mended them often, trying to make them last. Elfriede slipped on the only shoes she possessed that were remotely suitable for a date—the same brown heels she wore to work, issued by the Labor Service. *They're plain, but they'll have to do*, she thought as she opened her purse and counted out two and a half crowns for the tram fare.

They met on a murky street corner and walked into the shadows. Popular hot spots, like the beer garden called U Fleků, or the Deutsches Haus or Golden Fountain restaurants, were out of the question; far too many Germans frequented those places. Prying eyes must be avoided. Over the next several months, Kurt and Elfriede kept to the hazy back corners of smoky cabarets or small, out-of-the-way movie theaters, enjoying German musicals with generous amounts of tap dancing. The pair avoided the elegant Cinema Broadway where they were bound to run into acquaintances, instead favoring obscure nightclubs in the suburbs where jazz and swing music floated out into the night air each time the door opened. They stuck to places where mostly Czechs congregated and since they kept to themselves, the Czechs obligingly ignored them.

In August of that same year, the SS and police had been handed the authority to act against anyone resisting German rule as well as the Jews of Prague. There was always some kind of subversion afoot. By Himmler's orders, Kurt was kept busy cracking down on the most minor of infractions such as publicly making fun of or spreading rumors about the Nazi government or expressing dissatisfaction with the regime. He arrested people for listening to enemy radio broadcasts or making statements of loyalty to Christian churches, and he made sure Jews didn't try to enter public swimming pools, cinemas, theaters or stand on the banks of the Vltava, linger in parks or gardens or try to use taxis. He and his fellow officers had to police the city trams to be sure the Jews, as required, were standing at the back of the cars rather than sitting in seats. Kurt need only tell Emma that he was called out on duty and he was free to spend an evening with his paramour.

Elfriede would have loved to see the American *Broadway Melody* films shown in the larger movie houses downtown. Wagner's *Lohengrin* was playing at the German Opera House but dating Kurt meant Elfriede had to content herself with seeing obscure Czech films in tiny back-alley theaters. It didn't matter. She only wanted to be with him, to feel his arms around her and walk beside him in the shadowy streets even if they didn't dare join the other happy couples in Wenceslas Square.

Autumn and winter of 1941 were bitterly cold and the lovers possessed little privacy. Fuel was scarce and apartment buildings went unheated. Elfriede had only the barracks she shared with her Labor Service girls and Kurt had his family at home. Did they rent a room in a hotel or borrow the chilly apartment of an accommodating friend? Did they make love behind the shrubs of one of Prague's lush parks at night, trying their best to ignore the freezing temperatures, taking their warmth from one another?

Could they have set out to conceive a baby as a result of the indoctrination they had both received about presenting their Führer with a child, helping to raise the birthrate and thus serving the best interests of the Reich? To me, it seems unlikely, though by that time both were thoroughly steeped in Nazi ideology. The "new morality" confused many SS men who were taught on the one hand that strong marriages were one of the pillars of society and on the other hand encouraged to father children out of wedlock. These men, especially if they were older like Kurt, had grown up under more traditional views and tended to cling to those early, ingrained ideas, found unwed births scandalous.[29] It is far more probable that my parents were two people caught up in an age-old scenario of lust and loneliness. Official permission to have an affair and not fear the consequences of pregnancy was merely the background music to which they danced, the tape recording playing in the backs of their minds as they acted on their desires.

Their affair unfolded amidst an atmosphere of martial law. General Reinhard Heydrich was at that moment unleashing a wave of terror meant to shock and subdue the city of Prague. Appointed Deputy Protector of Bohemia and Moravia, that September he entered the city ready to kill. Within three days of his arrival, he had executed nearly 100 people and displayed their names on posters to strike fear in the hearts of the vanquished, who could only watch in mute horror as the travesty played out in front of their eyes. The terrorized Czech citizens wasted no time in dubbing Heydrich "The Butcher of Prague." Under his rule, Jews, forced to begin wearing the yellow star in September, had begun to be rounded up and deported to Łódź, Poland to be slowly starved to death in a sealed ghetto.

Heydrich's martial law was enforced all through the autumn and into January. During those months, 486 death sentences were handed down and 2,242 people banished to concentration camps, most of them members of resistance organizations. Thousands of people were arrested. Jews were deported to Chelmno where the Nazis, experimenting with more efficient methods of murder, killed many of them with car exhaust. In November, the Germans established the ghetto prison of Theresienstadt just south of Prague. Heydrich crammed it full not only of local Jews but Jews from many other European countries. Conditions and nourishment there were appalling, causing rampant disease.

Did Elfriede know or care that as an SS police chief squad leader, Kurt Novak surely had a hand in executing these roundups and deportations? After all, it was the police who cordoned off neighborhoods, raided houses and supervised the loading of trains with human cargo. Jewish families were forced to assemble in an area enclosed by barbed-wire near Stromovka Park. The police herded them at gunpoint through the streets to the Bubny station to board trains for Theresienstadt. As soon as they were gone, their property was divvied up amongst the Germans, all under SS supervision. Did it matter to her that Kurt and his fellow SS men functioned as Heydrich's hands and feet, doing his dirty work as he sat behind a desk up at Hradĉany Palace?

My mother had been fed a steady diet of Nazi propaganda from the age of 12, when Hitler took power and she joined the nascent League of German Girls. The Führer's frenzied voice shouting through the radio was as familiar to her by now as a family member's. Germans were superior and meant to rule the world. Jews and Slavs were less than human. This had been conveyed to her in countless ways, over and over again throughout her most impressionable years. Her lover was a man at the apex of society, the cream of the crop, an Aryan elite. He belonged to her only in the evenings and she cherished those stolen moments. Whatever he did during the days didn't concern her and was no more than his sacred duty to his Führer and the Reich.

In early February, Elfriede suspected she was pregnant. By March, suspicion had given way to certainty. Foods she had once enjoyed and eaten with gusto now nauseated her. Her complexion paled. Determined, she worked on, knowing she possessed the ability to push through physical weakness in order to fulfill her responsibilities. But one thing she couldn't control— her belly was beginning to protrude. Soon her clothing would become uncomfortably tight around her waist. On her slender, petite frame, a pregnancy couldn't be hidden.

Ironically, even though certain National Socialist leaders were preaching a new morality and the importance of providing the Nazi state with illegitimate children, the official stance of the Reich Labor Service concurred with society's traditional views and clung to the old morality. Girls discovered to be pregnant out of wedlock were immediately dismissed from their posts.[30]

What was she to do? Return to her father's household? The thought only increased her nausea. That hypocrite, Paul Kober, would surely rather cut his daughter off completely than see her return home pregnant and unwed even though he had fathered Gertrude before his own marriage to Martha Heide. Even if he did allow her under his roof, Elfriede knew she would never subject a child to his tyrannical rule. Curled up on her bunk after lights out, she agonized over her prospects. First of all, she had to tell Kurt.

The *SS Hauptscharführer* took the news stoically. Undoubtedly his police training had taught him to conceal emotion. When he finally spoke, the sudden coolness in his tone extinguished the glimmer of unrealistic hope to which Elfriede had been clinging. "Of course you realize I will never leave my family," he said succinctly. "I'm devoted to Emma and the boys."

Stung by his candor, Elfriede didn't answer. Instead she stared at her hands lying in her lap, especially at the right fourth finger, so naked without a gold wedding band. Had his wife been infertile, Kurt could have dissolved the marriage easily, for the Nazis had expanded the grounds for divorce to include infertility. But Emma had borne him two sons. Even if he had wanted to divorce her to marry Elfriede, serious obstacles stood in his path. With the usual contradiction that characterized Nazi policy, the Marriage Law of 1938 upheld the idea that in the case of a divorce caused by adultery, re-marriage could not take place between the adulterer and the person with whom he had committed that adultery.[31] This law pertained despite Himmler's encouragement to father children outside marriage. It was the children resulting from an affair the Nazis were prepared to support, not the dissolving of fertile marriages in order to form new domestic alliances.

Deep in her heart of course, Elfriede had known that Kurt truly loved Emma. Even in her most passionate moments she had sensed on a primal level that her devotion to the relationship surpassed his. Nevertheless, it hurt to hear the words spoken aloud. Against her better judgment, she had fantasized about an enduring love. She had simply lacked the sophistication to recognize that to Kurt she was a mere diversion, a casual dalliance.

He regarded her with a mixture of fondness and pity. "What are you going to do?"

So it was all on her shoulders.

"An abortion is out of the question," he reminded her. "The government is absolutely opposed to it; if the SS found out, I could be severely punished. But there are homes, special hospitals, where women pregnant by SS and policemen can go to give birth."

Elfriede had heard rumors of such places, some of them wild and preposterous sounding, about genetically selective breeding and "stud farms." She wasn't quite sure what to think of Kurt's suggestion. Did he regard her as a mere breeder? Did he see their unborn child as merely a "gift to the Führer," to be handed over to the state and then forgotten? If she entered one of those Lebensborn places, would she be kept there against her will, forced to have sex with other SS men and bear baby after baby? Or were those only crazy rumors?

In a subdued voice she replied, "I'll think about it."

Leaving Kurt that night, she knew the relationship was over. Now, when she needed him most, he had little to offer her and seemed only to want to extricate himself from the tangled mess they'd woven. Strangely, she felt very little resentment toward him. Rather, she reproached herself. Kurt hadn't taken advantage of her; she'd given herself willingly, caught up in the dangerous excitement of an illicit affair. She had been stupid, and now she must pay the price.

Elfriede did a little discreet asking around and learned that the rumors surrounding the Lebensborn program were grossly exaggerated if not downright false. One of her Labor Service colleagues slipped her a pamphlet, whispering, "Don't worry, Lebensborn will keep your secret completely! But all the Lebensborn maternity homes are overcrowded. The most luxurious of the homes is Heim Wienerwald, near Vienna. It's practically impossible to get a place there if you aren't associated with a high-ranking SS officer. They play favorites, you see."

Austria sounded like the perfect hideaway. Why should Elfriede want to be shut away in a bare-bones clinic somewhere when a place like Heim Wienerwald existed? She determined to give birth there despite the difficulties of securing a bed. She would make it happen even if she had to do so under false pretenses. Marshaling every ounce of resourcefulness within her, she concocted a plan.

Elfriede Kober, age 21

If we waited until civil morality changed, for the old-fashioned guardians of morality to die off, more generations of unwed mothers would suffer in purgatory. No, we cannot wait…

The Lebensborn homes shall replace the families of expectant mothers, and in fact Lebensborn is one big family, into which an expectant mother can enter to escape her unsympathetic environment.

—Official SS newspaper, *Das Schwarze Korps*

CHAPTER 5

Kurt Novak occupied a low rung on the SS ladder. His rank of *Hauptscharführer* was merely that of an SS enlisted man, not that of an officer. Seriously doubting whether he had adequate clout to pull any strings and get her admitted into one of the so-called "elite" maternity homes, Elfriede's thoughts turned to an old friend, another Kurt from the village of Thommendorf where she had attended school. Kurt Huebler was several years older than Elfriede. As a handsome young Army officer-in-training who'd returned home for a visit, he'd unwittingly been the object of her teenage crush. Kurt had done his family and community proud by rising swiftly in the ranks of the Wehrmacht. She hadn't seen him in years, of course. But according to the last bit of gossip she'd heard back in Aschitzau, he was, even though barely into his late twenties, already a lieutenant colonel and serving under Rommel in North Africa.

If, as Elfriede felt certain it would, the Lebensborn organization was willing also to cater to the girlfriends of high ranking Wehrmacht officers and not just those of SS men then Kurt Huebler was the perfect man around whom to build a falsehood. She reasoned that since he was safely out of reach in the North African desert, the unsuspecting officer couldn't dispute her claims and was probably next to impossible to contact.

Elfriede's thoughts now alighted upon her regional camp group leader in the Reich Labor Service. An older, no-nonsense woman, she was unlikely to approve of unwed pregnancy. Yet despite her brusque manner, there was something motherly about her; she seemed trustworthy, as if she might muster a bit of compassion and keep a secret. The organization's official policy was to dismiss unwed mothers from its ranks, but Elfriede sensed a sympathetic spirit in the woman and hoped she might skirt around the policy and allow her to return as an employee after the baby's birth. What was more, she struck Elfriede as well-connected. By the time Elfriede was able to arrange a private meeting with the woman, her belly was already straining at the elastic waist of her skirt. Buttoning her uniform jacket was becoming close to impossible.

My mother wasted no time in getting to the point. "I'm pregnant," she informed the camp group leader. "I know it means dismissal from my job, but I have nowhere to turn and you seem like a person I can trust." She pushed the Lebensborn pamphlet across the desk. "I've heard there's a home near Vienna where women like me can go to have their babies and that the home will keep my secret. Maybe you've heard of it—Heim Wienerwald, at Pernitz."

The elder woman perused the pamphlet. "For shame, Elfriede. I thought better of you."

Hanging her head contritely, she admitted, "I was stupid...."

"Well, we all make mistakes, and it certainly does look as though the Lebensborn program is your only option at this point."

Elfriede perked up. "Would you please be so kind as to call the home at Pernitz and recommend me? I feel so alone." She hastened to add, "You see, the father of my baby is Wehrmacht Lieutenant Colonel Kurt Huebler. I've known him for a long time; he's from my hometown in Silesia. But he's away in North Africa and unavailable to help me make arrangements."

"If he's away in North Africa, how did you get into this condition?"

Lying was coming easily to her now. "He came to visit me here when he was on leave for Christmas."

"You'll need his family history," the woman informed her, revealing she knew much more about Lebensborn than Elfriede realized. "Proof of his Aryan blood."

"Oh, of course!" she bluffed. "Yes, I can get those documents. I just need someone with more authority than myself to speak to the administration at Heim Wienerwald to persuade them to reserve me a bed. I've heard it's hard to secure a place there but I'm sure if they knew that the father of my baby was a high-ranking

Wehrmacht officer, they'd find a place for me."

The camp group leader gazed firmly, but not unkindly, at my mother from across her desk. "I'll do my best to persuade the Pernitz home to make room for you. But I can't do so until I've verified your claims."

"Wha-what do you mean?"

"It must be established that this Wehrmacht officer is indeed the father of your child."

"Well you'll just have to take my word for it. He's way out in the Sahara desert."

"We have ways of contacting him."

"I'm showing already! I don't have time to wait for a letter."

"That's obvious. I'll speak to the Wehrmacht Administration here in Prague and ask them to put a call through to his field headquarters."

Elfriede blanched. Clever though she was, she hadn't anticipated this turn of events. Of course Huebler would deny paternity, deny even having laid eyes on Elfriede since she was a blushing teenager. Still, she had faith in her scheme. Keep calm, she told herself. Act natural. "All right then. But I beg you to be discreet. You see, he's married, and I know he wouldn't want his staff, or his wife, to know about this baby."

"Very well, Elfriede. Try to conceal your pregnancy for a little while longer, and come back next week."

Hoping the violent trembling in her limbs wasn't noticeable, my mother left the camp group leader's office. As she walked in a daze back to the quartermaster's depot, her mind raced. Her plan now seemed doomed to fail, and she must come up with an alternate. Huebler would surely deny paternity. Yet she could insist he was lying. So many men refused to accept responsibility for children they fathered that it would hardly strike the camp group leader as unusual. Would her superior ask him if he had passed through Prague on his Christmas leave? It was certainly possible that he had done so, but what if he hadn't? She might have to insist he was lying about that too. Then she would have to write him a letter, explaining why she had told such terrible falsehoods about him, and hope against hope he would forgive her. Of course, the best case scenario would be that Kurt was simply un-contactable, in the throes of battle somewhere in Algeria or Tunisia. All she needed was permission to show up at the Lebensborn home; after that, she would leave him out of it.

The following week, Elfriede returned to the camp group leader's office. She was ready for anything—a shaming lecture, abrupt dismissal, even begging Kurt Novak to set her up in a rented room somewhere until she could think of some other solution. But against all odds and to her immense surprise, she learned her plan had succeeded.

"An Army radio operator dispatched a message by radio teletype to Huebler's field headquarters. A radio operator in Sicily spoke with one of his aides. As I instructed, he asked whether the lieutenant colonel knew you or not, and whether he was from your home village in Silesia. The operator also inquired whether he had been home on leave over the holidays. The aide found Huebler, asked him the questions, and relayed the answers through Sicily back to Prague. It was then reported to me that the lieutenant colonel answered yes to all three of them."

Her lips going white, Elfriede waited for the woman to announce they had asked Huebler whether he'd fathered her child, whether he'd rendezvoused with her in Prague. She never did. Apparently trying to be discreet, uncomfortable with sending such a blunt, personal inquiry over Army radio, the prim and proper camp group leader had been entirely satisfied that Elfriede was telling the truth on the basis of those three questions alone.

"I've already made the call to Pernitz, explaining your circumstances. The home director said there is a bed available, and to put you on a train as soon as possible. Lebensborn is a good solution for you. You're one of our best leaders, Fräulein Kober. You've been careless, but it would be a shame to lose you over an ill-timed pregnancy. Your secret will be safe with me. I see in your file that you suffered a bout of rheumatic fever in your teens and have a mild heart murmur because of it. If you like, I can write in my official report that we had to send you down to Austria for treatment. Then, if you want to continue with the Reich Labor Service after your baby is born, nothing will stand in your way. You'll be allowed to return...provided, of course, that you don't keep the child."

Elfriede felt her whole body sag with relief. She rose and cupped her superior's hand in both her own. "Thank-you! You've saved my life and reputation!"

She told her working girls, as well as her family through letters, that a routine physical examination had turned up a heart problem necessitating a medical leave. The Labor Service was sending her to a facility in Austria where the matter could be further looked into. Sadly, the girls watched her pack her belongings. They respected Elfriede and would miss her; she had been tough but sympathetic, working every bit as hard as they. Of course they understood her need for rest and recuperation. She'd been so pale lately. Her body appeared bloated as if it were retaining water. Some heart conditions were known to cause that, weren't they? If any of the more worldly-wise *Arbeitsmaiden* guessed their leader's true condition, they remained respectfully silent, at least until Elfriede had buckled the leather straps on her suitcase, completed the obligatory round of handshakes and climbed into a taxi bound for the train station.

Kurt Novak met her on the platform. He handed her a large envelope. In it were mimeographed copies of his ancestral documents: birth, marriage and baptismal records dating all the way back to 1750. They came easily to hand for he'd had to submit them to the SS in order to apply for membership. Along with those was a signed acknowledgement of paternity and a pledge to pay the 1.50 *Reichsmark* per day it would cost Elfriede to live in the Lebensborn home until her baby's birth, then the 1.75 RM per day after that.

Had she been Kurt's wife, he might even now be putting in an order for the congratulatory brooch, decorated with SS runes, that all SS men were encouraged to give their spouses upon the birth of a child. But the SS had no brooches for unwed mothers and Kurt wasn't celebrating this particular baby. They kissed good-bye, but the passion had dissipated. There was no future for them as a couple, only a polite agreement to bring this child into the world in the most convenient and private way possible.

Rumors swirled about Lebensborn during the 10 years of its existence, and they persist even today. Sensational films and novels, as well as unreliable websites that make startling claims but don't back them up with evidence—over the decades these have breathed new life into the falsehoods and misconceptions from time to time. But the fact remains that Lebensborn was never a breeding program. It did not consist of stud farms where perfect Germanic specimens of man and womankind mated in order to produce children of the Master Race. Whispered innuendoes about "breeding" were especially rife during the war years, but there is no proof of their veracity. The secretive nature of Lebensborn and the lack of information disseminated to the public only served to fan the flames of the rumors. Even some SS men didn't fully understand what Lebensborn was and harbored suspicious thoughts toward it.[32]

In fact, the staff at the Lebensborn Central Administration in Münich regularly rebuffed requests made by lonely women who were looking for mates, or at least someone to father children with them. To all such letters, Lebensborn administrators replied that they did not run a matchmaking service. In a Germany where most of the young men were off at war, some women bypassed completely the search for a mate. Desperate to become mothers and having latched onto the rumors that Lebensborn was a breeding program, they inquired about artificial insemination. These women, too, were politely turned away. Heinrich Himmler, however, took these pitiable requests to heart and hoped that one day, once the Greater Germanic Reich had been established, he would be able to implement some kind of program to grant such childless women their wishes.[33]

What then, was the Lebensborn organization? It was Himmler's brainchild, a program designed to encourage and support the births of children whom the National Socialist state deemed racially valuable. Children conceived by Aryan parents, mostly out of wedlock—encouraged, not engineered—were to come into the world with the best of care as long as their parents met the organization's strict racial and health requirements.

Lebensborn was founded in 1935. Its first maternity home, in the Bavarian town of Steinhöring near Münich, opened in 1936. By 1942, nine homes had been established in Germany proper. Eleven homes were founded in Norway, two in Austria, as well as one home each in Belgium, Luxembourg, and France. In all these homes put together, no more than 10,000 babies were born.

By the time my mother entered Heim Wienerwald in 1942, Dr. Gregor Ebner ran the medical side of the organization and SS First Lieutenant Max Sollmann was its administrative head. Sollmann, an authoritarian leader answerable only to Himmler, expertly guided the organization into rapid expansion, with rigid discipline and well-defined goals. He listed those goals as:

- To support racially and genetically superior large families.
- To aid in the childbirths of racially and genetically valuable expectant mothers who can prove their own Germanic ancestry and that of their children's fathers, and thus bring valuable children into the world.
- To care for those children.
- To care for the mothers.
- To assume guardianship of these children if required by circumstances according to Lebensborn's own judgment.
- To assume guardianship of and support SS war orphans by mandate of the *Reichsführer SS*, Heinrich Himmler.[34]

Without revealing its name, Lebensborn placed discreet advertisements in the form of articles in newspapers and women's magazines, offering aid and refuge for women who, like my mother, had affairs with German men and found themselves caught between the "old" and the "new" morality. The articles implied that unwed mothers were regularly shamed and shunned by parents and scorned and dismissed by employers—victims of a prudish society stuck in the Dark Ages, a social system slow to catch up with progressive and tolerant National Socialist ideology and even slower to recognize that these girls were merely performing a sacred duty to the German nation by providing it with children of pure blood. For all such women, there was an address to which inquiries could be sent.[35]

So desperately did the Nazi government desire to shore up the birthrate that Heinrich Himmler designed the Lebensborn program, which functioned under the umbrella of the SS, in order to make it possible for unwed mothers to have their babies away from the disapproving and prying eyes of society. Visits from outsiders were restricted. Absolute secrecy was the greatest commodity Lebensborn had to offer. If a young woman so chose, a Lebensborn birth could be kept secret even from her parents. Himmler, anticipating societal backlash over this blatant usurping of parental rights, resorted to illegal actions in order to insure this secrecy. To sidestep the German civil requirements of registering illegitimate births at the mother's hometown registry office, he directed Lebensborn to set up its own separate registries in Berlin, Vienna and Münich to process unwed births.[36] Before long, Lebensborn answered only to Heinrich Himmler, who answered only to Adolf Hitler.

Unmarried women could now bring their babies into the world, provided they were pure-blooded Aryan babies, in the accepting and encouraging environment of comfortable, well-equipped Lebensborn maternity homes. These mothers could choose to keep their babies if they found employment or if their parents eventually came around and accepted the illegitimate offspring into the family. Perhaps the child's father would marry her. If he did, all the better. If he was single and available or willing to divorce his first wife, they could form a family but he was by no means required to do so. There were also many infertile German couples who longed for children.

The unwed Lebensborn mother who wished to relinquish her child for adoption could be assured that Lebensborn would find it a good home, with priority going to childless SS men and their wives or those SS couples who might already have children but wished to increase their family size. No Lebensborn mother need ever worry, for one way or another, Heinrich Himmler and the SS clan assumed the symbolic role of godparent for her child and would personally guarantee a good upbringing in the spirit of National Socialism.[37] Relinquishing mothers could emerge from Lebensborn homes with their reputations intact, their family and friends none the wiser.

Lebensborn means "spring of life" in Himmler's neo-pagan Germanic vocabulary. Yet it is a tragic irony that the Lebensborn program also stood for death.

Though Adolf Hitler and the zealous executor of his vision, Heinrich Himmler, wished to increase the population of pure-blooded Aryans, they also desired the annihilation of non-Aryans or "subhumans" such as Jews, Gypsies and Slavs. Out of the same "spring of life" issued the concentration and death camp system and the kidnappings of eastern European children with features judged to be Aryan.

Himmler oversaw these tasks with a meticulous attention to detail.[38] He presided over the SS and Lebensborn with the pride of a parent watching his beloved child grow, gain strength and conquer the world. For Lebensborn was his child through and through. The *Reichsführer SS* relished equally his roles as sustainer of life and mass murderer.

Who was this man, my symbolic godfather, who stood ready to guarantee my future and by whose stringent guidelines I and thousands of other Lebensborn children qualified to enter the world?

Heinrich Himmler, who eventually became *Reichsführer SS,* Chief of the German Police, Commander of the Reserve Army of the Wehrmacht and the Reich Minister of the Interior, was born into a Catholic Bavarian family in the year 1900. He was a socially awkward youth, unable to stop himself from boring his peers with constant irrelevant chatter, yet astute and perceptive enough to recognize that he had trouble connecting with others on an emotional level. This frustrated him deeply. He felt inferior, self-conscious of his receding chin and unimpressive physique. Haunting him was the awareness that he continuously alienated the friends for whose acceptance he so ardently yearned. As he grew into red-blooded young manhood, girls seldom reciprocated his interest.[39]

While a student in college majoring in Agriculture, Himmler developed a fondness for tales about Nordic-Germanic heroes and heroines, devouring novels that revolved around such themes. At the same time, he began to delve into anti-Semitic works like Artur Dinter's *The Sin Against Blood* and Friedrich Spielhagen's *Ultimo.* Later he consumed more anti-Jewish literature, such as Wilhelm Meister's *The Register of Judah's Guilt* and Stewart Chamberlain's *Race and Nation.*[40] Gradually he came to adopt racial theory, increasingly identifying himself as a true Aryan.

He became obsessed with the military. Its focus on rules and routine and its dictation of proper behavior appealed to him, for behind it, through strict obedience, he could camouflage his social clumsiness. To the end of his days, Himmler thought of himself as a soldier. Spartan in his tastes, he dressed in a simple gray uniform and avoided ostentatious display.[41]

He had been too young to take part in any significant way in the First World War. That disappointed him deeply; Himmler longed to become a career military officer, but in a defeated and humiliated postwar Germany, there weren't many opportunities for that. He had to satisfy himself with joining paramilitary groups during his student years in Münich and it was during those years that he developed an interest in politics. Especially appealing to him was radical rightwing National Socialism. Its tenets dovetailed nicely with his anti-Semitic beliefs. Originally belonging to the Party of German Socialists, a separate party from the one led by Adolf Hitler, Himmler entered Hitler's orbit when the two groups finally merged to form the Nazi Party. After reading some of Hitler's writings, Himmler jotted down in a note to himself: *He is a truly great man and above all a genuine and pure one. His speeches are marvelous examples of Germanness and Aryanness.*[42] The would-be warrior had found his guiding star.

Himmler's obsession with detail,[43] devotion to Hitler as a leader, and insatiable desire for control served him well as he took on a desk job at the party's Münich headquarters. With utmost zeal and efficiency he performed mundane but vital tasks: handling correspondence, sending out propaganda materials and coordinating the schedules of party speakers. Himmler himself became one of the most active of these speakers, delivering speeches laced with anti-Jewish rhetoric.[44]

From a distance, Himmler continued to both revere and fear the charismatic Adolf Hitler, whose star was on the rise and who had little time for the pale, bowlegged young man who worked so tirelessly on his behalf. Hitler did, however, acknowledge Himmler's efficiency by appointing him "Deputy *Reichsführer SS*" in 1927.[45] Thus, he gave birth to the life calling of which Himmler grew to be the most proud, that of building up and directing the SS. Under his guiding hand, it grew from under 300 members into a colossal, highly organized killing machine.

In his youth, Himmler practiced the Catholic faith with devotion, regularly attending mass and confession[46] until as an older teen he began to read anti-Semitic works. Perhaps it bolstered his flagging self-esteem to view himself as a true Aryan, a Germanic hero poised atop the pinnacle of racial superiority. In order to embrace this new identity and fully hate "inferior" races, he had to close himself off to faith in a merciful God. He accepted wholly the belief that the superior Nordic-Germanic race was engaged in a life and death struggle for survival against those inferior races. The Radical Right and its commitment to racial theory appealed to him so much that he chose to abandon his Christian faith in order to wholly identify with it.[47]

What, exactly, is an Aryan? In 1935, Himmler founded the German Ancestral Heritage Society to concern itself with that very question, as well as the study of Germanic genealogy. He hoped to create a scholarly base on which to prop up his racial theory indoctrination of SS men.[48] This fascination with Germanic origin and mythology with an anti-Christian twist, did not originate with the Nazis but had been in and out of vogue since the early 1800s.

The term "Aryan" comes from the Sanskrit word "*Arya,*" and simply refers to a member or descendant of the prehistoric people who spoke Indo-European languages. The Nazis used the word to define non-Jewish, Nordic Caucasians. According to Nazi racial theory, the Aryan race contains five sub-types: Nordic, Mediterranean, Dinaric, Alpine, and East Baltic; of these five, the Nordic race enjoys superiority. Since the Germans have a strong Nordic heritage, they constitute the Master Race.[49]

Himmler instructed German Ancestral Heritage Society scientists and scholars to spend their time researching, with a view to ultimately proving the validity of, some of the bizarre theories he personally embraced. One of these was Cosmic Ice Theory, which hypothesizes that suns and ice planets are at continual odds with one another in the universe, causing natural disasters.[50] Knowing most mainstream scientists found this theory bizarre and fantastical, he ordered the research to be kept secret.

Himmler was also greatly interested in the Myth of Tibet, which postulated that human life began and grew highly civilized in the mountains of Tibet, giving rise to the highly developed humans who populated the lost city of Atlantis. From this sophisticated Tibetan people sprang other elite peoples such as the Germanic Teutons and the Japanese Samurai. Himmler also shared a close relationship with an occult figure named Wiligut who claimed to channel the spirit of an ancient Gothic clan. The *Reichsführer SS* admired Wiligut so much that he made him an *SS Brigadierführer.* However, when Adolf Hitler expressed his disapproval, Himmler broke off the friendship.[51]

A pattern began to emerge in which Himmler became obsessed with wild theories, Hitler would disapprove, and Himmler, ever subservient, would then backpedal and step away from those theories, at least publicly. Yet privately Himmler pulled threads together from all these strange beliefs and practices to form his own religion. His new faith consisted of elements of Teutonic Cult, Volkish thought, astrology, astronomy, various theories of the earth's origin, German mythology, racial theory and pre-Christian Germanic religion.[52] He was free to use some of this in SS indoctrination, but he had to restrain himself and be careful lest, in Hitler's eyes, things got a little too weird.

Occult practices such as astrology, hypnosis, spiritualism, clairvoyance and telepathy fascinated Heinrich Himmler. In this he was not alone; such things exploded in popularity during the 1920s. After devouring books on the subject, he came to believe that it was possible to communicate with the souls of the dead. And to fill the void that his rejection of Christianity had left, he began to weave together a substitute religion, a mélange of the occult, racial theory and Germanic mythology.[53] Christianity, with its roots firmly grounded in Judaism and therefore hopelessly contaminated, became a special target of Himmler's hatred—a hatred equal to, if not stronger than, his hatred of the Jews and communists. Jews, Christians and communists were enemies of the Teutonic struggle to rise above all other sub-human races. Heinrich Himmler called Christianity "the destroyer of every nation," and "a perverse ideology that is alien to life."[54] Christian emphases on sexual morality and mercy clashed with Himmler's ever-evolving commitment to a new morality in which the propagation of the Germanic race took precedence over all else. In his amalgamated belief system, Aryan children must be born within or without marriage, and Jews must die without being shown pity.

Himmler's desire to revive the pagan Germanic religion in the Third Reich, to revere Norse gods like Woden, Thor and "Waralda the Ancient," and his fascination with Germanic Volkish subculture and myriad occult practices struck Adolf Hitler and other leading Nazis as insanely over-the-top, even harmful to the National Socialist cause.[55] Hitler believed in the racial superiority of Germans, but was not nearly as obsessed with Germanic heritage as Himmler. And although Hitler himself dabbled in astrology, his involvement paled in comparison to Himmler's outrageous beliefs. Furthermore, the Führer, while no believer in Christ, was astute enough to recognize that in the land of Charlemagne and Martin Luther, Christianity ran deep. Most Germans identified, at least nominally, as either Catholic or Lutheran. The last thing Hitler wanted was to alienate his people by publicly condemning their religious beliefs, however opposed to them he might be in private.[56]

To please his Führer, Himmler was forced to tone down his flaming displays of neo-paganism. He began calling himself *"gottgläubig,"* an ambiguous term that suggested belief in a higher power, whatever that power might be, and he declared publicly that members of the SS must also be so. To the public, he worked hard to give the impression that as an organization, the SS was tolerant of the Christian religion, and officially, SS men were free to attend church if they wished. Within the confidential confines of the SS organization, however, Himmler discouraged anything deeper than a superficial involvement with Christianity. Attending worship services was permitted, but absolutely not while wearing the SS uniform. SS men were strictly forbidden to take on leadership roles in their churches.[57]

Privately, Himmler adhered ever more strongly to his self-constructed religion. This belief system was continually shifting and evolving except for two constants: the goal of establishing the Greater Germanic Reich and the virulent loathing of Jews and Christians. In 1937 Himmler wrote: We live in an era of the ultimate conflict with Christianity. It is part of the mission of the SS to give the German people in the next half century the non-Christian ideological foundations on which to lead and shape their lives.[58]

Within the SS, he encouraged the Teutonic cult through indoctrination and the celebration of Yule and summer and winter solstices rather than Christian holidays.[59] Through the SS,

Himmler could live out at least some of his fantastical beliefs, especially that of the revival of an ancient Gothic clan whose pure blood would populate the coming Germanic Reich. The racial theory on which he based his belief in the superiority of the Germans was as mythical as Thor and Woden. Racial labels like "Nordic," "Dinaric," and "East Baltic" were concocted on the unfounded belief that prehistoric, primal races were traceable in modern times.[60] These beliefs gave purpose and meaning to his life. They became a fantasy world in which the awkward, weak-chinned youth disappeared and a Teutonic hero took his place.

Heinrich Himmler married a woman as thoroughly anti-Semitic as himself—Margarete Himmler, seven years his senior. They had a daughter together and gave her the ultra-Teutonic name of Gudrun. Himmler doted on his child. Nevertheless, in 1938 he threw off the last vestiges of the constraints of his Catholic upbringing and began an affair with his private secretary, Hedwig Potthast. The births of the two out-of-wedlock children she bore him coincided neatly with his command that SS men father children outside marriage, wherever and whenever possible.[61] Did his beliefs shape his lifestyle or did his lifestyle shape his beliefs?

Although Himmler was considered by most who knew him to have little personal charisma or warmth, both Margarete and Hedwig remained devoted to him to the end of his days.[62]

Heinrich Himmler

All along, we have been trying to pave the way to a new morality, only to be blocked at every turn.
To us it has always seemed obvious that
society's old-fashioned attitude toward unwed mothers and their children must undergo a profound change,
if only for the reason that children born out of wedlock in large numbers, if they are of pure blood,
are an asset to the Nation, helping to preserve it, and must be protected and supported.

—Rudolf Hess

CHAPTER 6

The name *Wienerwald* means "Vienna forest," and true to its name, the Lebensborn home lay nestled in the rolling green hills and woods of the Piesting Valley just southwest of the magnificent Austrian city. Founded in 1904 by Dr. Arthur Baer and Dr. Hugo Kraus, Jewish pulmonary specialists, it became world-renowned as a state-of-the-art sanitarium attracting tuberculosis patients from all over the world. Its most famous patient was, perhaps, the Czech author Franz Kafka, but neither he nor the wealthy Brazilian coffee plantation owners who convalesced there could have foreseen the sad fate of the brilliant and compassionate doctors who oversaw their treatment.

When Germany annexed Austria in 1938, the SS and Gestapo confiscated the sanitarium. Dr. Kraus, his life's work demolished, committed suicide. Dr. Baer was thrown into prison and forced to sign over the property after which he fled to Czechoslovakia and, stripped of the right to practice medicine as a Jew, died in poverty in 1941. Now the resort-like sanitarium, with its elegant, white-lacquered glass and marble furniture, Thonet dining chairs and arboretum housing exotic Mediterranean trees, belonged to the Nazis. They immediately set about stripping it of unnecessary frills so that it could function as a maternity home. Initially calling it Heim Ostmark, they soon returned to using its original name, Heim Wienerwald. It would go on to facilitate the births of 1,296 Aryan babies.

Lebensborn established other maternity homes in a similar fashion by forcibly ripping them out of Jewish or Christian hands. Heim Schwarzwald, which had been a Jewish-owned lung sanitarium in the Black Forest, became available after its Jewish patients were evicted and shipped off to concentration camps in 1942. Heim Taunus was a Catholic children's home until Lebensborn seized it. Heim Sonnenwiese housed handicapped people,[63] but when they were euthanized by the Nazi government, the building came up for grabs.

As a medical facility, Wienerwald was nearly perfect. Doctors Kraus and Baer had outfitted the building with a sanitary white tile and linoleum interior and a modern surgery room. It had an elevator and a dumbwaiter. A large wooden terrace on which TB patients had sunned themselves now held sunbathing expectant mothers and rows of bassinettes in which infants basked in the fresh air.

Elfriede couldn't keep from smiling the first time she entered Heim Wienerwald and gazed admiringly about. From the foyer she caught a whiff of strong disinfectant, but that was a good sign, surely. She thought of her mother and grandmother giving birth in dark, dusty farmhouses with the stench of manure wafting through the windows. Had she stayed in Silesia and married a country boy, she'd no doubt be doing the same. Well, thank God she hadn't. If she had to bear an unplanned and illegitimate child, this was the very best of circumstances in which to do so. How lucky she was to have stayed in the Reich Labor Service, to be bringing her child into the world in such a sparkling clean, modern facility!

She had come well prepared. In her purse she carried a doctor's report declaring her to be 100 percent Aryan. The Prague physician had only been able to pronounce her so after physically examining her and viewing copies of her ancestral records, which fortunately, Paul Kober had obligingly sent when she explained she needed them for advancement in the Reich Labor Service. Elfriede sailed through the psychological testing. Her heart and kidneys passed muster. The heart murmur that had served as her alibi for medical leave was judged either non-existent or extremely minor and inconsequential. Next, she'd filled out an extensive, even embarrassingly personal questionnaire and sent Lebensborn full-body photographs of herself. Questions about her extended family's health required answering in as much detail as possible, as well as inquiries about medical insurance and political party affiliation. Did she foresee marrying the baby's father? She had had to write *No*. If not, why not? She had confined her answer to a succinct two words: *Already married*.

Her phony story about Kurt Huebler had to stop here. There was no way she could ever perpetuate the ruse by obtaining his family documents. She prepared to offer up an apologetic explanation for her lie, to get on her knees and beg if she must. But to her astonishment, when on the entrance form she listed *SS Hauptscharführer* Kurt Novak as her baby's father and handed over his papers, no one made a peep. No mention was made of the phone call from her camp group leader. It then occurred to my mother that this organization prided itself on secret-keeping and concealing inconvenient truths. It seemed lies were so much a part of Lebensborn's infrastructure that her own fib hardly raised eyebrows.

"Now, Frau Elfriede," said the home director, SS Captain Norbert Schwab, a man chosen for his devotion to Nazi ideology as much as for his medical training,[64] "you qualify for Lebensborn to subsidize your stay here with a one-time sum of 400 *Reichsmark*. Beyond that, we will bill your insurance through the Reich Labor Service for all birthing and medical expenses, and the father of your child for the cost of room and board."

"Yes, I understand that," she replied. "But I'm not 'Frau Elfriede.' I'm a *Fräulein*. Unmarried."

"Of course you are. But in the Lebensborn homes, all women are addressed as "*Frau*" so as to avoid any discrimination between the married and the unmarried. We believe all children of good blood are valuable, not only those who are born in wedlock. And we use no last names here—only first names—to preserve anonymity."

A nurse showed her to her room, which contained two narrow beds, each with its own nightstand and clothes cupboard. The facilities weren't nearly as luxurious as she'd been led to believe although the place was faultlessly clean. Elfriede liked that. It didn't take her long to unpack; the Lebensborn rules had stipulated she was only allowed to bring underclothing, two or three dresses, slippers and one pair of shoes along with shoe cleaning materials, soap, shampoo, insurance papers and a set of baby clothes. Hoping her yet-to-be-met roommate didn't snore, Elfriede sat down on her bed and read through the daily schedule and list of rules by which she must now abide. For the duration of her stay, her life would be broken up into precise increments: room cleaning from

6:00 to 6:30 AM, coffee from 6:30 to 7:00, bathing from 7:00 to 8:00, and so on, until the lights were turned out at 9:00 PM. Once her baby arrived, a routine of breastfeeding and diaper changing would ensue. The Spartan accommodations and the regimented lifestyle were not so different from her life in the Reich Labor Service, and Elfriede had always thrived in such an environment. She only wondered whether she might not get bored with so little actual physical work to do, just sitting around twiddling her thumbs, waiting for the baby.

Did it occur to my mother as she settled into Heim Wienerwald that the organization that presented itself to her as a compassionate friend in need would have kicked her to the curb if she, or the man who fathered me, had shown even the slightest evidence of "impure" non-Aryan blood, or if her physical examination or questionnaire had turned up any trace of a hereditary illness, even so much as an aunt or an uncle with diabetes or a tendency toward severe depression? As a single mother, she'd been scrutinized extra carefully since there was a good chance Lebensborn would assume guardianship of her baby. Lebensborn portrayed itself as a charitable organization offering a safety net and dignity to unwed mothers who were rejected by society. Yet this was no charity. It was a program with a political agenda in which pure-blooded German babies were intended to serve as the building blocks of the future in Hitler's Thousand Year Reich.[65] Lebensborn was the means through which the Nazi government would gain influence in those children's lives in order to mold them into the Reich's future leaders, soldiers, workers and mothers.

In an undated letter, Heinrich Himmler wrote to General Wilhelm Keitel, head of the Wehrmacht:

> *In my opinion, we cannot afford to allow our women and girls of valuable blood to undergo abortion and sacrifice their roles as mothers of the German nation...If we can thwart such women from obtaining abortions, we bestow on the Third Reich each year more than 600,000 children who would otherwise not have been born. This means that in eighteen to twenty years' time, each year 200 more regiments will march. The strength of these soldiers and workers will contribute considerably to ensure the stability and expansion of a greater Germany. For these*

reasons, I founded the Lebensborn program in 1936. Lebensborn leads the fight against abortion by providing homes, scattered around German territory, in which pure-blooded German mothers can wait in peace for the hour in which they will serve their people.[66]

Men were dying on the battlefield, but if cradles could outnumber coffins, this loss could be mitigated. Abortion was opposed, not because it took the lives of helpless unborn babies, but because it prevented those babies from shoring up the flagging birthrate and filling Germany's cradles. Those cradles weren't to be filled with just anyone, however. In *Mein Kampf*, Adolf Hitler wrote:

> *The state must put the subject of race at the very center of life. It must take care to keep race pure. It must pronounce the child a valuable commodity to its people. It must see to it that only the healthy bear children, because it is a shame to reproduce one's own illnesses and deficiencies, bringing them into the world along with children. It is therefore a great honor to do away with such things.*[67]

And do away with them, Hitler certainly had. Having already been sterilizing those it considered unfit to reproduce since 1933, between September 1939 and August 1941 the Nazi government implemented a widespread program for the "mercy killing" of those German citizens afflicted with incurable conditions. Over 70,000 people were put to death in six psychiatric hospitals around Germany. The mentally ill, mentally retarded, and anyone with severe enough disabilities or deformities to need institutionalization or ongoing medical care that would not lead to healing, was judged by Adolf Hitler as not worthy of life. Especially in wartime, such people consumed scarce food supplies and took up much-needed space in hospitals and care facilities—space badly needed for wounded soldiers.

Deformed and retarded children were secretly killed by injections of phenol, then recorded as having died of pneumonia, presumably for the benefit of a wider society not yet ready to accept the "progressive ideas" of its National Socialist government.

Adolescents and adults were murdered by gassing. Even institutionalized, elderly patients suffering from no more than ordinary age-related dementia were killed. The families were given death certificates listing false causes of death. Although the official euthanasia program ended in 1941, many institutions continued on with the killing until Germany's defeat in 1945. The true number of euthanized victims may never be known.

It is doubtful that my mother gave even the slightest thought to such inconveniently sobering facts as she perused the Lebensborn pamphlets and rule sheets. After all, she had come of age in an era of sweeping National Socialist propaganda about the superiority of the German *Volk*. Innumerable times, she had heard speeches, seen posters, learned in the classroom and read in news magazines that the Germans were in danger of dying out, and that inferior races, especially Jews, were the enemy of her people's survival.

She had passed the racial test with flying colors and the fact that Kurt Novak had been accepted on the basis of racial purity as a member of the SS made examination of his ancestral records a mere formality. According to the brochure in her hand, Elfriede was one of only 30 women in 100 to be accepted into this elite program, through which elite children would enter the world. She read on:

> *Lebensborn will assume guardianship of children born out of wedlock. This is the best way to insure that the child has the best possible upbringing, whether the child stays with its mother or is fostered with another family...however, believing it is best for a child to be raised in its own family, Lebensborn encourages the parents of an illegitimate child to marry.*[68]

"No chance of that," she whispered sadly. At least Kurt had never misled her.

With relief, Elfriede slipped out of her too-tight Labor Service uniform. As she grew, the home would have to provide her with shapeless, smock-like garments to wear, for she had brought nothing like that. For now, one of the casual dresses she had brought along would do.

Now officially part of the Lebensborn family, she would live in anonymous community with others like herself for the next several months. Only Kurt and the Labor Service camp group leader knew of her exact whereabouts. If Kurt wanted to visit her, which she doubted, he wouldn't be allowed. Only the married women's husbands were allowed to stop by, but even they were required to make appointments in advance and confine their brief visits to a public sitting room.[69]

Elfriede was required to share light housekeeping chores such as dusting or folding linens with her fellow boarders, eat with them at a large dining table, forego the wearing of lipstick and nail polish and even plucking her eyebrows.[70] She must attend the required political indoctrination sessions and, together with her fellow expectant mothers, gather round the radio to listen to broadcasts of Adolf Hitler's and Joseph Goebbels' speeches, always accompanied by triumphant music and trumpeted fanfares. Indoctrination sessions called "Philosophical Education" took place three times per week. They included readings by the home director of portions of *Mein Kampf*, speeches on National Socialist ideology, lessons on German history from a Nazi perspective and lectures on the subject of racial theory.[71] These sessions could have left little doubt in my mother's mind about the political nature and agenda of Lebensborn. In my opinion, they had a deep and lasting, if repressed, influence on her. She came to regard herself as a racially superior woman giving birth to an elite child in an elite institution. Within her, this exalted self-view later warred with a deep sense of shame and guilt for having broken long-established moral codes and for having so closely allied herself with the despised Nazis.

Dr. Schwab ran the home with strict efficiency and didn't hesitate to dismiss a boarder for failure to adhere to National Socialist principles. He once took a mother to task for speaking too freely to the other women about things she had seen in the East, such as mass murder of the Jews by the SS.[72] Schwab was offended by her loose tongue, believing her words to be unsuitable subject matter in a home filled with emotionally vulnerable expectant mothers.

Wienerwald, like the other Lebensborn homes, was stark white and clinical. But Elfriede and the other expectant mothers found a cozy refuge in the dayroom where they read novels, played games and chattered together against a backdrop of classical music on the radio. In the evenings, they held sing-alongs together with the staff. If the weather was pleasant, they strolled along the winding pathways of the sprawling grounds. It suited Elfriede that they were encouraged not to divulge their last names or too-personal information to one another. Like most of the single mothers who desired to give birth in secret, she had chosen a Lebensborn home located as far away as reasonably possible from her hometown. Because the women had no friends in the vicinity, loneliness and shared circumstances drew them together. Mostly they confided in each other their fears of going through childbirth. What would it be like? None of them were allowed into the birthing section of the home, and most of the women who had already given birth had departed the home soon after. Those who lingered for one reason or other were kept to a separate schedule and were seen only at mealtimes during which no one wanted to divulge, let alone listen to, the gruesome details of childbirth.[73] Now and then an expectant mother caught a glimpse of the head groundskeeper carrying away a stillborn child in order to bury it somewhere on the property in an unmarked grave. The sight never failed to elicit a shudder.

The women wondered if they would be good mothers, and if breastfeeding was as easy as it looked. Yet they had little opportunity to observe new mothers caring for their babies in a natural rhythm because Lebensborn separated the infants, keeping them in a nursery and only allowing their mothers access to feed and change them according to a strict schedule. Those boarders who had come with older offspring relinquished temporary custody of those children to kindergarten teachers who oversaw them 24 hours per day. Children, mothers and staff all dined in separate rooms.[74]

Meals were simple but hearty, consisting of meat, potatoes, fish, eggs, milk, butter and bread. There were plenty of fresh vegetables. Real coffee was made available to Lebensborn homes even after the rest of the population couldn't get its hands on any. Himmler considered the nourishment of his elite mothers a matter of highest priority, and with the Reich Finance Ministry subsidizing Lebensborn, no expense was spared to provide the most nourishing of fare. Himmler took great personal interest in the women's diets, insisting they be given whole grain bread and doses of cod-liver oil, giving serious consideration to their complaints about too much cabbage causing colic in their breast-feeding babies, and personally requesting that the homes be sure to serve the women fiber-rich oatmeal for breakfast.[75]

Himmler also took a voyeuristic interest in the Lebensborn mothers' ability to bear future children for the Reich. From the home directors, he requested information on each woman's menstrual history in order to try to calculate how many childbearing years remained to her.[76] By keeping track of the women after they left the Lebensborn homes, he intended to keep them within reach for the coming day, after a total German victory, when his more controversial ideas about increasing the population might be safely realized.

The fact that Lebensborn never became an official breeding program does not mean that Heinrich Himmler and other Nazi racial theorists did not toy with the idea and even throw around the term "breeding." Medical professor Dr. Martin Staemmler wrote in 1934:

> *We want to cultivate the breeding of our race...Breeding requires selection, judging between good and bad, valuable and valueless, acceptance and rejection. We must set up standards by which to judge, in order to reach our breeding goals. The goal is the Nordic human being. This doesn't necessarily mean blond-haired, blue-eyed, tall and lean. It's more about inner qualities. Our goal is to produce warlike heroes—methodical, sensible, levelheaded, energetic and enterprising. Our goal is the inner qualities of honesty, sincerity—pure, Germanic humans....*
>
> *We openly acknowledge that the breeding of human beings is fundamentally more significant than the most meticulous breeding of house pets, and because of this we approach the task with all due reverence and a sense of responsibility for our people.*[77]

Himmler, who suffered from painful stomach cramps, found relief at the hands of a Finnish practitioner of Tibetan medicine named Felix Kersten. Kersten successfully used massage to relieve Himmler's pain. Relaxed under his trusted doctor's hands, Himmler waxed eloquent about his ambitions for the Greater Germanic Reich and his views on population politics. Kersten massaged away, listening carefully to every detail. According to the doctor, Himmler expressed his firm belief that infertile marriages were of no value and that if he had his way, the government would force such couples to divorce and try again with new partners.[78] Too few people, in his opinion, were taking advantage of the 1938 law that allowed divorce on the grounds of infertility.

"In three hundred or five hundred years," Kersten quotes Himmler as saying, "no one will ask whether Miss Müller or Miss Schulze is happy or not, for it will be of no consequence. What will matter is whether or not a superior race exists that is able to secure the ability of its heirs to govern forever. We must take a decisive step in that direction, even if it means incurring the wrath of the Church."[79]

For this reason, Kersten claims, Himmler confided in him that he believed the very nature of marriage needed a massive overhaul, and that bigamy was the best option for raising the German birthrate: "I personally am of the opinion that our development as a society is leading us to break with monogamy. The current form of marriage is a satanic work of the Catholic Church."[80]

Bigamy wouldn't be legal for everybody, of course. At least, not in the beginning. Once Germany emerged from the war triumphant, only those men who had distinguished themselves by service to the Reich would earn the right to take an additional wife. Himmler thought that a little healthy competition between wives could be a good thing; it would keep women from growing lazy or slovenly. It was unrealistic to expect a man to spend his whole life with just one woman. And of course, with two wives, each man could father twice as many children.[81] Himmler claimed that Hitler agreed with his views on the subject especially since so much land was opening up in the East and so many German men were dying in battle. Hitler's private secretary, Martin Bormann, recorded the Führer as saying, "The women who are left alone after the war will not receive their children from the Holy Spirit, but from available German men. Increased reproduction by each individual German man is the obvious solution."[82] However, Hitler wanted to wait until after the war to implement the changes. If the first experiment with bigamy succeeded then perhaps it would become the norm for everyone.[83]

Heinrich Himmler and Lebensborn head Dr. Gregor Ebner toyed with the idea of eventually establishing a registry where single men and women could be connected with "reproduction helpers," matched according to their racial and genetic profiles in order to produce children. In Himmler's mind, however, such a program would be entered into purely voluntarily, a solution at last for the lonely hearts who kept on writing to Lebensborn Central Administration as if it were a matchmaking service. But, hyper-aware of the swirling rumors about Lebensborn being a breeding program and having no wish to feed them, Himmler never took steps to set up such a registry. Like his other plans, it would have to wait.[84] When Nazi Germany had won the war and solidified its hold on all of Europe, popular approval or disapproval would no longer matter.

Dr. Leonardo Conti, the Reich Health Leader, wrote to Himmler in 1942:

> *We must increase the fruitfulness of existing marriages... here the use of artificial insemination could be important, even within marriage—using the sperm of another man, or impregnating a wife's friend with her husband's sperm, even choosing pairings rather than letting people choose their own partners.*[85]

Conti's suggestion was radical considering that artificial insemination was used only with farm animals at the time.

Even an enthusiastic Himmler recognized that such ideas were bound to offend the average German. Thus, he urged Conti to keep his ideas to himself for the time being. The time was not yet ripe for such sweeping moral changes,[86] but that time was surely approaching. Radical ideas were dreamed up, bounced around, discussed and envisioned as eventual reality, but were never actually implemented during the years of National Socialist rule. However, as much as Himmler might have liked to see them put into practice, they remained wild, utopian visions for a more "enlightened" time.

Along with her fellow boarders, Elfriede took courses in the care of infants, cooking and housekeeping, childrearing, child development, and sewing. This curriculum left her in little doubt that, in Nazi Germany, the ideal role of a woman was to marry, bear many children and raise them in a sparkling clean home complete with handsome SS husband—something she would have happily done if she could. As things stood, she regularly had to choke down her envy of the few single mothers who had confided in her that they were planning to marry their babies' fathers. The lucky ones, engaged to the SS fathers of their babies, got to take a special "bride course" without the diploma of which they would be unable to obtain a marriage certificate.[87]

But my mother was far from being the only expectant mother in Heim Wienerwald with broken dreams. A few of her companions in pregnancy had been so desperately lonely they had persuaded men to sleep with them in hopes of conceiving a child. Longing for purpose and companionship, they hoped against hope to be able to keep and raise their babies despite the fact that the fathers remained distant and disinterested. Between 1941 and 1942, nearly 65 percent of Lebensborn mothers were single and 30 percent of their babies' fathers were already married to someone else. A few men stubbornly refused to acknowledge paternity and had to be dragged into court, but only by those women brave enough and with enough financial means to do so.[88]

In that regard, at least, Kurt Novak had been more than cooperative. He earned a decent salary and with a little financial sleight of hand, he could keep Emma from noticing the disappearance of the *Reichsmark* needed for Elfriede's room and board. As a member of the SS, he was already required to contribute a small portion of his salary each month to the funding of Lebensborn. The fees for his mistress's room and board could easily be disguised as part of that. Elfriede wasn't sure whether he would continue to support her and the baby beyond her stay in Heim Wienerwald. Too late, she realized they hadn't really discussed it.

If Kurt experienced any twinges of guilt, any discomfort over his girlfriend's predicament, he had only to remember that

Heinrich Himmler had in his October 28, 1939 mandate, in which he'd encouraged the SS and police to father illegitimate children, stated that, "SS men need not fear these children won't be cared for."[89] It put Novak's mind at ease to know that the entire SS organization itself, with Himmler at its head, would assume the role of godfather and guardian to Elfriede's child.

In all Lebensborn homes, the boarders were encouraged to observe certain holidays that reflected Himmler's neo-pagan beliefs. Besides Mother's Day, so important to National Socialist population politics, summer and winter solstices were celebrated in June and December. Yule was Himmler's preferred substitute for the Christian Christmas. April 20 was Hitler's birthday. November 9 was the anniversary of the 1923 Putsch with which Hitler tried to topple the Bavarian government, the failure of which ended up working to his advantage by sending him, martyr-like, to prison and gaining him publicity. For each of these occasions, coffee and cake and special ceremonies were in order.[90]

As the months dragged on and Elfriede's belly grew, her restful interlude was disturbed by discord and discontent. All around her, boarders complained about gossiping nurses who stirred up dissention amongst the pregnant women and scolded them harshly for the slightest rule infractions.[91] Elfriede herself found the nurses cold and unyielding, and dealt with them only when absolutely necessary, preferring instead to enjoy the company of her fellow expectant mothers.

Lebensborn's ethos preached equality between the mothers. They all went by "*Frau*" and greeted one another with "*Heil Hitler!*" Yet wives of high ranking SS officers were allowed their own rooms while single women had to share. Married women were excused from chores. Some of them made a point of announcing loudly that they, unlike so many others in the home, had husbands, and if those husbands happened to be nearby, visitation rules were bent so the couples could spend more time together. These officers' wives had earlier shunned Lebensborn to avoid scandalous association with unwed mothers. Now, with the war's progression, they flocked eagerly to the homes where food was plentiful and the rural settings were unlikely to be targets of air raids. Their husbands were far away. Many of them had other children to care for, and the round-the-clock childcare in the Lebensborn kindergartens allowed them to enjoy the traditional seven days of bed rest after giving birth. But their open disdain for and refusal to mingle with the single mothers upset the atmosphere in the homes.[92] And as far as the unwed in Heim Wienerwald were concerned, the staff openly showed preference to the mistresses of high-ranking officers, proving to Elfriede that she had guessed rightly that her lie about Kurt Huebler would work to her advantage in her quest for permission to arrive at the crowded maternity home.

Some boarders hated the institutional atmosphere in Heim Wienerwald; others complained about this or that grumpy nurse. And it didn't take superior powers of observation to notice that tension was rife between the "blue" nurses and the "brown" nurses, forced to work together in close proximity but miles apart with regard to ideology. The brown nurses, those trained in National Socialist institutions, made up the vast majority of nursing staff in Lebensborn homes. Thoroughly steeped in Nazi ideology, they had a reputation of being unsympathetic, more focused on political and racial ideals than on the needs of the individuals they cared for. The blue nurses were trained in religious schools and mentally and emotionally connected to either the Lutheran or Catholic Church. In the SS and Lebensborn's starkly anti-Christian atmosphere, blue nurses were treated as inferior and unwanted, while the brown nurses threw their weight around, treating their blue colleagues as inferior, tossing them cutting remarks and looks of disdain. This undisguised warfare created feelings of unease among the vulnerable expectant mothers who looked to the nurses for comfort and reassurance. And many of the nurses, brown and blue alike, were young and genuinely shocked by the high volume of illegitimate births. Ironically, even the National Socialist Nurses' Association fired nurses who became pregnant out of wedlock.[93]

As Elfriede relaxed in the day room or strolled the lush grounds, she pondered the news she'd read in a recent letter from her sister Lisbeth, the only family member to whom she'd confided her circumstances. Not even Lisbeth knew Elfriede's exact location. Letters couldn't be sent directly to her at Pernitz; to preserve absolute secrecy they had to be routed through false addresses in Berlin, Münich or Vienna.[94] Unmarried Lisbeth had given birth to a daughter two years before. Elfriede wished her sister was on hand to answer her questions about childbirth and advise her on child care. The two had shared so much during their growing up years; it didn't seem right to be awaiting such a momentous event without Lisbeth close by.

Did my mother ever receive a letter from my father, perhaps exhorting her to have courage or assuring her of financial support? Did he put his SS training on child-naming to use by suggesting possibilities to her? Or was there a vacuous silence in which all contact with him disappeared forever? The latter seems more likely for while my mother, now unwieldy and bulky, awaited my arrival in the summer of 1942 amid the pastoral setting of the Vienna woods, Kurt Novak was engulfed in the conflagration that was just then consuming Prague.

Heim Wienerwald

Conquer and die—only we men can do that.
But there is also a women's conquest: their achievement is to
replace the soldiers who have died
in the front lines on the battlefield.
In other words, the birthrate of children of valuable blood
must not decline, as it has during previous wars,
but must rise to a number
that surpasses the loss of manpower.
We must take care that our future, greater living space
is filled up with our people and stays that way.

—Rudolf Hess

CHAPTER 7

Even though, on the surface, life in the city appeared to flow smoothly on, Prague harbored a restless undercurrent of resistance. A hodge-podge of socialist, Catholic, Protestant, communist and military groups, each with its own particular slant, worked separately to undermine German rule. They organized boycotts of German products, unleashed firebombs on buildings occupied by Germans, and cut telephone lines and railway brakes.[95] These subversive acts became more frequent in the fall of 1941, even as Kurt and Elfriede carried on their affair. It was in response to these rumblings that Hitler had sent SS General Reinhard Heydrich to assume the role of *Reichsprotektor* over the Protectorate. If anyone was capable of effectively clamping down on resistance activities, it was this cold and ruthless architect of death.

In late May of 1942, under the direction of the Czechoslovakian government in exile, a group of British-trained Czech soldiers parachuted into their homeland's countryside. Among them were two men, one Czech and one Slovak, who had come for the express purpose of assassinating Heydrich. Tipped off to his scheduled movements, they ambushed the general's car as it slowed down at a curve, throwing a grenade into it. Immediately after the attack, a state of emergency was declared. Prague ground to a halt. All traffic was stopped. Kurt Novak, along with over 20,000 other SS and Army men, fanned out through the city to search for the perpetrators, beating on doors with rifle butts, rousting people from slumber, tearing through their belongings and searching under beds. They came up empty-handed.[96]

It took Heydrich nine days to die of his infected wounds. Even before the *Reichsprotektor's* soul left his body, Hitler ordered the retaliatory execution of 10,000 Czechs.

After Heydrich's funeral on June 9, still having turned up no clues as to who had carried out the assassination, the police surrounded a small mining village called Lidice just northwest of Prague, where the people were suspected of aiding and harboring resistance fighters. They shot all the men, sent all the women to the concentration camp Ravensbrück in Germany, and shipped most of the children off to be murdered at the death camp Chelmno in Poland. A handful of these children, judged to have Aryan features, were sent to Lebensborn children's homes in order to be "Germanized." The village of Lidice was burnt to the ground.[97]

Was my father personally involved in this gruesome slaughter? It is more than possible. The policemen who destroyed Lidice were deployed from Prague. Certainly Kurt Novak's energies were diverted to the massive manhunt that continued to dominate the city after Heydrich's assassination. Finally in mid-June, a young boy broke under torture and revealed the assassins' whereabouts; they were hiding with two other resistance fighters in the basement of an Orthodox church in the center of Prague. The SS and police, after failing to dislodge them by storming the building, using tear gas and trying to drown them with fire hoses, finally knocked down a wall and launched grenades. All four men inside died, some by suicide.[98]

Reinhard Heydrich's death resulted in 1,331 executions and 3,000 Jews being transported from Prague to the death camp Majdanek, all in the name of revenge.[99] Did Kurt, so busy conducting searches and arresting people, pause to remember the woman awaiting his child 150 miles away? Did Elfriede comprehend the chaotic depths to which Prague had plunged and the even more sinister turn her erstwhile lover's career had taken? For his part, Kurt was secure in the knowledge that Lebensborn was 100 percent committed to keeping his identity as the father of Elfriede's baby a secret. Elfriede, confined in Heim Wienerwald and fed a steady diet of Nazi propaganda, heard only Hitler's lavish praise of Heydrich in a speech delivered at the funeral in Berlin.[100] The news carried reports of a previous funeral for Heydrich held at Hradĉany in Prague. Thousands of SS men lined the road leading up to the castle, holding torches aloft. Perhaps the father of her child stood among them.

I was born during a summer of death in a murderous year. Heydrich's assassination and its brutal aftermath were only one small thread in the fabric of 1942, woven by Nazi leadership in pursuit of their goal of a Jew-free, Greater Germanic Reich. After watching Jews being shot to death en masse at Minsk in 1941, Himmler had concluded that shooting was not an efficient method for mass murder. Furthermore, killing at close range with guns was psychologically harrowing for the killers. That spring, Heinrich Himmler held a series of secret meetings with Reinhard Heydrich. With Hitler's blessing, the two cohorts set in motion a plan to exterminate Jews on a grander scale than ever before, using poisonous gas. The General Government, a vast area under German control carved out of eastern Poland, contained a dense population of Jews. It had recently come under the direct control of Himmler, whose zeal and enthusiasm in killing them surpassed even that of Hitler. The Führer would have been content to wait until after he'd conquered all of Europe to do so.[101] Heydrich's sudden, untimely demise hardly slowed Himmler down. After mourning his comrade, the *Reichsführer SS* returned to the task with renewed determination and meticulous attention to detail.

In May and June of 1942, the largest death camp of all, Treblinka, was constructed in northeastern Poland where it joined the likes of Chelmno, Belzec, Majdanek and Auschwitz-Birkenau which were already gassing Jews efficiently and in unprecedented numbers. That same summer saw the establishment of another death camp called Sobibor. Beginning in July and lasting until November, a total of 53 transports carrying 1,000 Jews each rolled eastward from France to Auschwitz-Birkenau, where they were murdered upon arrival. The very first transport of Jews from the German Reich arrived at Auschwitz-Birkenau on July 18. These Jews had been rounded up in Vienna, just 25 miles from where my mother awaited my birth at Pernitz. Still, it wasn't enough for Himmler. One month before my birth, he requested one train per day, carrying 5,000 Jews, to leave the Warsaw ghetto for

Treblinka along with two trains from the Lublin ghetto to Belzec every week.[102]

Around the same time, he wanted to see for himself the effects of his handiwork so he paid a visit to Auschwitz-Birkenau, where he personally observed Jews being gassed. That night he dined with colleagues, drinking wine and casually socializing.[103] To Himmler's way of thinking, these murderous tasks were unpleasant but necessary in order to found the expansive Aryan Reich of which he and Adolf Hitler dreamed. He longed to unite all the Germanic peoples under Hitler—the ethnic Germans scattered around Europe, such as the Sudetens and Tyroleans as well as the Scandinavians, Flemish and Dutch.[104] In 1942, he succeeded in creating a smooth-running system of mass murder meant to empty the eastern territories and make room for the Germanic peoples with which he hoped to populate them. As far as Himmler was concerned, I and the other 1,296 babies born at Heim Wienerwald were meant to be among those Germanic colonists.

On August 12, my arrival was announced. My name, weight and length were reported at the expectant mothers' dinner table in Heim Wienerwald, eliciting a hearty round of applause. The birth had been difficult, for my head was unusually large. Even as my mother struggled to bring me into the world, something called the *August Aktion* was just getting into gear in which half the population of the Ukrainian city of Lviv, all Jews, were arrested and sent to Belzec to be massacred. Around the same time, Himmler officially ordered the SS to hunt down Jews under the guise of rooting out partisans whom he referred to as "bandits."[105]

In the midst of all this death, Himmler, just three days after my birth, took a little time off to encourage life—German life. On August 15, he decreed that any young men on the battlefield, single or married, who had not yet fathered a child would henceforth be called home in order to do so.[106]

My fifth day of life coincided with Himmler, whose headquarters were in the Ukraine that summer, making a tour of forced labor camps in the East. Immediately afterward, he flew to northern and western Germany to inspect air raid damage inflicted by the Allies.[107] The *Reichsführer* SS was riding high, gaining power, feeling a sense of accomplishment that was hardly diminished by the Allied landing in North Africa. He had long since taken over the job of developing and expanding the entire system of concentration camps. He implemented the use of triangle badges: green for criminals, red for political prisoners, black or brown for Gypsies, pink for homosexuals, purple for Jehovah's Witnesses to name but a few. Jews, of course, wore a yellow badge and star. By the summer of my birth, the camps were bursting at the seams.

It was for the charismatic, impassioned Hitler to be the public face of Nazism in Germany and the world, pounding the podium and whipping up the crowd's emotions. Heinrich Himmler, lacking in persuasive charm, contented himself to work behind the scenes directing those who operated the machinery of death, pulling the strings of the killer marionette. Doggedly he pursued his goal of wiping out all of European Jewry by the end of the year. Yet despite attacking the task with ever-increasing gusto, by autumn even he was forced to admit that the Reich's dire shortage of man power meant scaling back on his plans.[108] Among the Jews marked for annihilation were skilled workers who could prove valuable to the German war effort. For the time being, Himmler would have to spare them.

> *Just as all we Germans are privileged to be alive at such a time and do not think of ourselves as individuals but rather as part of the German Nation, so a German mother must lay no claim to her children. She has the great and sacred duty to raise her children to meet the demands of the State; what a lofty purpose for our German mothers!*[109]

So National Socialist activist Johanna Scholz was quoted as saying in 1936. According to Himmler, who stated over and over again that a child's value and worth had nothing to do with whether it was born in or out of wedlock but rather had everything to do with its pure Aryan blood, I deserved the best of all possible care for I was a gift to the German Nation. A thorough examination at birth showed me to be in strapping health. I was immediately separated from my mother, taken to Heim Wienerwald's nursery and placed under the care of the blue and brown nurses. From now on, I would see my mother only at intervals of three to four hours, five times per day, to breastfeed and have a diaper change. By Himmler's express order, breastfeeding was required for at least 10 weeks.[110] My diapers were changed an extravagant six times per day, one time more than in ordinary hospitals of that time.[111] I napped in the fresh summer air on a sunny veranda and was bathed regularly and thoroughly.

The only hiccup in those pleasant post-natal days occurred three weeks after my birth. On the night of September 4, Soviet *Petlyakov Pe-8s* flew a bombing mission over Vienna, prompting the Heim Wienerwald administration to roust the expectant and nursing mothers from their sleep and herd them to the cellar. The place was dark, cavernous and steamy from the boilers. Sweating and clutching me tightly to her breast, Elfriede began to feel claustrophobic. She struggled for breath.

"I'm going upstairs," she gasped to the young mother beside her. "If I'm going to die, it might as well be up there as down here in this hell-hole." Through the dark stairwell she carried me up to fresh air and was soon vindicated, for no bombs fell on Pernitz that night. The raid on Vienna was an isolated incident, not to be repeated until 1944.

Bombing scare aside, Elfriede enjoyed a speedy recovery, being allowed to turn over most of my round-the-clock care to the nurses. She ate and slept well and relaxed in the spa-like atmosphere, where locals were hired to cook and do laundry and prisoners of war from places like Poland, France, Holland, Czechoslovakia and Belgium performed the heavier chores such as maintenance, grounds keeping and renovations.[112] It was a veritable life of luxury for a girl who had worked hard her whole existence. In Heim Wienerwald, she felt elite. She felt valued. My birth was proof of her high status in the National Socialist realm and the very fact that she'd been accepted by Lebensborn and that I was judged to be a perfect specimen of Aryan flesh and blood confirmed it.

She couldn't know then that Lebensborn had exaggerated when it claimed that only 30 percent of applicants were accepted into its homes. Such false statistics were mere flattery, adding to the aura of the organization's "eliteness." The real numbers were higher, somewhere between 44 and 75 percent, since National Socialist desperation to increase the birthrate blurred the lines and allowed for many more women to enter than the organization admitted to.[113] The ideal Lebensborn mother was, of course, tall, blond-haired and blue-eyed, but smaller women with hazel or brown eyes and hair, like Elfriede, made up the majority of the women who gave birth in Lebensborn homes. Even the occasional woman with unusually dark skin or eyes could be admitted provided she could prove pure Aryan ancestry through family records.[114]

After my birth, Elfriede was relieved to learn that a disconcerting rumor she'd heard about Lebensborn wasn't true. The organization would not steal her child and hand it over without her permission to be raised in an intact SS family. She had a little time at least. Decisions had to be made, but not immediately. She could stay in the home for as long as six months if necessary, while pondering whether to keep me or relinquish me for adoption. Yet she was growing restless, eager to get out from under Heim Weinerwald's strict confines.

I'd like to think my mother fell in love with me immediately, as did many Lebensborn mothers once they held their newborns in their arms. Many of them defied society's disapproval and took their babies home, even to disapproving parents. The truth is, I don't know. Love me she might, but Elfriede was in no position to take me out of Heim Wienerwald to live with her. She planned to return as quickly as possible to the communal barracks atmosphere of the Reich Labor Service, a life in which there was absolutely no room for a baby.

If my mother had wanted to take me to live with her somewhere, find a male guardian for me outside of Lebensborn and legally pursue Kurt Novak for financial support, she would have to go through the German civil authorities. Lebensborn, in order to protect the fathers' privacy, tried to hinder such a step by asking the mothers to sign over guardianship of their children to itself. Many unwed mothers signed this document before their children's birth. In this way, Lebensborn assumed guardianship of fully half of the children born within its homes. Those women who refused were required to come up with a viable alternative, and most of them signed over guardianship to their fathers or fiancés.[115] As Elfriede had neither fiancé nor trustworthy father, she signed me over to Lebensborn. The organization would see to it that I had a proper upbringing, whether she chose to keep me or not. In this way the SS, through Lebensborn, was all set to legally secure influence over me. If Elfriede took me home and raised me herself, Lebensborn would hinder any attempt by her to seek child support from Kurt through the regular civil authorities. Instead, the organization would pressure Kurt to contribute to my support, albeit secretly, by adding to what he was already compelled to contribute through the SS. Lebensborn would try to keep tabs on us to make sure I was being raised in a clean, orderly and disciplined household. They would find work for my mother so that I could be well provided for. Later, when I was ready to begin school, it would provide me with a certificate of Aryan descent to ensure my enrollment and also aid in my being accepted into the Hitler Youth, entering university, and eventually joining the SS.[116]

If Elfriede married, Lebensborn would scrutinize her intended spouse to make sure he was a dedicated member of the Nazi party and able to adequately support us. Such a scenario was ideal for I would cease to be a financial burden for which the SS was responsible, yet would still be dependent upon it for my legal identification and the documents necessary to move forward in life. If my mother gave me up for adoption, Lebensborn would do its best to find me an SS family in which I was guaranteed to be raised "in the spirit of National Socialism."[117]

Among my tiny contemporaries, however, there were those to whom such options would never be made available.

Lebensborn babies born seriously ill or handicapped held absolutely no value for the Reich. Neither did those who evidenced very dark hair or skin make the cut. A minor deformity such as *Wolfsrachen* (cleft palate) or a clubfoot earned a child immediate dismissal from the home and a rescinding of Himmler's promise to assume guardianship if his mother was single. Rare exceptions were made for such children if their fathers were prominent Nazis or ranked high in the SS. Otherwise, all promises of concealing the pregnancy from society and help finding the mother employment after the birth were at that point declared null and void.[118] Such a mother, after being forcibly sterilized, found herself on her own with a child desperately in need of medical attention.

They were the lucky ones.

Children with handicaps judged severe and incurable, such as a girl named Sigune, born with Downs' Syndrome in Heim

Wienerwald just five months after me, were shipped off immediately to be killed. Sigune was shunted around from one clinic to another before landing in an institution near Dresden. There she was given an overdose of Luminol tablets and morphine shots. Her cause of death reads, "Lung infection."[119]

Some babies suffered from illnesses for which there was no cure at the time, and they would have died anyway. But others like Sigune, born with chromosomal abnormalities, microcephaly or non-life-threatening conditions such as lameness or blindness, were shown no mercy. Most ended up in the Görden Institute in Brandenburg near Berlin, to be overdosed with medication and slip into a coma. As their bodies' functioning slowed, they became vulnerable to lung infections which were allowed to progress to their inevitable end without medical intervention. Hence the death certificate reading "lung infection" as cause of death. The mother of such a child was not given an official death certificate, just a short note informing her of her child's demise and a small urn containing ashes.[120] To whom would she dare complain? These mothers were, after all, fully aware of the racial policies of the organization in which they had chosen to give birth.

It touches me deeply to know I shared a nursery, however briefly, with the ill-fated Sigune. I can only imagine the grief of the Lebensborn mothers whose infants were taken away for being "subhuman" when they were supposed to have entered the world as elite citizens. No amount of ideological brainwashing about racial superiority and the need to eliminate inferior human beings could, I believe, conquer that deep place in a mother's heart that harbors love and pity for the child of her womb.

My given name, Wolfgang Rüdiger Kober, was Elfriede's way of standing with one foot in popular culture and acquiescing to pressure from Lebensborn to give her child a Teutonic name taken from German mythology.[121] The name Wolfgang was popular and Germanic though not especially ancient. Rüdiger, an old Saxon moniker, fit the bill. Especially frowned upon from SS leadership were biblical and Christian names. After a visit to the Lebensborn home at Steinhöring in 1937, *SS Brigadierführer* Dr. Wilhelm Kinkelin wrote in an in-house memo:

What bothered me was that...Scandinavian names are not used correctly. It appears that the Scandinavian forms of Catholic names like Katharina and Karin are in style. This is a nuisance in SS Lebensborn homes, to see little Germans saddled for life with Christian names like Hans (Johannes), Peter and Sepp (Joseph). There should be some kind of regulation that requires mothers in these homes to give their children only Germanic names.[122]

I was never christened or baptized in any church as were most babies in Germany at that time, being born into a Catholic or Lutheran tradition. Despite having been confirmed in the Lutheran Church as an adolescent, my mother did not attend church and never evidenced any desire to affiliate herself with that or any other mainline denomination. Because great pressure came down on single Lebensborn mothers to take part, I believe it is highly likely that I underwent the SS Name Consecration Ceremony. Participation wasn't obligatory, but it was strongly urged.[123] Someone like Elfriede, who had spent time in the League of German Girls, worked from the age of 17 for the strongly Nazi-indoctrinated Reich Labor Service, became pregnant by an SS man and spent most of her pregnancy sitting under SS ideological teaching, was unlikely to refuse to take part in the ceremony on grounds of disagreement with SS beliefs or a preference to have me baptized elsewhere.

The Naming Celebration was designed by Heinrich Himmler as a substitute for Christian baptism, during which the offspring of the Aryan elite were welcomed into the SS kindred. Knowing that German society was not yet ready to accept such things, he asked that each Naming Ceremony be conducted in private, inviting only those sympathetic to his cause. In Himmler's detailed instructions for the conduction of the ceremony, he wrote:

In place of the cross, the swastika. In place of the Bible, "Mein Kampf." Instead of Christ's name, say "Hitler."[124]

Within each Lebensborn home, a large meeting room was festively decorated with banners, a bust or photograph of Hitler, flowers and candles. Chairs were set up in rows before an altar of sorts, draped with a large swastika flag. As in a church, the honored baby's mother sat holding it in the front row. Her fellow Lebensborn mothers joined her, filing into the rows of seats behind. Sometimes relatives were invited if they lived nearby, but even without them, the Lebensborn staff and a contingent of locally stationed SS men rounded out the guest list quite nicely. Whenever his schedule and travel itinerary permitted, Himmler himself attended these ceremonies to stand in physically as a symbol of his organization's guardianship.[125]

Although the order and details of the ceremony varied slightly from one home to another, the home director always officiated in an atmosphere of great solemnity. Music was played, SS mottoes and portions of *Mein Kampf* were recited and a brief oration delivered about pride in one's Aryan ancestry or the importance of bestowing Germanic first names on one's children. Often, as per Himmler's instructions, the home director read the words:

> *We believe in the God of the universe, and in the mission of our German blood that springs eternally young from the German soil. We believe in the nation, the bearer of this blood, and in the Führer whom God has given us.*[126]

Just which god Himmler was referring to can only be guessed at since he so openly reviled Judaism and Christianity. Yet his use of the socially accepted term "God" rather than "Waralda the Ancient," "Thor" or "Woden" reveals an attempt to tone down the ceremony's language in order to make it more palatable to the people involved.

Unvaryingly, the mother carried her infant forward and laid him before the altar, then took her place beside an SS man. This man, often someone completely unknown to her, represented the SS's guardianship over her child. At this point, they were asked three questions:

"German mother, do you commit yourself to raise your child in the spirit of National Socialism?"

"Are you, SS comrade, prepared to give your personal protection to this woman and child when they are in need or in danger?"

"Are you both prepared to insure that this child is raised in the ethos of racial purity as set forth by the SS?"

To all these questions, the participants gave assent with a handshake.

At this point, the home director laid an SS dagger on the child's belly, saying, "I hereby take you under the protection of our kindred and give you the name _____. Bear this name with honor."

Since the SS man who stood beside the child's mother was merely symbolic, he knew he was not personally responsible to care for this mother and child and in fact, had no intention of ever doing so. Rather than fall under the care of one particular man, we Lebensborn children were intended to be absorbed into the SS community in general, to feel throughout all our lives its influence over our development and our education, to one day make up its elite membership.

Even if a woman intended to give up her child for adoption, the ceremony's questions still applied, for in bestowing on her baby a Teutonic name and surrendering it for adoption by an SS family, she was still agreeing to do what was necessary to raise her child in the National Socialist spirit.

Lastly, the mother was presented with a Naming Certificate and a silver coffee spoon. Children born on October 7, Himmler's birthday, were particular targets of his largesse. They received his personal promise of guardianship along with an engraved silver cup. The ceremony closed with an anthem called, "*Treue Lied*," a song extolling loyalty to the SS. Coffee and cake were served in the dining room, sometimes followed by a concert or a special dinner. If enough SS men were in attendance, a dance was in order. If amidst the laughter, twirling and flirting, new liaisons formed, so much the better, especially if more Aryan children resulted.[127]

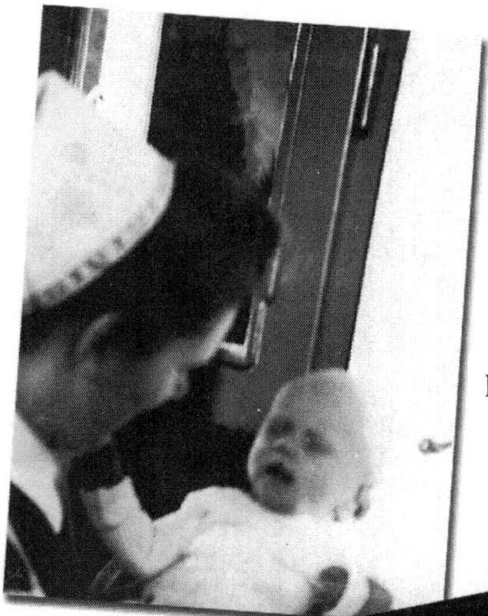

David with Lebensborn nurse

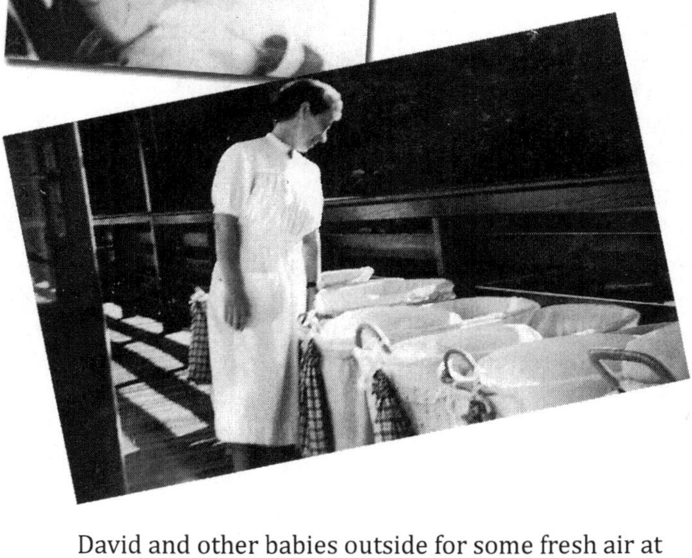

David and other babies outside for some fresh air at Heim Wienerwald. Photo taken by Elfriede.

Whatever we find in the way of good blood
from our race we will take, if necessary
by stealing children and raising them ourselves.

—Heinrich Himmler

CHAPTER 8

At eleven weeks of age, I was left behind in the Heim Wienerwald nursery with other infants whose mothers had departed. The realities of German society at that time meant there were many Lebensborn children who shared my fate. Unwed mothers were given until two years after their babies' births to get their lives in order and arrange a way to bring them home to live with them. After that point, foster or adoptive families were automatically sought. Though I never found the courage to ask my mother about her initial intentions for me, I'd like to believe that in those first few months after my birth, she never wavered in her determination to keep me by her side. But the realities of the situation are far more nuanced. Her decision to re-enter the Reich Labor Service meant a communal and barracks lifestyle in which there was no room for a baby. She had already signed guardianship of me over to Lebensborn, as did most unwed mothers, the fathers of whose babies were not prepared to take on a parenting role. Some unwed mothers made their own fathers guardians of their children,[128] but Elfriede had no desire to take me anywhere near Paul Kober, whose last name I legally bore.

This transfer of guardianship to the Lebensborn organization was done with utmost secrecy. Civil laws of registration and legal guardianship had to be surreptitiously skirted. By assuming the role of guardian, the SS, through Lebensborn, secured what it hoped would be a position of lasting influence in my life. If my mother couldn't claim me by two years of age, I'd be fostered out or adopted into an SS or other Nazi-affiliated family. Such adoptions were swift and uncomplicated. Within the bosom of a dedicated Nazi family, I was guaranteed to be raised in an ardent National Socialist atmosphere. Should I instead go into foster care, Lebensborn would remain my legal guardian until I reached legal adulthood.

In theory, the Lebensborn maternity homes could function as a bottomless supply from which childless couples would select tiny Aryan bundles of joy, and the secrecy of our parentage made us all the more desirable, for then everything was less complicated. All documents detailing our true ancestry were locked away in a file cabinet in the Lebensborn Central Administration office in Münich, the only facility allowed to store them. More than half of the unwed mothers who gave birth in Lebensborn homes requested that the birth of their children be kept secret.[129] Those who wished to relinquish their babies felt secure in the knowledge that both their and the babies' fathers' identities would be forever guarded under lock and key.

Raised by devoted Nazis, we would be well-prepared to step into our roles as young men and women of the Reich—the men to work and fill the ranks of the military, the women to fulfill their sacred duty of giving birth to babies of pure Aryan blood. The ever-expanding Germanic Reich, as its borders moved eastward and eventually into Asia, after eliminating or enslaving the "useless sub-humans" who already occupied those territories, would need to be populated with pedigreed people like me and my eventual offspring. As I grew, the SS would issue me, through the Lebensborn Central Administration, all the documents necessary for a successful life. On none of these documents would the name of my father appear, and my birth place would read simply, "Pernitz."

Had my mother chosen to relinquish me, my chances of actually landing in an adoptive home were slim at best. As the war dragged on and food became more and more scarce, with the ever-increasing dangers of Allied bombing raids, most SS couples failed to buy into the government's propaganda about raising large families. Early on, the Nazi policies had succeeded in elevating the birthrate; now no amount of tax breaks, Mother Crosses, celebratory coffee parties and congratulatory plaques could persuade couples to add more mouths to feed around their tables. Conceiving children wasn't even possible in many cases since men and women were kept apart by war. While husbands were away fighting, their wives were struggling to raise children alone. Despite Himmler's mandate to reproduce at a great rate, SS families, just like other German families during the war years, stubbornly insisted on having no more than two or three children. Stringent racial requirements made for more paper-work and ended up discouraging many couples from adopting. Those willing to take in foster children preferred girls over boys. Perhaps the prospect of raising a son, only to send him off one day as cannon fodder, repelled them.[130] A snarky, popular quip on the streets during the Nazi era perfectly encapsulates this attitude: *Räder müssen rollen für den Sieg, Kinderwagen für den nächsten Krieg.*[131] (Wheels must roll for victory; baby buggies roll for the next war.)

In theory, Lebensborn's ethos didn't encourage the raising of children in institutional settings. Such an upbringing was neither healthy nor suitable for the newest generation of the Master Race. Yet so many of our mothers couldn't take us out into the world with them and the organization was left with no choice. Maternity homes gradually turned into children's homes as more and more of us were left behind.[132] The nurses and kindergarten workers did their best to care for us all with a Germanic commitment to order and cleanliness insofar as it was possible. Heinrich Himmler took time out of his busy schedule of organizing mass murder to inquire after our well-being. He requested regular reports on how we were faring and paid attention to them in detail, and he made sure we continued to receive shipments of high quality food even as other Germans were hungry, experiencing devastating shortages due to the war. He saw to it that we received little gifts from time to time,[133] tokens of his godfatherly esteem.

But no amount of special favors could keep most of the Lebensborn homes from overcrowding as more and more women flocked to them and left their babies. Nurses, both brown and blue, were overwhelmed. Sickness swept through at an alarming rate. A doctor named Wilhelm Pfannenstiel made an inspection of Heim Taunus in 1940 and wrote in his report:

> *Almost all the children had snot-encrusted noses, many scratches on their faces and hands. The infants were poorly-washed, gray, scraggly diapers; some of them lay in soaked diapers that appeared to have been wet for hours.*[134]

Whooping cough was especially prevalent along with pneumonia. With no penicillin available, mortality rates in the Lebensborn homes climbed.[135]

Life in a crowded institution, with its lack of personal attention for each child, also retarded some children's development. They were late in reaching the milestones that so delight mothers and fathers, such as holding up the head, taking first steps, speaking first words. In the kindergarten, which included any child over the age of six months, group living resulted in constant squabbling among children and a pecking order being established—the strong bullying the weak. Bodily functions became group activities with mass potty sittings, group walks in the fresh air, the doling out of food at long tables lined with hungry toddlers who slept in dormitories in rows of bed after bed.[136]

A high rate of turnover in staff meant that babies and toddlers attached to a certain caregiver only to one day find her gone and a new person in her place.[137] Knowing what recent studies have shown about the importance of attachment between mother and child during the first year of life, I cringe to think of my own start in this world. But in the 1940s, the prevailing belief among child psychologists was that a child remembers nothing and is unaffected psychologically by conditions during the first two years of life.[138] This is why, for the Lebensborn organization, two years was the cut-off point by which a child must be either taken home by its mother or placed in a foster or adoptive family.

Yet can I or any other Lebensborn child truly complain? To do so would be to trivialize the genuine suffering of so many others. We were the cream of the crop as far as the regime was concerned, worthy of the very best efforts at daily care and nurturing even if those efforts were severely curtailed because of overcrowding. The staff was allowed to punish us for misbehavior but they weren't allowed to hit us and could be dismissed for doing so. They were forbidden to force food or drink down our throats should we turn our mouths away and refuse to eat what we were served.[139]

Yet just as one half of the world basks in sunlight while the other gropes in darkness, children abducted from Eastern Europe experienced a completely different side of Lebensborn. The racial theory embraced by National Socialism taught that the Germans had a right to rule over Slavs. Thus, the Slavic people were earmarked for slavery in the coming Germanic Reich. According to Heinrich Himmler's plans, they would be educated only until the fourth grade, ensuring they acquired the ability to count to 500 at most and perform other simple tasks required for a lifetime of servitude, such as writing one's name, obeying Germans without question, working hard and behaving docilely.[140] There was no reason for them to learn to read.

Some Slavs, however, possessed facial features that qualified them to be "Germanized." For instance, if a Polish forced laborer in Germany became pregnant by a German, or a German woman conceived a child with a Polish man, which happened often, despite the fact that under National Socialism, sex between Germans and non-Aryans including people of Slavic, Baltic, Latin, Jewish and Celtic origin was technically illegal, doctors examined her closely to determine if her baby might stand a good chance of possessing an Aryan appearance. If that were found to be the case, she was allowed to give birth to the child, then compelled to turn it over to a German family. If her own features (or the features of the Polish father) were judged too Slavic, she was forced to abort the fetus. If by some negligence of the German authorities such a pregnancy managed to escape notice and reached full term, the baby, if born to a mother judged too non-Aryan in appearance, was put in a facility where there was little chance of survival. Many thousands of such children died in this way.[141]

As far as the Nazis were concerned, a veritable goldmine of children with Aryan potential existed in the conquered eastern territories. In 1942, with the Germans well entrenched in Poland, the Soviet Union, Czechoslovakia and the Balkans, the tempting opportunity presented itself to seize "orphans," or the children of parents accused of resistance to the German occupiers, who had been either executed or sent to prison camps. Himmler called such people "bandits" and considered their children war booty. Some children from ordinary families were taken as well, along with babies fathered by German soldiers if they caught the eye of social workers trained to distinguish between Slavic and Nordic features. All such children were hustled off to special homes in Bobruisk and Kalisz or gathered in holding camps to be evaluated closely for Aryan appearance. Possibly they carried some vestige of Nordic blood in their veins. If judged worthy, they were then sent on to Lebensborn children's homes in Germany to begin the process of Germanization. The first shipment of these children into Germany took place when I was one month old, in September of 1942. They were sent to the Lebensborn homes Steinhöring and Bad Polzin.[142]

These unfortunates, most of who came from Poland, were stripped of their original identities, given German names and forbidden on threat of severe punishment to speak their native languages. Torn from family and familiar surroundings, desperately homesick and terrified, they were schooled in the German language and forcibly molded into young Nazis. They were issued falsified birth certificates. Those between the ages of two and six were adopted out to German families whenever possible, but this ended up being only a small minority. As the war progressed, the hardships it brought meant fewer people were looking to adopt. Unlike Lebensborn's Aryan children, for whom an institutional upbringing was considered substandard and undesirable, most kidnapped children from the East became wards of Lebensborn and languished in "boarding schools" where they suffered a brutal regimen of brainwashing and harsh discipline if they failed to cooperate with the Germanization process. And unlike those of us born to German parents, they were punished with hitting and denial of food. After suffering the psychological damage of kidnapping and brainwashing, only a small percentage of these children were able to return to their home countries after the war. Some became lost in the system, their records destroyed. Others had been with their German families long enough to bond and refused to return to their country of origin, much to their biological parents' or other surviving relatives' grief. Some German adoptive families took advantage of the general chaos at war's end and managed to elude the Red Cross workers who sought to locate and return kidnap victims, determined to hold onto the children they now considered fully theirs.[143]

Elfriede left Heim Wienerwald just as soon as she had fulfilled Himmler's breastfeeding requirements. Walking out the front door with suitcase in hand, she had no idea that, along with all the other Lebensborn mothers, she had undergone a secret evaluation by the home leadership, the report of which was laid directly on Himmler's desk. The evaluation covered her racial appearance: did she look Aryan enough? It covered her political leanings: did her ideological views line up with National Socialism or had she been heard to utter anything negative about Adolf Hitler and his government? Regarding her intelligence and character: did she show signs of a low IQ? Had she whined and complained during the physical discomforts of advanced pregnancy? Himmler wanted to know all this and so much more about the mothers of his elite children. It concerned him greatly whether or not these women truly embodied SS principles. If a single woman was judged unworthy according to this evaluation, she stood in danger of losing Lebensborn's support as she raised her child.[144] Knowing my mother, so stoic in difficult circumstances and devoted to hard work, I have no doubt she passed with flying colors.

Fortunately, her former camp group leader pulled strings to get her reassigned to a nearby Labor Service post where she would be close enough to visit me. Every Sunday, she came to Pernitz and wheeled my stroller along the wooded pathways of Heim Wienerwald's grounds, or into the tiny neighboring village of Feichtenbach. These weekly visits were encouraged by Lebensborn, whose goal was to foster a close connection between mother and child, which they believed to be in a child's best interests. Minimal as they seem in retrospect, I believe it was these weekly outings that strengthened Elfriede's mothering instincts and solidified deep down the feeling that I belonged to her completely.

By December, she had confirmed the decision to keep me. This meant she must leave the Reich Labor Service and take advantage of Lebensborn's proffer of help in finding work for its unwed mothers. The organization did its best to fulfill this promise, often hiring young mothers into the Lebensborn system itself as cooks, housekeepers, secretaries and kindergarten helpers. This phenomenon only added to the false impression of Lebensborn as a breeding program, for when local farmers and merchants delivered fresh milk, bread and other groceries, or tradesmen were called in to repair plumbing or electrical wiring, they couldn't help but notice most of the female employees had babies in tow—and no wedding rings.[145] Sometimes SS men were seen visiting the homes for Naming Celebrations or other holidays, giving rise to the question, "Just what are they doing there on that secluded property?"

At that point, there must have been no position available for Elfriede within the Lebensborn organization that would have allowed her to keep me with her and care for me herself. Instead, a job was secured for her as a salesgirl in a fine-handcrafts shop in Berlin. But how would she care for me there? With her minimal salary, she could hardly afford to pay a full-time babysitter. She had no choice but to leave me at Pernitz.

In different circumstances, Elfriede would have relished the excitement of Berlin, the pulsing heart of the Reich. But in those days, men were scarce in the city. She had no date to accompany her to cabarets on the Kurfürstendamm or the chic underground bars and nightclubs featuring jazz, a style of music forbidden by the Nazi regime but secretly flourishing. Even if she'd had a boyfriend, her feet ached after a long day's work. She was still struggling to fit into her pre-pregnancy clothing. Clothes were strictly rationed; in order to be eligible for new garments she had to prove that her old ones were worn out, and the no-nonsense Reich Labor Service uniform was simply indestructible. Her stockings had gaping holes in them. Finding new stockings was becoming impossible, and Elfriede felt juvenile in the ankle socks she was advised to wear instead.

On January 30, even as radios all over the country were broadcasting propaganda minister Josef Goebbels' speech celebrating the ten-year anniversary of Hitler's rise to power, Elfriede heard a thunderous noise. She ran out of the shop to see British *Mosquito* planes roaring overhead, releasing whistling bombs. The air smelt of smoke. Soot began to coat her mouth and throat. Hurriedly Elfriede and her co-workers locked up the store and filed down to the basement to wait out the air raid. The speech, replayed over and over, ad nauseum, later that day as if nothing had happened, touted Germany's imminent victory in Russia.

The next day, the German Sixth Army surrendered at Stalingrad.

Elfriede's section of Berlin had been spared damage and she remained hopeful. Spending her days among porcelain figurines, designer light fixtures and hand-painted vases had its charms compared to the utilitarian atmosphere of the quartermaster's depot where she had previously worked in Prague. She enjoyed interacting with the customers, unpacking and arranging pretty things on shelves. The pay was minimal but the work was light. If she could just hold on a while, prove herself as invaluable to her new employer as she had to the Reich Labor Service, she might be promoted to manager or to a larger store, thus earning enough to support me too. However, it was not to be.

In February of 1943, in response to the stunning defeats of the previous autumn at El Alamein and Stalingrad, Adolf Hitler declared "total war." At his instruction, Josef Goebbels made a speech to the nation demanding each and every German devote himself fully to the desired victory. The *Volk* must make sacrifices. War production must be raised; the entire population of German males between the ages of 18 and 60 would be mobilized.[146] Goebbels, in a frenzied shout, ended his speech with, "Now people, rise up and let the storm break loose!"

Severe food rationing was introduced. Luxuries had no place in an austere Germany so fully dedicated to victory. Frivolities such as the finely handcrafted items in the shop where Elfriede worked must wait for better times. One day, with hardly any warning, the shop was ordered closed. My mother found herself unemployed and alone in a strange city. Feeling buffeted by the whims of war, she abandoned hope of earning enough of a living to support us both in a home of our own. She felt as if someone had cut her tether; she was free-floating and aimless, missing her son. It struck her that now was as good a time as any to return to Pernitz and extract me from Heim Wienerwald. The future looked grim; she might as well face it with a baby in her arms.

Her sister Lisbeth was living in Görlitz with her three-year-old daughter, Inge. Little Inge's father was a first lieutenant in the Wehrmacht. Before Lisbeth had even realized she was pregnant, he'd been sent East and died in the Pripjet Swamps of Byelorussia. The two had never married. His parents, who owned a pharmacy in Berlin and might have taken her in or at least helped her out financially, had both been crushed to death beneath the rubble of their apartment building during a bombing raid.

Elfriede had earlier written to Lisbeth explaining that a heart murmur was not the real reason she had gone to Pernitz. Lisbeth knew all about what it was like to bear a child out of wedlock; she would never criticize or turn her sister away. Lisbeth had struggled along as a single mother until meeting a young Navy officer called Hans Becker. They'd married in the summer of 1942. Elfriede knew through her sister's letters that Hans was now serving as a machine specialist on a submarine in the North Atlantic, kept away at sea for long periods of time. Surely Lisbeth would be happy for her sister's company. The two could combine resources, prop each other up through difficult times.

Elfriede scraped together train fare to Vienna and returned to claim me from Heim Wienerwald. She found me in the kindergarten section of the home and bundled me up for the journey, reassuring herself that a child belongs with its mother despite her uncertain prospects. Together we left Pernitz for Vienna and from there, boarded a train for Görlitz.

"Friedel!" cried Lisbeth, genuinely thrilled to see her sister. Elfriede gasped. Below where Inge sat shyly in her mother's arms, Lisbeth's belly protruded sharply. "You should have told me!"

The two women laughed and exclaimed over each other's offspring before sitting down to steaming cups of ersatz coffee made from roasted barley.

"Wolfgang's father is an SS policeman," Elfriede confided to her sister. "He was so much older than I, and married…but I really cared for him."

"I understand, Friedel," Lisbeth reassured her. "I loved Inge's father too, and we were planning to marry. Then he went missing in the swamps. To this day, they haven't found his body." Sighing deeply, she lay both hands on her swollen belly. "Ah well, we don't have the luxury of grieving. We have to keep going. I'm so lucky that I found Hans."

Elfriede put a hand on her sister's forearm. "Listen," she said, "I'm not planning on telling anyone else in the family about Kurt. You might have married Inge's father if he hadn't gone missing but that was never a possibility for me. Everyone will ask me why I haven't married Kurt and I don't want to tell them he was married to someone else. I'm going to say I was raped."

"I don't blame you," said Lisbeth. "If you told the truth, our father would call you a whore and everyone else would stare down their noses at you. You can stay here with me but you'll have to register at the town hall."

Elfriede registered as a single, unemployed woman, leaving off the inconvenient fact of her illegitimate son. Lebensborn's policy of absolute secrecy meant there was no civil record of my birth and she need not fear the authorities discovering her omission. The extra rations allotted me would have been helpful, but she didn't relish facing all the explanations and red tape and looks of scorn. Besides, at seven months I didn't consume much food.

She soon recognized her mistake. An official looking letter arrived at Lisbeth's address, calling Fräulein Elfriede Kober to report to an air raid observation post in Koeslin, Pomerania. That very January, the Nazis had begun requiring all women without young children as well as non-pregnant women between the ages of 17 and 45 to register for work, both for the war effort and at jobs that men had abandoned when sent to the front. With no choice but to obey, my mother left me in her sister's care and departed.

Her stay at Koeslin was brief however. Dutifully learning the identifying characteristics of British and American planes like *Spitfires, Mustangs, Hurricanes* and *Lightnings,* Elfriede once again proved herself a valuable asset to the Reich. But whether through the stress and fear of keeping a constant lookout for approaching enemy aircraft, or a cunning ruse requiring skilled acting, my mother's increasing heart palpitations and claims of a previously-diagnosed heart murmur persuaded a doctor to release her from duty. Immediately she returned to Görlitz.

Soon she was reassigned as a typist in the finance department of Wehrmacht headquarters on the east side of town, close to Lisbeth's home. The work pleased her. It brought back pleasant memories of earlier days manning Herr Brocke's office desk, only now she was surrounded by a sea of desks, ringing telephones, a hum of voices and the constant coming and going of smartly uniformed co-workers.

By this time, luxuries like chocolate and most citrus fruits and bananas had disappeared and meat was extremely difficult to find. The sisters pooled the ration cards they were issued every two months, handing in the tear-out coupons for minimal amounts of basics like bread, eggs, cheese, butter, margarine and oil. Also rationed were jam, sugar and canned goods. Thanks to Lebensborn, Elfriede was receiving a small amount of financial support from Kurt. This together with her Army salary helped to buy local fruits and vegetables and a few coveted items from the black market. She relished the role of breadwinner, secure in the knowledge that Lisbeth was taking good care of me at home.

Bolstered by each other's company, the sisters shrugged off the annoying inconvenience of war shortages. Together they laughed about the strange tasting, chalk-like powder with which they were now forced to brush their teeth instead of toothpaste. They tried to be creative with cooking, disguising bland foods with sleight of hand. Being in close proximity again felt good after the years of separation. When Lisbeth's son Peter was born, Elfriede was able to take time off work and manage the household during her *Wochenbett*, the traditional week-long hospital stay for new mothers. The two siblings, who had survived a dismal home life together, had emerged strong and would continue to thrive with each other's support. Never again would they ask their father for a single penny. They wanted nothing to do with him. He hadn't changed one bit. Recently he had abandoned Grete and his son with her, Manfred, and taken up with yet another woman. Although Lisbeth and Elfriede were not sorry to see the back of Grete, they felt sorry for their ten-year-old half-brother and were sickened by their father's callous behavior.

Something wonderful happened in Görlitz, something that gave Elfriede hope. She caught the eye of a young Army payroll officer. First Lieutenant Rudolf Kobsch was a local boy just two years older than she. He looked so handsome in his green jacket with braided shoulder boards adorned with gold stars. Rudi had wavy brown hair, a finely shaped nose and a disarming smile. His forehead was just high enough to give him a look of intelligence, his shoulders broad enough to lend him a manly air, yet there was also something sweetly boyish about him. His parents owned a textile shop in downtown Görlitz. When he took her over to meet them, his mother, Elisabeth, greeted her warmly. His father, Walter, studied her as if trying to determine whether she passed muster. Despite it making her feel a little uncomfortable, Elfriede understood. Rudi was, after all, his only child.

Happily, Görlitz remained untouched by air raids. The quaint city, with its pastel-painted Gothic, Renaissance, Baroque and Art Nouveau buildings, felt like an island of peace floating on the roiling sea of war-torn Germany. The two lovers walked hand in hand along the banks of the Neisse River and strolled through the market squares across cobblestones glistening in the rain. While crossing a bridge from the eastern to western part of town, they paused to gaze down at the river and watched first spring blossoms float away beneath them then as time passed, autumn leaves. Situated just outside of town was a large POW camp called Stalag 8A, but its grim presence hardly dampened the atmosphere in lovely Görlitz. Ducking into cozy cafés together, sharing sappy messages through the Whispering Arch on the Via Regia, Elfriede and Rudi giggled like school children caught up in the heady emotions of romance. That summer of 1944, the British and American armies invaded the Normandy coast. "Our Rommel, our Desert Fox will beat them back!" came Joseph Goebbels' confident voice through the radio.[147] Wanting desperately to believe it, Rudi and Friedel, as he called her, continued gazing dreamily into each other's eyes. The French coast was so very far away from Görlitz after all. When, by mid-October, the Desert Fox was dead, forced by Adolf Hitler to commit suicide as punishment for supporting the plot to assassinate him, Rudi and Elfriede's love had grown stronger than ever.

Elfriede and Rudi

Elfriede with David during one of her Sunday visits to Heim Wienerwald. She is wearing the hat of the Reich Labor Service.

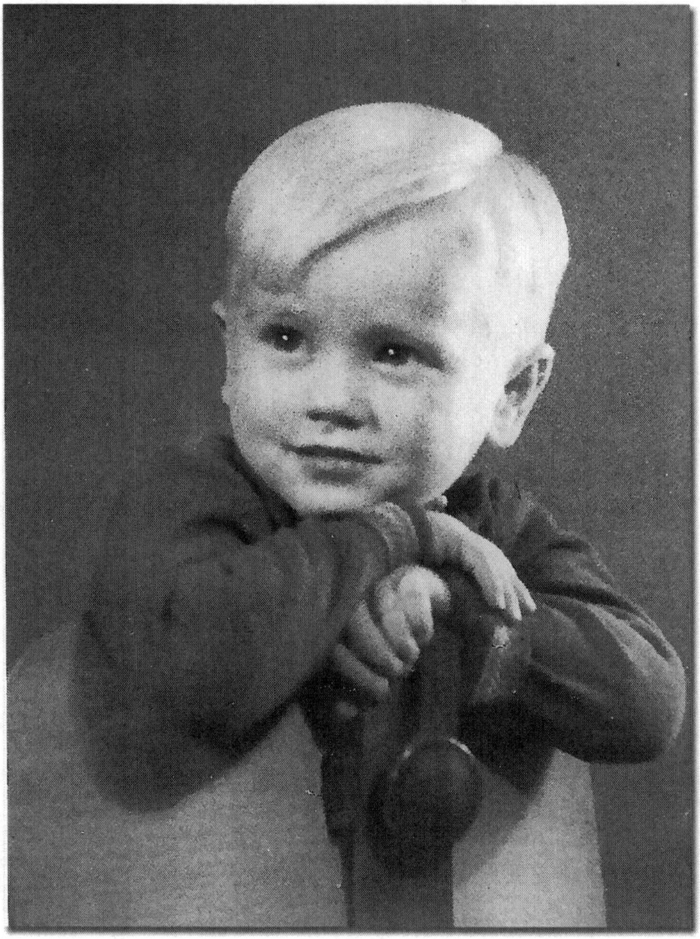

Bub

I don't care in the least what happens to the Russians or the Czechs...Whether other nations are prosperous or die of hunger only interests me in so far as we have slaves for our culture; otherwise it doesn't interest me.

—Heinrich Himmler

CHAPTER 9

Just when did Elfriede tell Rudi about me? Did she opt for full disclosure right away, or wait until she knew she had captured his heart completely? At some point, he came to Lisbeth's house, met me and accepted me fully as Elfriede's child. Had she been tempted to tell Rudi that I was the product of a legitimate marriage and she a war widow, she might very well have gotten away with it. Young German husbands and fathers were falling in battle all over Europe at that point; her story would have been plausible and almost impossible to refute without digging up records in some town hall or other. Many of those town halls had been bombed and their records destroyed, making secret-keeping possible. Yet there is little doubt that she told him the truth about my being a product of an affair and born in a Lebensborn home. Two things convince me of this.

First, the abhorrence Rudi's father displayed toward me later on. Had I been a legitimate war orphan, I don't believe Walter Kobsch would have felt disgust, but rather pity and acceptance. As things stood, I was a bastard, a shameful appendage to the loose woman his only son insisted upon loving, and though he came to accept Elfriede and forgive her moral lapse, he simply could not forget my sketchy origins nor consider me worthy to join his family.

Secondly, Rudi was unable to marry my mother because the Wehrmacht, no doubt to the immense frustration of progressive Nazi thinkers like Heinrich Himmler, held fast to its tradition of refusing to allow its officers to marry unwed mothers, even if the officer in question was the child's father. Such a marriage was considered a disgrace and a condoning of immoral behavior unfitting for Army officers.[148] This convoluted logic, meant to uphold traditional moral standards, unfortunately prevented many a young couple from legitimizing a child or legally establishing their commitment to one another. In order to marry Rudi with the Army's blessing, Elfriede would have had to give me up for adoption even if I had been Rudi's child. Had she met him during her pregnancy or when I was still in Heim Wienerwald, she might have been tempted to relinquish me, but by the time she fell in love with Rudi, Mother and I had bonded.

This is why, after one and one-half years of togetherness during which a sexual relationship had developed and after being repeatedly rebuffed in his attempts to persuade the Army to grant him exceptional permission to marry his lover, Rudi sat down and penned the following letter to Elfriede:

Görlitz, January 1, 1945

My beloved Friedel!

If you are now reading this letter, it means you are filled with great sorrow; but it should not mean the end of your young life. You must live on in a manner seemly for a German woman, and continue in the task of motherhood for the German people. Sadly, we were only allowed a short time of happiness together, but during that time we gave each other everything that those who love one another possibly can. You have added so much to my young life and made me very happy. I want to thank you for that. Unfortunately I don't know whether we will have the happiness of having a child together—a child through whom I can live on for you. If you turn out to be pregnant then I did not live in vain. How sad it is that I am unable to enter into the commitment of marriage with you, but it is nevertheless my desire that you and my child should bear my name. Take my letter as proof; it shall take the place of my verbal marriage vow should you encounter difficulties. My parents will stand with you as witnesses before the authorities. I am confident you will raise any child of ours to be an upstanding German citizen. Therefore I bequeath to you, as my wife, two-thirds of my property and one-third to my parents, to whom I am also thankful, for it is through them that I came to be all the things I was to you.

I wish you now, in your future life, as well as the life of our child, health and happiness.

Again to you, dear Friedel, my thanks and my greetings.

Forever your Rudi

It is no surprise that Rudi had the fathering of children on his mind. His girlfriend's sister, Lisbeth, had given birth that very December to her third child, a delicate little girl named Rosel. Rudi had watched Elfriede fuss over her pregnant sister, had observed her skills in homemaking and handling young children during Lisbeth's *Wochenbett*. Seeing her like that confirmed his hunch that she would make an excellent wife and mother of his children.

Rudi, like all Wehrmacht soldiers, had been subject to the same pressure to produce offspring as were SS men. Since 1942, Himmler had been urging all childless soldiers to return from the battlefront in order to father some and prevent their family lines from dying out. He must have sincerely hoped to contribute a child to his nation as he took the letter to be mimeographed. The original was notarized and sealed in an official envelope which he turned over to his parents. Solemnly he handed Elfriede a sealed envelope containing the copy, explained its contents to her, and instructed her to open it only in the event of his death.

Their time together was fleeting. In the eyes of the regime, a desk job no longer sufficed for a strong young man like Rudi. To beat back the Russian advance, a desperate Germany needed even skilled accountants to don fatigues and take up weapons. He was to be shipped eastward along with other reinforcement troops to repel a Russian attack rumored to be slated for mid-January. The pair had only a few hours together before he had to depart. Rudi told Elfriede with all the confidence he could muster that he felt sure she would never have to open the envelope he'd just given her. When the war ended and he was honorably discharged from the Army, they would be free at last to marry and raise a family together.

However, the winter of 1945 was an inauspicious time to predict a happy future. War fortunes had shifted irreparably. Soviet forces were holding a steady line on the eastern front, having encroached on the *Lebensraum* into which the Germans were supposed to spread out and establish their massive, everlasting Reich. The year 1943 had seen the Germans caught unawares with armed uprisings in the Warsaw, Bialystok and Glubokoje ghettos and mass breakouts from the death camps Treblinka and Sobibor. As a result, those two murder facilities had to be permanently dismantled. Jews who had been rounded up, starved and terrorized, shocked and unsettled their captors with their irrepressible will to live and to fight as they took down as many Germans as they possibly could with the scant weapons they managed to get their hands on. The Germans responded by ruthlessly ramping up the scale of murder with a zeal made all the more potent by the knowledge that the Allies were gaining the upper hand on all fronts.

In Prague during the summer of 1943, my father, Kurt Novak, took part in a sweeping wave of arrests ordered by Himmler. The *Reichsführer SS* was ever zealous in his ruthless oppression of anyone opposed to Nazism. Any Czech officials and civil employees who appeared to be slacking in their commitment to serving the Nazi overlords were to be apprehended. Five hundred random Czechs were also arrested and sent to a concentration camp as an object lesson to their fellow countrymen of what happened to anyone who opposed Nazi rule in even the slightest way. Czech troublemakers and saboteurs, as many as 100 per month, were hanged on the spot without trial.[149] Such death sentences continued unabated, keeping Prague police and SS men exceptionally busy.

With the Allied landing in Normandy in June 1944 and the assassination attempt on Adolf Hitler's life a little over one month afterward, Germany's predicament was looking more and more hopeless. But even as the Reich's fortunes waned, Himmler's powers increased, for Hitler considered him one of the few men he could trust after the betrayal of his would-be assassins, most of who served in the Wehrmacht. At this critical point, Hitler appointed Heinrich Himmler Chief of the Reserve Army. Himmler used this new power to press ahead with his plan of sweeping genocide. He increased the use of terror tactics in conquered territories, killing more civilians. Jews were forcibly taken from Hungary and Slovakia, where they had thus far been protected by those governments' unwillingness to hand them over to be slaughtered. In a speech to Wehrmacht officers over whom he had been awarded command, Himmler said in July 1944: "All your training, selection and skill have been in vain if it is not founded on unshakeable faith in the German prerogative and German victory. I base this faith on the merits of our... race. I am convinced that we are of greater worth than the others."[150]

Wehrmacht leadership, long sickened by his brutality as displayed through the murderous actions of the SS, had no choice but to submit and show deference to Himmler as a Führer-appointed superior.

Surely the young lovers saw the end coming despite the nearly constant barrage of propaganda to the contrary. By Christmas of 1944, the Soviet advance had been stalled for several months just east of the Vistula River. The Russians were known to be amassing ammunition, equipment and manpower for a coming offensive. They were also known to have two and a half million men. They possessed a deep reservoir of supplies and equipment but Hitler, who was by this time showing signs of losing his grip on reality, refused to believe intelligence reports and thus did not allow his generals to take the necessary actions to regroup and prepare. German troops, pressed by the Allies in the West and South and spread too thin along the eastern front, were running out of supplies and manpower and demoralized by Hitler's harsh criticism and threats to strip them of their decorations and regimental insignia if they could not prevail against overwhelming odds.

No sooner had the New Year dawned than Rudi and his comrades were loaded onto eastbound trains. Standing on the platform with other weeping young wives and lovers, Elfriede watched him go. She felt as if her heart were ripping in two. That same day, Adolf Hitler greeted his countrymen over the radio with a jubilant message of certain victory. Everyone knew it was a farce, but if they said so, they risked denunciation and arrest for "defeatist talk."

Rudi and his fellow reinforcement troops joined the Fourth Panzer Army battalions located along the Vistula at a place called Sandomierz, or the Baranov Bridgehead, 300 miles east of Görlitz. There, on the frozen landscape, General Harpe ordered them to take their places in anticipation of the Russian attack. Rudi and his compatriots had no illusions. They realized they were heavily outnumbered. Still, they hoped and prayed their *Panzerfausts*, or hand-held anti-tank missiles, were up to the task and that the motto on their belt buckles, *God With Us*, would prove true.

Early on the morning of January 12, the Soviets unleashed their attack. It caught the Germans by surprise. Soviet Marshal Ivan Konev's First Ukrainian Front hammered the outnumbered Wehrmacht with artillery for six hours before rolling his tanks forward. In blinding snow, they mowed down their dazed and exhausted opponent and beat a hasty westward path toward Berlin. By the end of January, the Russians stood less than 50 miles from their goal.

"Friedel! Friedel! Open up!" Lisbeth stumbled to the door in the pre-dawn hours and opened it to one of my mother's Army Administration co-workers. Ruth stood there, disheveled and trembling, clutching her two small children by the hands. Lisbeth led her to her sister's room.

Elfriede rolled out of bed, rubbing her eyes. "What is it? What's happening?"

"It's the Russians," Ruth panted. "They've broken through our defense lines. Friedel, they're headed this way! They're moving fast, destroying everything, raping every woman in their path. The Army is evacuating its employees. A train is waiting to take us further west, to Dresden. Hurry! Wake up little Wolfi and come with me, now."

Lisbeth gasped and began to cry. Elfriede clung to her sister. "If only I could bring you along!" Both knew it was futile; the Wehrmacht could not offer civilians space on its precious trains.

"Don't worry about me, Friedel," Lisbeth insisted. "Just go!"

Lisbeth shook with terror as Elfriede stumbled around on trembling legs grabbing pieces of clothing and shoving them into a satchel. The racial overtones of Nazi propaganda had continued unabated even at this late stage of the war. Goebbels' radio speeches bombarded terrified Germans with the news that the French and American armies, utterly degenerate and hell-bent on the destruction of German culture, were advancing in the West with wild black men among their ranks. On the other hand, the Russians, advancing from the East, were nothing more than Mongol hordes and Asian barbarians.

Pulled from the warmth of my crib and hastily dressed, I toddled sleepily alongside my mother to the train station. Elfriede and Ruth jostled for space on the crowded platform where they huddled with their children and nearly 40 other female Army employees beneath a heavy sky that threatened snow. Stacked high beside them were crates filled with Army Administration documents. When at last they and the precious Army files were loaded onto a train headed for Dresden, they breathed a collective sigh of relief, having no way of knowing that a journey normally lasting a handful of hours would drag on for two torturous weeks. Shunted from track to track, unloaded only to be reloaded, shifted repeatedly from one train to another, my mother and I, along with her co-workers and their children, finally reached a small town on the outskirts of Dresden in early February. But instead of continuing on into the city, we were ordered to evacuate the cars.

"What! Why?" the women looked at each other in dismay. Their goal had been Dresden's central station; some sighed and others cursed under their breath as they reluctantly hauled their luggage and children off the train and onto the platform. Failure to reach the longed-for city of refuge frustrated them deeply. The fact that they could see its church spires in the near distance made their disappointment all the more palpable.

Thus it was that we were spared from perishing in one of the most hideous events of the entire war.

Our little group of 39 made up only a minute fraction of the hordes of refugees straggling toward the overcrowded city. Rumor had it that the Allies had promised the Red Cross that Dresden would not be an air raid target. There was every reason to believe it was true. Although the city had a few factories, it was mostly a bastion of culture, its greatest contribution to the war effort being its position as a railway hub for transporting German troops to the East. Fueled by Nazi propaganda detailing the horrors that awaited anyone caught in the path of the Red Army as it marched toward Berlin, as well as terrifying testimonies of survivors who had seen Russian atrocities toward civilians first hand, endless columns of ethnic Germans from the East, mostly women and children, straggled into Dresden, relieved to have found a safe haven. Their journey had been hellish. Smoke billowed into the frigid winter sky as they fled their burning homes and barns. Lifeless bodies lined the icy roads. Biting snowflakes pelted their faces as they passed abandoned towns that lay in ruins. Three years' worth of pent-up

Russian rage had been unleashed on these *Volksdeutsch,* the first actual Germans the Russians had managed to get their hands on since the Nazi invasion of their homeland in 1941.

With the influx of eastern refugees, Dresden's population of 350,000 swelled to an estimated 650,000. The natives did their best to absorb and put up with the displaced hordes, knowing the war was grinding toward its inevitable end. Surely relief was imminent, they thought.

No one in Dresden expected the raid. There were no warning sirens. Just after 10:00 PM on February 13, the first British bombers flew over, releasing red candle flares that dropped like falling stars in the pitch-black winter sky. Their explosions rocked the city center and lit up the night, waking the population to a nightmare worse than any their slumbering minds could conjure.

Mercifully, our group of Army employees had been billeted in temporary lodging well outside the city limits, but the ferocity of the attack sent even them running for cover. My mother, clutching me, fled into the dark street despite her companions shouting at her to follow them to the basement.

"No!" she screamed. During her brief time in Berlin, she'd heard too many tales of people who sheltered in basements only to be buried alive in rubble, dying of asphyxiation before help could arrive and dig them out. Or they drowned when water mains broke and flooded their low-lying dens of refuge. She would rather be obliterated by a direct bomb hit than suffer such a fate.

"Elfriede!" someone called, and then she heard footsteps pounding toward her. Ruth and another co-worker seized her by the arms and pulled her down to safety, insisting she had a child to protect. "Think of little Wolf! You must take shelter!"

In the dark belly of the building, she could feel the earth shake from the force of distant bombs. Those brave enough to venture upstairs and peek saw bright flashes illuminating the horizon. During that first wave, British *Lancaster* bombers dumped over 2,000 tons of explosives on the city, but when the planes disappeared across the night sky, the horror was far from over. Throughout the rest of the night and the following day, British and American aircraft unleashed a special brand of hell upon Dresden.

It was like nothing Elfriede had witnessed in Berlin. These bombs were phosphorous incendiaries, bursting into flames that spread over the city, whipping up an inferno that sucked up and fed off oxygen, thereby growing in intensity and power. The explosions shattered roofs, walls and windows. In the city center, the luckiest victims were killed by the bombs' impact. Thousands of those less fortunate were consumed by the fiery tornado as it generated winds up to 100 miles per hour and sucked its victims up into a vortex. Some tried to save themselves by jumping into lakes and ponds but drowned or burned to death when coming up for air. Temperatures peaked at somewhere around 1,800 degrees Fahrenheit. Street asphalt melted, scorching people's feet as they ran. When it was finally over and traumatized survivors streamed out of the city, American planes flew low and strafed them with gunfire.

Deep within the city, basement shelters rocked violently. Walls grew hot and all the air seemed to be sucked outside. People soaked pieces of cloth in water or beer and held them over mouths and noses to keep out poisonous fumes. When terrorized survivors emerged into daylight with the help of medical corps workers, they were confronted by a burning shell of a city, its contours nearly indistinguishable through the smoke. Trees were still on fire. Charred bodies lay everywhere. The wind carried bits of debris and the stench of burning flesh. Estimates of Dresden's dead numbered between 35,000 and 135,000, but because of the influx of refugees, no one will ever know the exact death toll. Eight square miles of the city were completely destroyed. Dresden burned for seven days and smoldered for weeks as SS guards from a nearby camp piled up as many bodies as were still intact and set them alight. Thousands upon thousands of victims were dumped into mass graves.

Dresden's bombing was a final death blow meant to bring an already staggering Germany to its knees. It also served as a warning to the advancing Russians, showing them that the Americans and British would be a postwar force to be reckoned with.

Why it happened mattered little to Elfriede. Far more pressing was the question of where to go from there. Dresden was supposed to have been a haven for us and now it lay in smoldering ruins, the stench of burning flesh heavy over the surrounding countryside. Gazing up at the smoke-filled sky, my mother felt sick to her stomach and wracked with worry. She didn't have long to wait, however. Within days, the little band of Army Administration employees and their children were ordered to move farther west to Chemnitz. We were crowded into a boxcar recently occupied by cattle. Another car was filled with the Army documents. The trip was agonizingly slow and in the fetid, overcrowded boxcar the bacteria from cow manure proliferated, causing the passengers to become feverish and nauseous. Shivering, watching her breath emerge in puff-clouds in the freezing train car, Elfriede thought of Rudi. *Oh please let him be safe,* she prayed to a God she hardly believed was listening. *A Russian prisoner of war camp can hardly be a picnic,* she thought, *but at least there he'll be safe from combat, and they'll release him once Germany surrenders.* Such hopes carried her through until we arrived in Chemnitz. Immediately, our entire group was hospitalized and treated for exhaustion and illness.

With Germany now teetering on the brink of collapse, the Wehrmacht administration employees split up and sought their own survival, abandoning the Army documents. When my mother and Ruth recovered sufficiently to leave the hospital, they put their heads together and formed a plan.

"Let's pool our money," suggested Ruth, "and buy train tickets. We'll ride as far into the countryside as we can get."

Elfriede readily agreed. The Allies were merciless in their bombings and cities like Chemnitz were prime targets. As long as they stayed there, they would spend their nights in fear, huddled in crowded basements. They had children to feed, and prospects were better in rural areas where farms abounded. Even as Germany unraveled, its farmers continued to sow and reap.

Mother and Ruth, spending their last *Pfenning*, bought tickets that took us 35 miles southeast to the small town of Neundorf near the Czech border. Its remote location promised to hold no attraction for Allied bombers. But they knew absolutely no one there. No one awaited us. When we stepped off the train, it was 10:00 at night and bitterly cold. As the train pulled away, Mother and Ruth gazed forlornly about. The station was dark, its ticket office closed up for the night. Farther down the platform, a young girl about nine years old stood shivering. She seemed disappointed, as if she had come to meet someone who never materialized. Despite her own desperate straits, Elfriede felt a surge of motherly concern for the child and struck up a conversation with her.

"Do you have a place to stay?" the girl asked after assuring my mother she was all right.

"No," replied Elfriede and Ruth in unison.

"Then come home with me."

The two women glanced doubtfully at one another. The child's impulsive generosity was heartwarming, but were her parents willing to house complete strangers? Yet the girl insisted and the women knew their children would freeze if they spent the night on the exposed platform.

Mother never disclosed whether the girl's father, a baker, made her feel welcome or if he only grudgingly humored his daughter by allowing us all to bed down in the hay in his barn. Whatever his and his wife's personal feelings, they selflessly shared fresh-baked bread with us and allowed us to occupy the barn until a couple of other families in town agreed to take us into their homes. The two women were thankful to have a roof over their heads, however rustic. And in that temporary shelter, Elfriede found enough of a respite to at last contemplate what she had been suspecting for the past few weeks. She hadn't menstruated lately, an all-too-familiar nausea gripped her and she was growing tired quicker than usual, even for a war-weary woman on the run. Rudi's wish had come true. Elfriede was pregnant.

Rudi's parents, Walter and Elisabeth Kobsch, had refused to flee Görlitz, determined to protect their livelihood—the textile shop. Disrupted by the chaos of war, the mail was unreliable but Elfriede managed to send Rudi letters through military field post. She wanted him to know that she was safe, that he need not worry for her sake. She also confided to him that a child was on the way. These letters were forwarded to Rudi's parents. If they wrote to her in reply, the letter was lost in a disintegrating postal system. Elfriede was left to fret with no news of the man she loved. As if to symbolize the wintery nightmare of defeat engulfing Germany, the spring remained bitterly cold with frost covering the ground well into April.

All around us, atrocities on a spectacular scale were unfolding. As the Reich collapsed and its enemies drew nearer, the incriminating concentration and prison camps were evacuated. German guards fled the encroaching Allies, but rather than abandon their tortured and emaciated prisoners to bear witness to their atrocities, they commenced herding them at gunpoint on a series of aimless death marches. These forced treks were characterized by unimaginable cruelty.

On March 27, 1945, 14,000 male and female prisoners of Flossenburg, a slave labor camp holding mostly prisoners of war and political prisoners, and incidentally the camp where theologian Dietrich Bonhoeffer was hanged, set out at gunpoint for Regensburg, 50 miles to the south. However, with no good reason except the hope of killing off the prisoners through extreme physical exertion, lack of food and inadequate clothing against the cold, their captors forced them on a northward route. Many had no shoes. On their northernmost stretch, these unfortunates passed a mere stone's throw from where we sheltered at Neundorf. At nearby Lengenfeld, they turned south again. What should have been a 50-mile journey stretched into 250 needless miles. Stragglers were shot. Others dropped dead in their tracks and were left to rot in the frost and mud. Few survived.[151]

Another death march passed a mere 18 miles from us that spring. The marchers set out from Berga, a slave labor camp that held political prisoners, Jews and Russian and American prisoners of war. Aiming for Plauen, only 25 miles to the south, the prisoners covered 170 miles in a roundabout route designed to kill. Komotau, my father's home town, lay along their path. Their merciless captors denied them rest and food even when sympathetic German villagers tried to share with them. Hundreds collapsed and were shot along the way.[152]

These forced marches reflect the chaos into which the Reich was descending. Authority was disintegrating. Many of the guards had no idea who was in charge anymore. They also reflect the depth of hatred for Jews that ran through the captors, who at this point could have easily let them go without repercussion from a soon-to-be defunct Nazi government. In fact, Heinrich Himmler, intuiting that negotiations with the Allies might stand a better chance of success if Germany stopped all the killing, ordered the prisoners released into the countryside, but the years of Nazi propaganda, on top of centuries of anti-Semitism, had had their effect. The brutality continued.

A little farther to the south of us, a column of women trudged along at gunpoint. Forced out of the Helmbrechts camp wearing rags and given no food for the journey, over 1,000 women marched out the gates guarded by 45 male and female armed Germans. The Germans soon abandoned the Russian and Polish women, leaving them in a fairly decent state of health. For the Jewish prisoners, however, the march took a sinister turn. Having begun the trek in a state of starvation and ill health, they straggled southward through the Sudetenland. Their guards ate well, but only occasionally tossed the women a few miserably inadequate scraps of bread or doled out watery soup. They prevented sympathetic villagers from giving sustenance to the victims. Desperate, driven by whips and rifle butts, the starving women devoured grass and rotting animal fodder wherever it could be found. American troops were coming nearer. In order to outrun them, the Germans drove the women increasingly harder, allowing them rest only during the freezing April nights. Most of them lay on the ground in the open, exposed to the elements. Those lucky enough found barns to sleep in, but even they often died in their sleep. Finally the guards abandoned them. A mere remnant of skeletal survivors was discovered by American soldiers in Volary, Czechoslovakia in early May. The Americans lined up the dead in a neat row and forced the local Sudeten Germans to file past and behold the Nazis' handiwork.[153]

All of the death marches were led by, and their crimes perpetrated by, members of the SS.

Elfriede (at head of table) with Wehrmacht colleagues

Elfriede with Rudi and his mother Elisabeth

If the war is lost, the people will be lost also…
It is not necessary to worry about what the German
people will need for survival….
In any case, only those who are inferior will remain
after this struggle, for the good have already been killed.

—Adolf Hitler

CHAPTER 10

Back in Görlitz, the spring months brought a never-ending flow of refugees from the East, desperate to keep one step ahead of the advancing Russians. The quaint, historic city could hardly house them all. Having no choice but to camp in the city parks, they suffered from typhus, many dying without even basic medical attention.

Rumors circulated that the Führer was almost ready to unveil a *Wunderwaffe*—a miracle weapon that would turn the tide and give Germany the final victory. It was said that scientists were working on it around the clock somewhere up on the Baltic shore or maybe down south near the Bodensee or deep in the Black Forest. Supposedly this weapon contained enough power to wipe out huge swaths of England and destroy that nation's industrial centers. Yet Adolf Hitler seemed to be the only one left in Germany delusional enough to fully believe in such fantasies. Even while his war-fatigued people circulated the rumors, they remained unconvinced. Those who lived in Germany's eastern-most parts could hear the thunder of Russian artillery drawing nearer every day.

It was at this point that Elisabeth Kobsch decided to set out for Neundorf to find Elfriede. She had to piece together her journey by riding the few trains available, trudging on foot, and hitching rides on farmer's wagons. There was no gas for Walter's car; using precious fuel for private automobiles had long since been banned. She determined to hurry. Dear Friedel was carrying her only grandchild from her only son. Both she and Walter worried night and day about the young woman. They hoped to reach her before the Russians did and somehow protect her. Perhaps there was time to find her and bring her back home to Görlitz before the Red Army arrived, but the onus was on Elisabeth to accomplish the task. For Walter to accompany his wife was out of the question. Their entire livelihood was wrapped up in his textile shop; he must stay in Görlitz and guard it with his life.

With all the men off at war, Neundorf was mostly inhabited by women, children and old folks. Elfriede never knew how the baker had managed to avoid being called up to join the Army. Perhaps it was for health reasons. The old men formed a town watch and devised a system of warning should Russians approach. Wild rumors were circulating about Red Army soldiers raping every woman they could get their hands on. These stories had a ring of truth about them; they were verified by the ragged, disheveled refugees from the East who passed through Neundorf pushing and pulling carts loaded with all the earthly belongings that remained to them. A haunted look darkened their eyes, as if they had seen the devil himself. Watching them straggle past, Elfriede felt the urge to flee but knew it was best to stay put. Here, at least, she had food and shelter, and should the Russians come this far west she could hide in nearby fields and woods.

One night the old men sounded a warning. Mother grabbed me and followed the other women to a nearby bridge. Shivering with cold, trembling with terror and aware that rape would be their fate if they were discovered, the women concealed themselves beneath the bridge, cupping hands over their children's mouths. Hours dragged by. At last, with the sun's rising, Mother knew she had dodged a bullet. We straggled back to our temporary lodgings where she heard the sobering news that a group of women hiding in another part of town hadn't been so lucky.

Life had to go on. Rising early each morning to help our host family with household chores and taking her turn in the kitchen as well as looking after me, Elfriede felt soothed by the familiar rhythms of small town life. Routine, however mundane, was reassuring in a world gone mad.

Sometimes as she peeled potatoes or plunged her arms into scalding dishwater, she permitted herself to imagine the impossible: herself standing beside Rudi before the altar in the Lutheran church in Thommendorf, he in smart dress uniform, she looking like Marlene Dietrich in a draped, low-backed lamé gown, clutching a cascade of flowers, ribbons and greens. She fancied a summer wedding, one in which she could wear white sling-back heels with peep toes. The Wehrmacht had denied her this dream, but soon the war would end and Rudi would be discharged. If only she knew where he was! She had no reply from his parents and she didn't dare try to make her way back to Görlitz with Russian brutes roaming about.

One late April day, a woman jumped down from a wagon, thanked the farmer who had given her a lift and knocked on the door of our house. In one hand she clutched a letter listing this place as the return address. "Is Elfriede Kober here?" she asked our hostess.

When Elfriede recognized Rudi's mother, she rushed to her and seized her by the hands. Questions tumbled out faster than she could organize her thoughts. "How did you get here? Why isn't Walter with you? Where is Rudi?"

At the mention of her only son's name, Elisabeth began to weep. "Oh Friedel, I bring you such sad news." From her travel satchel she pulled an envelope. She would have opened it but Elfriede snatched it from her, ripping out its contents and devouring them with hungry eyes.

February 14, 1945
Dear Mr. Kobsch,

I have the sad duty of informing you that your son, Ordinance Officer Rudolf, fell in battle during the massive Russian attack on the Baranov Bridgehead near Ziçing on January 12, 1945. He was struck in the head, and according to his comrades, who immediately came to his aid, died immediately.

May the certainty that your son gave his life for the enduring greatness of the Fatherland comfort you in your deep sorrow. Through his heroic death, the Regiment has lost one of its finest, who remains an unforgettable example of fairness and justice to his comrades and fellow men.

Because of the severity of the battle and the enemy's quick advance, we were unfortunately unable to bury your son.

Heil Hitler!
Yours,
First Lieutenant and Adjutant Lange

Elfriede's expression went blank as she struggled to absorb the letter's contents, then crumpled as she finally comprehended. Rudi's letter spiraled to the floor as she clung to his mother and sobbed.

On the eighth of May, the Russians finally reached that part of Görlitz that lay east of the Neisse River, the part where Lisbeth and Elfriede had lived before fleeing in January. They renamed it Zgorzelice, declared it part of Poland, and set about crossing to the western side, an act made difficult by the fact that the Germans had blown up every bridge before departing. When they finally crossed over and began to occupy the city, Walter and Elisabeth Kobsch's textile shop was plundered until hardly a scrap of fabric remained.

During that last winter of the war, Heinrich Himmler was headquartered in the Black Forest in southwestern Germany working out of a fancy saloon wagon on a train near Triberg. In the autumn, with Allied troops occupying almost the whole of France, he had organized the *Volkssturm*, to which all available men between the ages of 16 and 60 were called up and formed into ragtag, ill-outfitted guerilla warfare units. In an October radio speech, he declared, "Our enemies must be taught to understand that every kilometer they advance into our country will cost them rivers of their own blood. Every building in the town, every village, every farm, every forest will be defended by men, young and old and—if necessary—by girls and women too." Rather than unleashing terror on a large scale, however, these *Volkssturm* units mostly helped frightened, war-weary civilians evacuate towns and villages when Allied troops approached.[154]

That fall, Himmler had also organized secretive sabotage units called "Werewolves," charging them with the task of wreaking havoc behind enemy lines.[155] The boys and men of "Operation Werewolf" were slightly more successful at sabotage, but in the end could do little to halt the Allied advance.

Brutal and ideologically driven to the end, Himmler decreed that any civilian overtures of surrender to the Allies, such as flying a white flag, would be punished with death.[156] As the Reich collapsed, however, even he admitted defeat, much to the disgust of a delusional Adolf Hitler. Hitler blamed Himmler for Germany's military losses late in the war and their relationship imploded. When the Führer learned of Himmler's attempts in April of 1945 to negotiate directly with General Eisenhower, he stripped him of all his authority and expelled him from the Nazi party.[157] It was one of Hitler's last official acts before putting a gun to his head in his Berlin bunker.

Himmler was stunned at this betrayal by the man he had served so slavishly. For a short time, he clung to the delusion that he and his beloved SS would be needed to help guide Germany into a postwar world. Reality soon slapped him in the face. Rejected by Grand Admiral Dönitz, whom Hitler had appointed his successor and who only wanted to surrender to the Allies unburdened by association with rabid Nazi ideologues, Himmler attempted to disguise himself and escape the Allies' notice, disappearing into oblivion in a country turned upside down.

Even as my pregnant mother, Rudi's mother and I awaited the end of the war in our remote hideaway near the Czech border, the former *Reichsführer SS* was captured by the British. They recognized him immediately, even though he had donned civilian clothing and was stubbornly insisting his name was Heinrich Hitzinger.[158] Eventually he realized the game was up. Unwilling to face justice, the man who had promised to provide for me and my fellow Lebensborn children committed suicide by biting down on a cyanide capsule.

Announcement of Germany's unconditional surrender to the Allies brought relief, but little comfort to Elfriede and Elisabeth. Heartbroken, plagued with uncertainty, they lingered in Neundorf until their hosts hinted strongly that since one month had passed since the surrender, it was time for them to be moving along. And they wanted to go. It was just that the Russians were out there prowling about the whole northeastern part of Germany, ravaging any women they happened upon. People were saying they didn't even spare grandmothers and young girls, subjecting them all indiscriminately to humiliating gang rapes. It was whispered about in the village that women who dared to resist would suffer mutilation, torture, even murder. Fueled by vodka and an insatiable craving for revenge for the German atrocities inflicted on their own people, these bestial acts hadn't stopped with Germany's surrender. So far, the occupying Soviets had taken only sporadic notice of tiny Neundorf, but they were bound to assert their presence more strongly in the future.

Elfriede and Elisabeth whispered together late into the night. How would they cover the 90 miles back to Görlitz? That particular train route had been bombed. Other forms of public transportation were paralyzed. There was no fuel for buses. They would have to walk, but the prospect seemed like a suicide mission. Left with little choice, they asked a local farmer if they might take one of his old wooden vegetable wagons. He agreed. On a sunny June morning, they loaded me into the wagon together with their few belongings and set off.

Keeping to narrow farm roads and forest paths, Elfriede and Elisabeth took turns pulling me in a northeasterly direction along the Czech-German border. With wary eyes, they kept constant watch for the pea-green uniforms of the Soviets. Since the summer landscape was bursting with shades of green, it was a difficult task.

"If only they wore red!" sighed Elfriede.

Whenever they thought they saw movement in the distance, they crouched low, hearts racing, clapping a hand over my mouth. At dusk, they knocked on the doors of farmhouses asking for water, a little food, and permission to shelter for the night. Most of the farmers took pity and gave what they could. Some merely waved us away. There were so many displaced people wandering the countryside in those days, first fleeing westward, then trudging eastward after war's end in an effort to get back home, exactly as we were doing.

One evening my mother rapped on the door of an isolated farmhouse at the edge of the forest. The farmer regarded her wearily, as if he had seen too many just like her and would be happy to see no more. He might have turned her away if he hadn't caught sight of the blond toddler in the wagon and the bedraggled, grandmotherly woman standing beside it.

"Go ahead, sleep in the barn," he growled before slamming the door.

That night, Elfriede collapsed in the straw and began to weep inconsolably. Neither Elisabeth's gentle reminders that she was upsetting me, nor her admonitions to be thankful that we at least had a roof over our heads and had so far evaded the Russians, could mollify the grieving young woman.

"I'm hungry and so tired, and I can't walk another day," Elfriede sobbed.

Elisabeth stroked her hair and felt her own heart break all over again. Rudi's Friedel was nearly seven months pregnant now. Her skirt wouldn't even button over her belly and she had to tie it with string where it gaped open. Her ankles were swollen. Remembering her own pregnancy and the ever-present fatigue of carrying another human being within, Elisabeth pitied the girl deeply. She felt utterly helpless. Elfriede needed more food than usual, yet some days all they had were raw dandelion leaves and milk surreptitiously squeezed from the udders of grazing cows, the owners of which were none the wiser. Friedel needed rest and an extra measure of understanding. Elisabeth could not provide her with food and rest, but she could offer sympathy, encourage her to keep going and not give up. Already they had covered more than two thirds of the journey home. Walter was eagerly awaiting them. His textile shop would bring in much needed money, especially now that the war was over and people could at last think of sewing new clothing and curtains.

Elfriede allowed herself to be comforted and eventually she quieted. But long after Elisabeth and I had fallen asleep, she wrestled with dark thoughts. Across the barn, a cow lowed, its plaintive voice providing accompaniment to her grief. Rudi had handed her his sealed letter on New Year's Day. Less than two weeks later, just six days shy of his twenty-sixth birthday, he lay sprawled in the mud and soot while Russian tanks rolled over his body and pressed him into the earth—the only burial he would ever have. It was devastating to think of the man she loved that way, rotting anonymously in the Polish countryside. And here she was awaiting his child, the one he had so hoped for. She hadn't realized how badly Rudi wanted a baby until Elisabeth arrived to break the tragic news, and the two women sat down together and opened his letter.

Relief washed over her to know that he would have rejoiced in her pregnancy, inconvenient though it was. She herself had no stomach for abortion. Yet she knew other women who, traumatized at the thought of another mouth to feed, had obtained one illegally at great personal risk. For in 1943, the Nazi government, in response to most Germans refusing to comply with its wishes by producing large families and stubbornly continuing to limit births, had declared abortion a capital crime punishable by death. A harsh measure, certainly. But necessary, thought Heinrich Himmler. German lives must be preserved at all costs. Conversely, that same year, on October 4 in Posen, Himmler commended SS men for their fortitude in the face of the psychologically taxing task of murdering Jewish men, women and children:

> "Most of you will know what it means to see 100 bodies lying together, when 500 are there or when there are 1000. And...to have seen this through, and—with the exception of human weakness—to have remained decent, has made us hard and is a page of glory."[159]

These obscene contradictions were far from Elfriede's mind as she lay silently weeping in the straw. The government that had wanted all those babies and even promised to help provide for and rear them, was now defunct. Imagining bringing a baby into the hell of a shattered, Russian-occupied Germany terrified her. She had managed to avoid being raped so far, but for how long would her luck hold? Advanced pregnancy was hardly a deterrent to the animal-like Russians, and it only made her more vulnerable, less able to fight or to run. What would life be like in Görlitz with those green uniforms lurking behind every corner?

She had allowed herself to dream of a life with Rudi. That was a huge mistake. Elfriede's grief was all the more visceral for having dreamt. If she was going to survive, she would have to harden herself. She would have to get about the business of feeding and clothing two children while surrounded by and submitting to the enemy. Practicality and stoicism would be her best weapons. If she could master her emotions, beat them down and learn to focus on getting through one day at a time, there just might be a chance of overcoming.

As precarious as my future was as I rolled in the wagon toward Görlitz, I was fortunate compared to many children born in Lebensborn homes. I had spent only four motherless months in Heim Wienerwald. Now we were together and Elfriede was determined to raise me herself. A home awaited us in a town that had escaped bomb damage. Although I had narrowly missed out on gaining a stepfather who loved my mother and accepted me completely, he'd left me a sister and thereby increased my little family by one third, strengthening it and giving me a sense of belonging as I grew.

Other Lebensborn children had lived through and were still suffering far greater trauma than I. When the Allies began bombing northern Germany in 1940, the nurses and mothers in Lebensborn facilities such as Heim Hohehorst near Bremen, snatched babies from their cribs and rushed with them into cellars and shelters. This harrowing ordeal was repeated for weeks on end. Staff, mothers and children were plagued with exhaustion and unquenchable fear. Finally evacuating the danger zone, Lebensborn shipped the pregnant mothers, infants and nurses to other homes around Germany, many of them on Heinrich Himmler's private airplane. Later, when the danger had passed, Heim Hohehorst resumed its work. When the British arrived in 1945, they found over 50 toddlers who had been abandoned there by their mothers.[160] At Heim Sonnenwiese near Kohren-Sahlis, the Americans found 93 such children.[161]

As the Allies made progress in the West, the Lebensborn homes in France, Belgium and Luxembourg had to be evacuated, along with several other homes in western Germany. Their mothers and children were divvied up among the few remaining Lebensborn homes within Germany.

Later as the Russians gained ground in the East, the occupants of Lebensborn homes there, including children who had been given up for adoption and were still awaiting families, were loaded into trains and also sent to Heim Steinhöring near Münich. Southern Bavaria was Hitler's alpine stronghold, intended to be a last holdout against Allied attack. Never to be denied the best of what Germany had to offer, these Lebensborn children were supplied with plenty of food for the journey and an SS escort to keep hungry citizens from attacking the train.[162]

The Allies bombed Münich many times but the damage inflicted in January of 1945 was by far worse than any previous. When the Lebensborn Central Administration offices on Herzog-Max Strasse were destroyed, executive director Max Sollman fled the city and took up residence at Heim Steinhöring. He'd managed to salvage all the Lebensborn files, among which were the names of thousands of illegitimate babies' fathers, and store them with him on the grounds of the last Lebensborn refuge. By the time the Americans closed in, Sollmann had fled. The SS men left behind to guard the property built bonfires and tossed the files into the flames.[163] They had been ordered by Sollmann to destroy every last scrap of paper associated with Lebensborn.

In May 1945, American troops walked into a chaotic scene at Steinhöring. They found 162 babies and toddlers, scores of terrified pregnant women, some of who were German, many who were from places like Norway, Denmark, Belgium, France and Holland and had been brought to Germany from the besieged and abandoned Lebensborn homes in their own countries, where they were supposed to have given birth to children fathered by German soldiers. At the very end, even the SS guards assigned to protect them had deserted them,[164] leaving behind the smoldering ashes of the children's documented heritage.

The Norwegian women at Steinhöring had endured a particularly long and painful odyssey. When the Germans invaded Norway in 1940, SS General Friedrich Wilhelm Rediess sent out an internal SS memo reading:

It is desired that German soldiers father as many children with Norwegian women as possible, whether legitimate or illegitimate.[165]

Why? Because Nazi racial theorists believed Norway contained the most perfect specimens of pure Aryan blood. It wasn't necessary to rape Norwegian women in order to achieve the desired result. Understanding that relationships between occupying soldiers and women in the countries they occupy develop quite naturally, the Nazi occupation government did all it could to facilitate such liaisons. SS and Army soldiers were encouraged to attend open air concerts, dances, nightclubs, to mingle with the local women in cinemas, pubs and restaurants. Nothing was forbidden: visits to prostitutes, one night stands, longer-lasting affairs, even marriage. The strategy worked. So many young Norwegian women became pregnant that Lebensborn set up 11 homes in Norway. The women who entered those homes were desperate for a place to turn, for though their countrymen might turn a blind eye to flirtatious romance with German soldiers, something about one of their own bearing the enemy's child got under their skin.[166] It was perceived, in fact, as the ultimate act of collaboration.

Those Norwegian women whose families allowed it gave birth at home and kept their babies, but many desperately needed the refuge of a Lebensborn home where the Germans rejoiced over each new little Aryan life and encouraged the women to take their children and settle in Germany or give them up for adoption by German couples. Many a young woman, deeply in love or simply infatuated with her baby's father, envisioned marriage and a happily-ever-after with him in Germany, failing to grasp that for him it was just a war-time fling endorsed by his government.[167] The men had merely enjoyed the license given to them by Himmler's new morality, pursuing pleasure while simultaneously serving their country by fathering Aryan children. For them, service in Norway had been something of a dream job.

In all, around 8,000–10,000 Norwegian women gave birth to babies fathered by Germans. Only 1,200 were born in Lebensborn homes and the rest entered the world either in Norwegian medical facilities or at the women's family homes. But 8,000 registered with Lebensborn because it offered them financial help and the possibility of either leaving for Germany or taking the babies off their hands in a society where they were taunted with epithets like "Whore!" and "Collaborator!" Norwegian women who entered the homes weren't offered the same secrecy privileges extended to German women. Because a woman couldn't check in until six weeks before her due date, her pregnancy was obvious to all. Shunned and scorned by their countrymen, coming to the painful realization that the handsome soldiers they'd fallen for had no intention of marrying them, many Norwegian women chose to give their babies up for adoption. Such babies were sent by ship to Germany where some were adopted and others lived out the war in Lebensborn children's homes. A few of these were claimed by their fathers.

Plenty of Norwegian women kept their babies, choosing to raise them in Norway as single mothers or to try their luck in Germany where they at least would not be vilified as collaborators. Around 2,000 of them traveled to Germany. They had spent their last pennies to get there and found heartache and disappointment awaiting them. Often, the German men who had proposed marriage were not willing to deliver on that promise. Either they were already married or simply disinterested in pursuing the relationship. German women were jealously possessive of the few men left after the war and hardly welcomed the presence of single foreign women to compete with.[168] Their hopes shattered, many managed to scrape together enough money to return to Norway with babies in tow, resigned to facing their society's disapproval. Those who couldn't manage to return stayed in Germany by default.

Walter Kobsch almost collapsed with relief when Elisabeth and Elfriede straggled through the door of his apartment. The two women had waited until dark and approached the building stealthily, ducking out of sight of any Russian patrols. Walter had done his best to clean up the damage, but the marauding Russians' handiwork was still painfully in evidence in the form of smashed doors, broken dishes, gashes in the walls made by bayonets and rifle butts. They had looted his textile shop so thoroughly that hardly a scrap of fabric remained. All the fine linens and laces had disappeared. But now our little almost-family was together again, and together we would find a way to survive.

Rudi and Elfriede December, 1944

Transcript of Rudi's letter to Elfriede

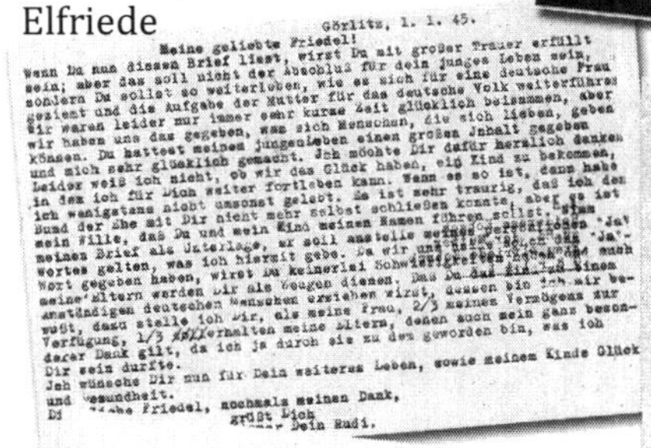

Görlitz, 1. 1. 45.

Meine geliebte Friedel!

Wenn Du nun diesen Brief liest, wirst Du mit großer Trauer erfüllt sein; aber das soll nicht der Abschluß für dein junges Leben sein, sondern Du sollst so weiterleben, wie es sich für eine deutsche Frau geziemt und die Aufgabe der Mutter für das deutsche Volk weiterführen. Wir waren leider nur immer sehr kurze Zeit glücklich beisammen, aber wir haben uns das gegeben, was sich Menschen, die sich lieben, geben können. Du hattest meinem jungenleben einen großen Inhalt gegeben und mich sehr glücklich gemacht. Ich möchte Dir dafür herzlich danken. Leider weiß ich nicht, ob wir das Glück haben, ein Kind zu bekommen, in dem ich für Dich weiter fortleben kann. Wenn es so ist, dann habe ich wenigstens nicht umsonst gelebt. Es ist sehr traurig, daß ich den Bund der Ehe mit Dir nicht mehr selbst schließen konnte, aber es ist mein Wille, daß Du und mein Kind meinen Namen führen sollst. [illegible] meinen Brief als Unterlage, er soll anstelle meines [illegible] 'Ja'-wortes gelten, was ich hiermit gebe. Da wir uns [illegible] auch Wort gegeben haben, wirst Du keinerlei Schwierigkeiten [illegible] meine Eltern werden Dir als Zeugen dienen. Das Du das Kind zu einem anständigen deutschen Menschen erziehen wirst, dessen bin ich mir bewußt, dazu stelle ich Dir, als meine Frau, 2/3 meines Vermögens zur Verfügung, 1/3 erhalten meine Eltern, denen auch mein ganz besonderer Dank gilt, da ich ja durch sie zu dem geworden bin, was ich Dir sein durfte.

Ich wünsche Dir nun für Dein weiteres Leben, sowie meinem Kinde Glück und Gesundheit.

Di[illegible] Friedel, nochmals meinen Dank, grüßt Dich [illegible] Dein Rudi.

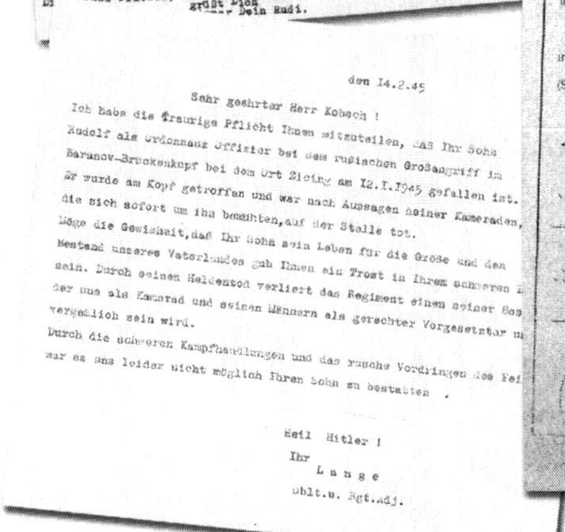

den 14.2.45

Sehr geehrter Herr Kobsch !

Ich habe die traurige Pflicht Ihnen mitzuteilen, daß Ihr Sohn Rudolf als Ordonnanz Offizier bei dem rußischen Großangriff im Baranov-Brückenkopf bei dem Ort Ziciny am 12.1.1945 gefallen ist. Er wurde am Kopf getroffen und war nach Aussagen seiner Kameraden, die sich sofort um ihn bemühten, auf der Stelle tot.

Möge die Gewisheit, daß Ihr Sohn sein Leben für die Grosse und den Bestand unseres Vaterlandes gab Ihnen ein Trost in Ihrem schweren [illegible] sein. Durch seinen Heldentod verliert das Regiment einen seiner Bes[illegible] der uns als Kamerad und seinen Männern als gerechter Vorgesetzter u[illegible] vergeßlich sein wird.

Durch die schweren Kampfhandlungen und das rasche Vordringen des Fei[illegible] war es uns leider nicht möglich Ihren Sohn zu bestatten .

Heil Hitler !

Ihr

Lange

Oblt.u. Rgt.Adj.

Letter to Walter Kobsch informing him of Rudi's death

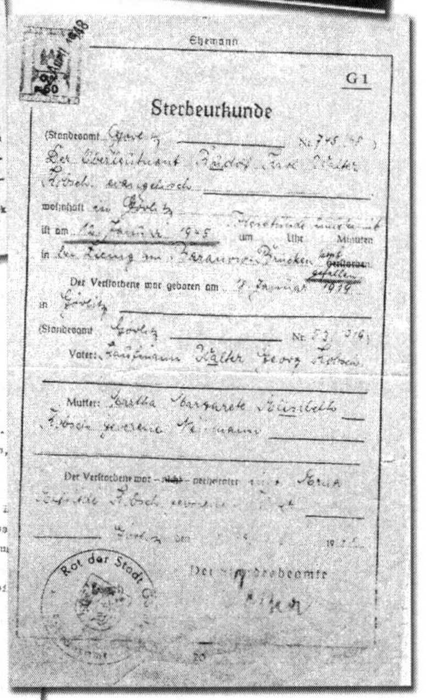

Ehemann

G 1

Sterbeurkunde

Rudi's death certificate

Der Winter ohne Kohlen, die Schuhe ohne Sohlen,
die Lehrer ohne ABC.
(Winter without coal, shoes without soles,
teachers who don't know their ABCs.)

—1940s graffiti scrawled on the *Ratskeller*
in Hoyerswerda, East Germany

CHAPTER 11

Chaos and confusion reigned when the Russians marched into Görlitz. The townspeople cowered behind closed doors, unsure of exactly who was now in charge. Soviet military commanders could barely control their men, to whom the ordinary trappings of everyday German life looked like wanton luxuries. Dazzled by an abundance of niceties they rarely saw at home, they simply helped themselves to bicycles, fur coats, jewelry, sausages, cheeses, furniture, pianos and liqueurs. They had a special fascination for wristwatches; some Red Army soldiers stole enough to wear two or three on each arm.

"Fortunately," Walter told Elisabeth and Elfriede, "it looks as if the Russian military commanders are starting to be replaced with administrators who actually know how to run things. What it all means for the future remains to be seen. With any luck, the occupation will last a year at most, perhaps two. Maybe after they've thoroughly humiliated us, they'll have had enough and withdraw." For the time being, the inhabitants of Görlitz simply had to accept the harsh reality that they were living under the thumb of those they considered to be Slavic barbarians. The fact that Walter had owned his own business and Rudi had been an officer in the hated German Army made the Kobsch family particular targets as capitalists and Fascists.

Walter Kobsch had been truly conflicted over Rudi's romance with Elfriede. It was no trifling thing for a man of his generation to discover that the son he adored had fathered a child not only out of wedlock, but with a woman who appeared to make a habit of such behavior. Yet Rudi was lost to him now. All that remained of his beloved only child was the unborn baby in Elfriede's womb, a treasure beyond worth. Was that not reason enough to embrace the girl, to treat her like a daughter? No question remained; he must protect her at all costs.

Kobsch sat the women down and minced no words. With his own eyes he had seen Russian soldiers drag mattresses out of apartment buildings, order German women to lie down on them and line up to abuse them in full view of passersby. If husbands, brothers and fathers objected, they were shot on the spot. In fact, the Red Army had requisitioned the entire ground floor of this very apartment building and six soldiers were bunking down there. Elisabeth and Elfriede could not risk going outside or even down the stairs, at least not until things changed, if they ever did.

"The Russians go on drunken rampages at night," said Walter. "They break into people's apartments, looking for women. As long as the weather is warm, I insist that you both sleep on the roof. I'll run any errands that need running." Walter alone would deal with the Russians if they required something. He laid a gentle hand on my mother's arm. "You're carrying our grandchild, Friedel," he said, "and that child is all Elisabeth and I have left of Rudi. I will do my very best to protect you, but you must promise to do everything I say. If you have to go outside for any reason, put on baggy clothes and pull your hair up into a cap to disguise the fact that you're female."

So we remained behind bolted doors. It wasn't difficult to comply with Walter's wishes at first; Elfriede was exhausted from the journey and had no desire to go anywhere. When she peered out from behind lace curtains, she saw Russian soldiers everywhere, crossing the street below, lingering on corners, swarming the railway platforms at the train station across the road. Watching their movements, she felt trapped in a cage, yet there was little she could do to free herself. Her body was becoming more and more ponderous. I was fretful and clingy, insecure in my new surroundings. In quiet moments, my mother solaced herself by re-reading Rudi's letter. Clearly he had wanted what she also desperately wanted—for his name to legitimize her coming baby. However precarious her future, she desired to face it as Rudi's widow, not a "loose woman" with two illegitimate children at whom society was sure to look askance.

Before the war, the Nazis had imposed strict guidelines on couples wishing to marry. If either man or woman was found to carry genetic defects, a couple was denied a license and the promised marriage loan of 1,000 *Reichsmark*. This exclusionary policy backfired, lowering the marriage rate and making things problematic for a government that supposedly stood for marriage and traditional family values. In an attempt to remedy the situation, during the war the government relaxed its standards somewhat. Beginning in 1939, a soldier and his fiancée could take their marriage vows long distance, and a blind eye was turned to minor genetic defects or family illnesses.[169]

Still, the marriage rate fell. Life during wartime was so uncertain that young people postponed marriage, unsure of what tomorrow would bring. With so many men falling in battle, a more radical policy was needed to shore up plummeting marriage statistics and raise sinking morale. In November 1941, Hitler decreed that postmortem marriages would henceforth be allowed. The new policy allowed women like my mother, who had been denied the opportunity to marry their still-living Wehrmacht fiancés, to finally legitimize their children and collect military widows' benefits. The Nazi government didn't want the policy to become widely known and tried to keep its existence hush-hush, a privilege only for the military. Yet word of it leaked. People who got wind of it snidely called it "corpse marriage."[170]

Rudi had known that as a Wehrmacht officer, only in death could he marry Elfriede. He had written her the letter of January 1, 1945 as a way of proving his intent and giving her what she needed to seal the bargain.

Now, almost six months later, she determined to put the letter to work. Before leaving for the eastern front, when Rudi had given his parents the original notarized and sealed letter, he instructed them to turn it over to the civil magistrate at City Hall. They had done so as soon as possible and its contents were processed on January 11, one day before his death. Even under Russian occupation, local governments still functioned and German civil law remained in effect concerning matters of marriage. Together with Walter and Elisabeth, Elfriede risked going out in public for this all-important errand without which her coming baby would be doomed to illegitimacy, like me. They took me along, hoping a toddler's presence would deter rape in broad daylight, for the Russians, if dangerous to women, were known to be fond of and even downright indulgent toward children.

At the marriage registry desk, Rudi's letter was dug out of the files and compared with Elfriede's copy. His parents stood by her side as witnesses to her verbal vow of marriage with their dead son. The letter was transcribed; documents were signed and stamped. When the sad little ceremony and its attending bureaucratic ritual were completed, Elfriede applied for a widow's pension. Afterward, the newly forged family returned home, the women keeping their heads down and Walter one eye behind him.

I have no recollections of Christmas or birthday celebrations in Görlitz. Hunger is my most pervasive memory during those postwar years. An ever-present gnawing sensation and the constant scrounging for food loom large in my memory, but otherwise I was too young to notice the gradual changes taking place as the Russians tightened their grip on eastern Germany.

Believing that Germany owed their nation war reparations and perceiving the only way to get them was to simply seize them, the Russians systematically dismantled factories, down to stripping out the plumbing and wiring, and sent them home to be reassembled. They ripped up railroad ties and took those along with the trains. Tram cars, trucks, machinery, coal, iron ore and steel left Germany and made their way to the Soviet Union. All this looting dealt a death blow to the German economy in the eastern zone. With textile factories disassembled and shipped away, Walter Kobsch had no way of replenishing the stock in his textile shop. His car was also confiscated and sent to Russia.

Trainloads of German grain, sugar and alcohol were shipped to the Soviet Union. Local crops were requisitioned to feed the Russian soldiers. Amidst this staggering loss, the Germans sank into a passive state of depression. Thousands of German soldiers, captured by the Russians during the war, were still being held in camps in the East while those who returned from western POW camps were whisked off to undergo political "re-education" before being allowed to return to their families.

If through her "corpse marriage" my mother hoped to secure a respectable position for herself in a post-Russian German society, she was sadly mistaken. It soon became clear that the Soviets had no intention of releasing their hold on Saxony and the other eastern German states. With the passing of time, they became more firmly entrenched, rendering her marriage to a deceased Wehrmacht officer a strike against her rather than an advantage. The Russians despised everything having to do with the hated Nazi regime and were quick to punish anyone with any connection to it.

At least Rudi hadn't been an SS officer. SS butchers had committed atrocities all over Russia and were especially despised. Elfriede had held onto all of Kurt Novak's ancestral birth, death and marriage records but they weren't incriminating in and of themselves. My mother didn't know that the Lebensborn records listing my father's name and SS rank had gone up in flames, but she did rest in the knowledge that they were safely tucked away in the American-occupied sector of Germany. As far as the taint of my SS parentage was concerned, she felt safe.

Daily life grew harsher. The black market thrived despite severe penalties for anybody caught dealing in it. Those wanting extra food to supplement their meager rations had to bribe Russians and many women offered up their bodies in order to feed their families. Immediately after the war ended, an election of dubious authenticity was held which placed in power a German communist government. This new government was merely a puppet whose strings Stalin pulled; thus, eastern Germany entered into the process of being "Stalinized." Private farms became collectives; privately owned factories were nationalized. The man I began to call "Opa" was allowed to reopen his shop, but there was little left for him to sell. He gathered together the few bolts and remnants of fabric the marauding Russians had left him and tried to eke out a livelihood.

When my sister, Heiderose, was born in September, Kobsch Oma and Opa were thrilled to see the reflection of their departed child in her lovely features. The fact that she was female, however, dashed Opa's hopes of a male to carry on his family name. This cemented his hatred of me. With my thoroughly Nazi origins, my presence was a constant reminder of the delusional Führer whose imbecility and mishandling of the war had killed his only son. As far as a male heir was concerned, Walter Kobsch was left with nothing but the son of a faceless SS officer, a product of a married man's promiscuity, no less.

Was it he that forbade my taking Rudi's—and his—last name, or was it simply a bureaucratic impossibility? When the posthumous marriage took place, my mother became Elfriede Kobsch. She had no birth certificate for me. This would have made things difficult, but surely many such documents were lost in the chaos of the war's end. All over Germany, with registry offices bombed and records burnt, allowances and adjustments had to be made. Elfriede could have explained her situation and requested to have my name changed too, thus officially including me in her new little family. Did she even try? If she did, did Walter Kobsch object? If he had, she was unlikely to cross him. Rudi's father was her lifeline to survival. He provided a roof over our heads and a sense of security, however flimsy. This possibility is less painful for me to accept than to entertain the idea that she intentionally excluded me.

Whatever the reason, I remained Wolfgang Kober. Throughout my childhood, whenever I tried to call myself Wolfgang Kobsch, I was corrected with, "No, your last name is Kober." Later, as a schoolboy learning to write, I tried to spell out the name Kobsch and was told, "No, erase it. Your name is Kober."

Oma and Opa, whom I believed were my own as well as Heidi's, cooed and smiled at the little bundle, their own flesh and blood, a living thing arising out of the grave. I hadn't known Opa was capable of such a smile since I was never on the receiving end of one. Mostly he ignored me and avoided eye contact with me. He made silly, playful faces at Heidi, cuddling her and covering her soft cheeks in kisses. When we worked or picnicked in the garden plot, Opa watched protectively over Heidi. Was she warm enough? Was she secure in her little seat? Why was she crying—could she be hungry? Was her diaper wet? Never once did he play or laugh with me, tickle me, show the slightest interest in my comfort or safety.

Walter and Elisabeth Kobsch had also taken my mother's sister Lisbeth and her children under their wing. After we fled Görlitz with the Army employees in January of 1945, Lisbeth had bundled up her own three children and joined the westward exodus from the city. Accompanied by her mother-in-law, Frau Becker, she had made it to the countryside outside of Dresden just in time for the heinous bombing. The little family sheltered on a farm that night as the horizon glowed from the doomed, blazing city. Once back in Görlitz, the two sisters joyfully reunited. Lisbeth's husband Hans was now in a British POW camp in Northern Ireland. For Elfriede's sake, Rudi's parents treated Lisbeth as part of the family, welcoming her children into their apartment and their garden on many occasions. Kobsch Opa showed them nothing but kindness, constantly asking about Hans' well-being, expressing how he hoped the young father would soon come home. Perhaps this was his way of filling the void left by his dead son.

There was a limit to Walter's emotional largesse, however, and I stood just beyond it. For me, he had nothing but loathing.

All this I accepted as the unchangeable reality of my life. My mother was never within hearing distance when Kobsch Opa hissed a furious, "I can't stand you!" at me. Despite not knowing why he spewed such vitriol my way, I never questioned his right to do so. This was simply my role in the family, at least where Kobsch Opa was concerned—that of the despised child. There was nowhere for me to turn, especially when my mother disappeared for several weeks. Only much later did I learn that she'd crossed alone into the western zone on a mission to buy socks for me and Heidi, an item that for some reason was impossible to find in the Russian zone. She returned empty-handed. At the border, coming home, she was arrested, accused of theft and detained in a jail cell. With her indomitable charm, she managed at last to befriend one of the guards. One day, for no apparent reason and without so much as an explanation, he unlocked her cell and told her to leave. She hurried home to us, deeply shaken.

Our garden *Laube* was a welcome escape from the green uniforms patrolling the streets, the constant fear of police knocking on the door and dragging us away. In the city, I was still too small to play outside by myself, so during the day I remained shut up in the Kobschs' second floor apartment at Sattigstrasse 26, where the balcony provided my only escape. When Lisbeth brought Inge, Peter and Rosel over to visit, they would round the corner and glimpse me on the balcony. "Bub!" they called out, waving excitedly. Ecstatic at the prospect of being with my cousins, I would press my face through the iron grill and shriek with delight.

The balcony overlooked the train station. On lonely days, peering down for hours on end, I began a love affair with trains that is still going strong today. The clanging of the cars connecting thrilled me; even more so the ear-piercing whistle, sparks flying upward out of the chimney and steam blasting out the sides. My heart picked up speed as the wheels of a departing train began to turn, the chugging sound working a hypnotic effect on me. Here was a powerful beast, magical and free and utterly entrancing to a puny, caged boy.

Görlitz had come through the war virtually unscathed. Living conditions were decent: we had electricity and running water in our intact houses. Mother and Oma no longer feared being raped by the six Russians downstairs; they turned out to be officers who were ashamed of their countrymen's behavior. In fact, the rapes, though still occurring sporadically, subsided significantly once the Russian soldiers were segregated from the German population and made to live in compounds.

Conditions were livable but the Kobsch apartment was crowded. Mother, Heidi and I slept together in one room. There was no yard in which I could play and burn up energy. Itching to be the mistress of her own turf, Elfriede applied to the housing authority and asked for permission to live with Heidi and me in a small apartment she had found in a suburb of Görlitz, called Rauschwalde. Under communist control, rents were cheap and with her widow's benefits, my mother could easily manage. Permission was granted.

With a living room, kitchen and two bedrooms on the ground floor of a four-story building, it was perfect for our needs. I, and later Heidi, could run in and out to play in the yard which had a swing set and most delightful of all, other children. From that yard, I often stole away to the train tracks at the edge of town. My hair whipped in the wind as the trains flew past, first the shiny red and black steam trains with bright lights then as time went on, the pea-green East German electric and diesel trains that looked so drab in comparison, with their lights glowing a dull yellow hue. Those trains just didn't have the pizzazz of the war-era steam engines. They lacked an aura of excitement and adventure as they lumbered along, pulling freight. Today, in my home, I model German trains in G scale and as I lovingly assemble them, I once again become that small boy waiting along the tracks, utterly enraptured.

On those occasions when Heidi was allowed to toddle outside with me, I had to stick close to the building and keep an eye on her. We would play with the other apartment children, making piles of leaves and jumping in them, pushing each other on the swings, digging in the dirt or playing tag. No matter how absorbed in my play, however, I snapped to attention whenever our kitchen window flew open.

"Wolf! Bring Heidi inside, right now!"

Knowing the penalty for failing to obey my mother would be a hard swat with a broom, I hastened to grab Heidi's little hand and lead her inside.

"Both of you, get under the bed and stay there!"

Sure enough, whenever that happened, a siren sounded along with an approaching motor and the slamming of car doors. *Volkspolizei*, trying to look official in their pieced-together combinations of old Army and police uniforms and carrying billy clubs, would knock on a neighbor's door and haul someone away for interrogation, then arrest them for "reasons of security." All too often, that unfortunate soul was never seen again.

I have never been able to figure out how Mother knew. Did a network exist by which neighbors alerted one another to the approach of the dreaded communist police? Myself oblivious, I learned to trust her instincts. At the age of five, I understood that I lived in a dangerous world in which unquestioning obedience was vital to our little family's survival. Heidi and I clung to our mother; she was all we had. She protected us and fed us what scant bit of food she could get her hands on. Alone with her, I felt equally as loved as Heidi, but in the city with Opa and Oma, I knew I was only tolerated, and that just barely.

With little food available in shops and the last of our garden's produce used up, Elfriede was reduced to foraging and begging for sustenance. When she wasn't working at one of the temporary jobs she managed to find, standing in line for meager bread rations and begging became a full time job of sorts. Whenever possible, she gathered stinging nettle to boil into soup. Mostly she left us with Oma and Opa while she made the rounds knocking on doors, attempting to trade small items for food.

In the autumn, she took Heidi and me out to farmers' fields where she showed us how to follow along after the harvesters and glean potatoes they had missed. One chilly October night, she left Heidi and me asleep in bed and trudged out, knife in hand, to steal a pumpkin right off the vine. Struggling to carry it home, she hoped that by its sheer size it would insure us several days' worth of food. We watched her wrestle with the corpulent vegetable as she plunged the knife in and out, peeling, chopping, scooping. She cooked it in every way she could think of: grating it onto salads, mixing it with flour and baking it, stretching it thin by puréeing it into soup. On the day that she ladled out the last of the soup, she dissolved into tears.

"Mutti, why are you crying?" I felt so unsettled, seeing her like that.

"Because winter is coming, Wolf. There are no more pumpkins where that one came from."

How odd it felt to be living in a modern apartment building with nice furniture and have absolutely no food in the cupboards. In the eastern zone, people began to sing irreverent words to the tune of the German national anthem under their breath:

Germany, Germany, without everything,
Without butter, without fat,
And our little bit of jam
Is gobbled up by the government.
During the Kaiser's reign we had it good—
We had pork to eat.
When old Hindenburg ruled,
We had beef roast.
With Hitler and Göring
We at least had a herring.
But under the current regime,
We only read about food in the newspaper.[171]

Mother dragged us with her to various outlying farms, hoping our skinny, saucer-eyed presence would elicit pity. Any baby fat I'd carried had long since vanished, leaving me with bony elbows and kneecaps protruding from stick-like limbs.

"Please, ma'am," she would say as soon as the door opened, holding out both hands in supplication. "I have a spool of thread and a sewing needle from my father-in-law's shop. Would you trade with me for a potato, or an egg, or both? I'll even take a wilted carrot or a few cabbage leaves."

"Leave us alone. You have ration coupons, just like everyone else," some replied curtly. Money didn't tempt them; there was nothing to buy with it anyway. People wanted *things* in exchange for food—things no longer available on store shelves.

"We're city people," she retorted, "and the rations are meager. You can supplement them with food from your farm, but we can't!"

Some of the farmers' wives, in a gesture of pity, traded with her whether or not they actually needed another needle or spool of thread. At such times, we carried our priceless treasures home with utmost care, afraid to break an egg and diminish the size of our next meal. Eventually I began slipping outside and wandering into the field across the road from our apartment building in hopes of spying an overlooked potato or cabbage leaves drifting in the wind.

It was finally determined in the summer of 1948 that Rudi's entire inheritable net worth was 200 *Reichsmark*. Divided between his parents and his wife in a black market economy where one cigarette sold for the equivalent of a working man's weekly wages, it managed to buy only a few extras to supplement our starvation diet before it disappeared into thin air.

School might have distracted me from the constant nagging fear that our little family of three might be separated and one of us dragged away in the night. But I never attended school in the Russian zone. Mother didn't want to send me to school only to have me indoctrinated. Besides, conditions in the eastern zone schools were horrendous. No chalk, no blackboards. Cold, dark classrooms with few light bulbs available to illuminate them. Teachers dressed as poorly as their ragged pupils. Textbooks were in short supply. Most teachers at the time were former Nazis who had gone through a three week "anti-fascist" training. Tired of an oppressive communist regime and the political role they were forced to play in indoctrinating children, they kept slipping away to the West. This made the teacher-student ratio such that classrooms were hopelessly overcrowded.[172]

We often spent time with Oma and Opa in town. Walter's shop was still technically open for business, but with textile factories shut down he could hardly replenish his stock, and even the few remaining factories were up against a shortage of raw cotton and wool. In 1946, the Soviets had made the seizing of his business legal by passing a vote in Saxony that the property of war criminals and those who had been active Nazis would pass to ownership of the people.[173] So far, the regime had allowed him to keep his shop open but began to demand he turn over his profits. Opa Kobsch fit the Soviet definition of a war criminal merely because his shop had continued to turn a small profit during the war. It mattered little to the Russians whether he had wholeheartedly embraced the tenets of Nazism or not. He felt helpless. The shop would have to be given up; he saw no way to continue on with it. There was now little hope that the Soviets would withdraw from the eastern zone. In fact, word on the street was that the Russians were preparing to create a new East German state, cementing its separation from the rest of Germany and ensuring forever its commitment to communism. Walter and Elisabeth found the very thought unbearable but, now in their sixties, felt they had no choice but to stay put.

"How does one start over at our age?" Opa kept saying, shaking his head.

Elfriede, on the other hand, was 27 and hoped for many years still ahead of her. Life was bleak in the Russian zone for a young woman who craved a little fun in order to forget her misery. During the exceptionally cold winters immediately following the war, most stage theaters and music halls were closed down for lack of fuel to heat them. Cinemas, also cold and drafty, stayed open but the Russian films they showed were poor quality and had somber political themes. Their tendency to portray Russians as heroes and Germans as evil villains grated on German audiences.[174]

Elfriede was growing alarmed watching Heidi's and my ribs become visible through our pale skin. Confronted with the specter of starvation, she began to fantasize about spiriting her little family out of the Russian zone and into the West. If she was going to do it, she had to act soon, while I was still young enough for her to make excuses about not enrolling me in school. The more she thought about it, the more sense it made and the more it seemed the only option. Communism, as practiced by the occupying Russians, obviously didn't work. We and everyone around us were growing thinner by the day and lived in constant fear.

She had other motivations too. One day, I overheard a conversation between her and Opa.

"We're next," he said.

"What do you mean, Walter?"

"The Americans! They dropped that nuclear bomb on Japan at the end of the war, and now they hate the Russians every bit as much as they hated the Japanese. Don't you see, Friedel? We are Russians now, as far as the Americans are concerned. I wouldn't be surprised if one day soon they bomb us into oblivion!"

This careless speculation in front of a five-year-old sent me into paroxysms of fear. Every time I heard the jet engines of the *Messerschmitts* at the airfield a few blocks away from our Rauschwalde apartment and whenever violent thunderstorms broke over us, as they often did, I began to shake uncontrollably, diving for shelter under my mother's bed, certain that bombs were falling.

Opa's prophecies of doom, fed by Russian propaganda, did not seem irrational or far-fetched to Elfriede and she took them into consideration. More than ever, she wanted out of the Russian zone. She wondered who could possibly help her. In earlier days, through her work at the Wehrmacht Administration, she had enjoyed the acquaintance of many high-ranking military men. Her natural charm and beauty had drawn them to her like bees to pollen. Now, in this communist environment, to admit she had a connection to any of them would damn her. They were powerless to help her or even themselves now, scattered as they were and trying to pick up the pieces of their shattered lives or even to mask their identities. She felt utterly alone.

"I want to leave here and go to the American zone," she confided to her parents-in-law.

"Leave us? Haven't we been kind to you, Elfriede?"

She couldn't deny that they had. Kobsch Opa had grown to love my mother because Rudi had loved her and because she had delivered Heidi, Rudi's parting gift. If he could only do more for her, he would. The thought of losing Heidi tormented both Walter and Elisabeth, but try as she might, Elfriede could see absolutely no future in Görlitz. If she stayed much longer, her hope would be utterly depleted. It was humiliating to be young and strong and willing to work, yet reduced to a beggar's life. The elder Kobschs' love for Heidi was palpable, but Heidi couldn't eat love. My mother had willingly cast in her lot with Rudi's parents but not even their unflagging support could make life under communism bearable.

"You've been so very good to me," she admitted. "But do you want Heidi to live like this—always hungry? We can't even get coal to heat the apartment! If I could just get a good job doing some kind of physical work, our rations would increase, but how can we Germans find jobs when the Russians have taken all our factories?"

"I'm going to file a complaint to the local commissar and protest my status as a war criminal," Walter told her. "They seem to be easing up a bit. If we can just ride it out until my complaint is processed, a court will surely decide in my favor."

Frankly, she didn't believe it. To Elfriede, it was evident that Walter was clinging to false hopes. "Those Soviet 'courts' take forever to process anything," she scoffed, "and even then, they aren't likely to favor you. You'll have to bribe someone."

"Bribe them with what?" Walter dropped his head into his hands. "I have nothing left. Just wait a few weeks, Friedel," he urged unconvincingly. "Things might get better."

"Things won't get better, Walter. You'll always be a Nazi to them, and a capitalist. They'll find ways to stop you no matter how hard you try. I'll wait only as long as two weeks, just to give it a chance. But I'm not the slightest bit optimistic."

As soon as she'd spoken, she regretted the outburst. But Walter was already beginning to second-guess his optimism. "*Ach, ja.* You have to do what's best for yourself and the children, Friedel," he conceded. "All Oma and I can do is wait to see if things here will improve. But you're young; you can make a life for yourself in the West. If things don't change for the better soon, Elisabeth and I won't stand in your way."

Kobsch Opa

Walter and Elisabeth Kobsch in front of their textile shop

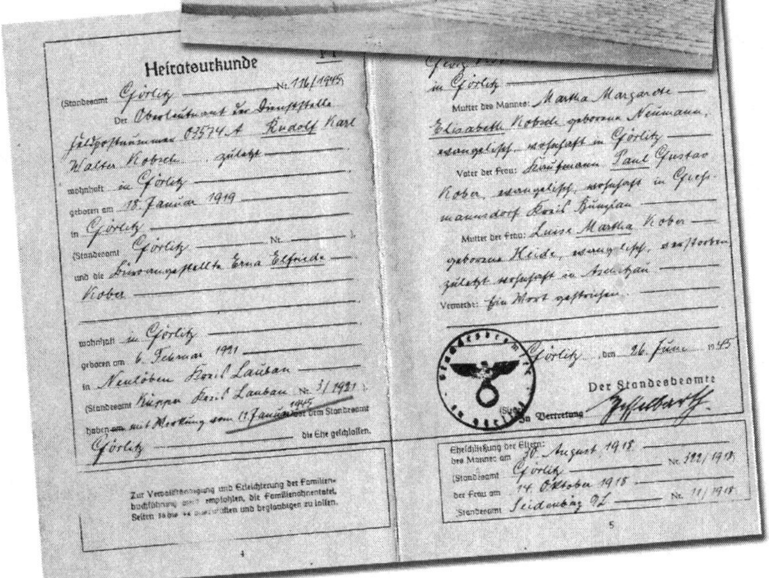

Heiratsurkunde

(Standesamt Görlitz Nr. 116/1945)

Der Oberleutnant der Dienststelle Feldpostnummer 03574 A Rudolf Karl Walter Kobsch, zuletzt

wohnhaft in Görlitz

geboren am 18. Januar 1919

in Görlitz

(Standesamt Görlitz Nr.)

und die [illegible] Erna Elfriede Kober

wohnhaft in Görlitz

geboren am 6. Februar 1921

in Neulöben Kreis Lauban

(Standesamt [illegible] Kreis Lauban Nr. 3/1921)

haben [illegible] 1945 vor dem Standesamt Görlitz die Ehe geschlossen.

Zur Vervollständigung und Erleichterung der Familienbuchführung wird empfohlen, die Familienahnentafel, Seiten 36 bis 44 auszufüllen und beglaubigen zu lassen.

4

[illegible] in Görlitz

Mutter des Mannes: Martha Margarete Elisabeth Kobsch geborene Neumann, evangelisch, wohnhaft in Görlitz

Vater der Frau: [illegible] Paul Gustav Kober, evangelisch, wohnhaft in [illegible] Kreis [illegible]

Mutter der Frau: Luise Martha Kober geborene Heide, evangelisch, verstorben, zuletzt wohnhaft in [illegible]

Vermerke: Ein Wort gestrichen.

Görlitz, den 26. Juni 1945

Der Standesbeamte

(Siegel) In Vertretung [signature]

Eheschließung der Eltern:

des Mannes am 30. August 1918 (Standesamt Görlitz Nr. 192/1918)

der Frau am 14. Oktober 1918 (Standesamt [illegible] Nr. 11/1918)

5

The posthumous marriage certificate of Elfriede and Rudi

Welcome liberators! You take from us eggs, meat,
butter, cattle and feed.
And also watches, rings, and other things.
You liberate us from everything,
from cars and machines.
From all this rubbish—you've liberated us!

—Popular song in Halle, East Germany, 1940s

CHAPTER 12

Far from improving, Elfriede's prospects took a decided turn for the worse. Stalin, who was eager to develop atomic weaponry, had as early as 1946 decided to exploit the natural deposits of uranium in the Erzgebirge region near Görlitz. Since then, thousands of unemployed men and women had received orders to report to the mines, where conditions were appalling. Miners stood for hours at a time in knee-deep radioactive slime with no protective boots. Leaving the cold and drafty mines at the end of the day, they returned to makeshift barracks and tents to share cots in shifts or sleep on the ground with no bedding or blankets. Skin diseases broke out, as did venereal disease. If a worker escaped, he was hunted down and forcibly returned.[175]

Women were generally not forced to enter the mines, but they had to operate heavy machinery and work in mills and laboratories where exposure to dangerous quartz dust and radon was high. This exposure resulted in lung diseases, leukemia, decalcified bones and the wasting away of internal organs. Horror stories abounded about beatings and faulty, outdated machinery, hazardous conditions and fatal accidents.[176] In the late spring of 1949, my mother received orders to report to work for the SAG Wismut mining company. So far, she had managed to elude Wismut's grasp, but clearly her luck had run out. She needed work, but this was more like a death sentence.

Convinced that she would never return from the Erzgebirge alive or even in decent health, Walter now withdrew his request that his daughter-in-law wait things out. He promised that he and Elisabeth would do whatever it took to help her make her way to the West. Elfriede, who had been secretly negotiating with a woman named Frau Schönich, had already devised a plan.

One by one, pieces of our furniture disappeared. It happened so gradually it hardly fazed me. Then on a summer evening, we packed up some extra clothing, locked up our Rauschwalde apartment and went to spend the night in the downtown home of Opa and Oma Kobsch. Early the next morning, Mother shook me out of a deep sleep and told me to dress quickly. We left Heidi sleeping in her little bed and entered the living room. Oma and Opa waited there, looking nervous and concerned.

Mother hoisted a fat leather satchel over one shoulder. She shook hands with Opa and gave Oma a lingering hug. In turn, Oma hugged me while Opa merely looked past me out the open door. Mother took me by the hand and led me downstairs, across the street and onto a train platform. I could hardly believe my luck! Was I really to ride one of those magnificent machines?

"Yes, Wolf," Mother said, guessing my unspoken question. "We're riding the train to Plauen today to visit a friend of mine. I need you to speak to no one, sit quietly, and look out the window. There will be lots to see."

Her orders weren't hard to obey at first. Sitting on that green DDR train, feeling it shudder and begin to chug along, I impatiently waited for it to move faster and faster until it blew like the wind across the countryside. I waited for the landscape to streak by, an abstract blur. But disappointingly, the train never reached a high speed. It seemed stuck eternally in slow motion, chug-chugging along as if in no hurry whatsoever to reach its destination. Out the window, there wasn't much to see but fields and the occasional farmhouse with a cow or two thrown in for good measure. Houses would appear, first one then two then in thick clusters just before we screeched to a halt at a small station. There we would sit for long, boring stretches before finally moving on again.

Three times *Volkspolizei* boarded the train and demanded that Mother show them papers of some kind. They never smiled. After perusing her passport and documents, they always handed them back to her with the same question, "Why are you going to Plauen?"

Feigning innocence, she chirped, "I have an old friend there I want to visit. My seven-year-old son needs fresh air and a chance to run around on a farm, and I really need a vacation!" This chattiness was her way of creating the impression that she couldn't possibly be planning to slip over the border. Each time they responded with suspicious looks. Undaunted, she smiled brightly up at them until they handed back her papers and moved along to the next passenger.

"Wolf, put your head down and rest," she said, patting the leather satchel. "It's going to take a long time to get there."

I dozed on and off, but was always awakened by the whistle and endless jerking motions of the train. The third-class benches were hardly conducive to sleep. I kept popping up to peer out the train window then plopped back down again, disappointed at seeing nothing of great interest. Time dragged.

In the late afternoon, we finally arrived in Plauen. Mother helped me off the train and led me at a brisk pace along unfamiliar streets. We passed other pedestrians and several houses, but she looked resolutely ahead, striding confidently, trying to appear as if she belonged there. Only occasionally did she glance furtively behind her to make sure no one followed. At the edge of town she found a wheat field. We plunged into it and came out the other side next to a small farm road. Mother pulled a large kerchief from her satchel before tossing it into the stalks to hide it. Together we sat down in the grass at the field's edge. She tied the kerchief around her head in the manner of a farm woman then pulled some bread wrapped in paper out of her pocket.

"If a policeman comes by, don't look at him," she instructed, handing me a slice with a thin spreading of butter on it. "If he stops and asks us what we're doing, I'll say we're having a picnic, just for fun. This is our field; we've been out weeding it and now, since the weather is so fine, we're eating our *Abendbrot* outside instead of at home."

I chewed my bread silently, suppressing my usual talkative nature, for I sensed something strange going on. Since when did my mother do anything with me just for fun? What was so special about the edge of this wheat field that it merited a picnic, when our garden *Laube* back home in Görlitz was far nicer? Indeed, several green-uniformed border policemen rode by on horseback, pistols on their belts, patrolling the insignificant little road. They had smart uniforms, much nicer than those of the ragtag *Volkspo-*

lizei. Each time one passed us without comment, I saw my mother relax visibly. We stayed there after we finished our bread, waiting for nightfall. But daylight lingered long on a June evening and eventually we stood and began to stroll along the road, leaving our satchel concealed in the wheat. Finally, when day began to blend into dusk, we returned to the field, reclaimed the satchel and made our way to a modest farmhouse.

Mother knocked on the door. While we waited for a response, my curious eyes took in the courtyard. It contained a pair of empty wooden wagons with their handles propped up on rusty hinges as if they hadn't been in use for a while. A pungent smell emanated from the open barn door. The house had a stone foundation with three steps leading up to the entrance.

The door opened a crack then pulled wider. A woman stood there dressed in a shapeless ankle-length garment and with a scarf tied around her hair. A wide cloth belt was wrapped around her waist. She wasn't much older than my mother, but her skin was leathery, her hands rough and calloused. I saw no evidence of a man about the place.

"Frau Kobsch!" she gasped. Her eyes darted warily out at the street. "You're far too early. You should have waited for nightfall."

"I couldn't wait any longer, Frau Schönich. The sun sets so late this time of year. I feel conspicuous. We don't belong here in Plauen and my satchel gives me away as a traveler."

"Well, hurry inside," she said, giving our shoulders an impatient nudge. Across the room, her teenage daughter darted an anxious look in our direction. "Follow me." Frau Schönich led us down a dark hallway to a back bedroom. It had whitewashed stone walls and a big feather bed. "Stay in here and don't come out, not even to pee. I'll get you a chamber pot. At 2:00 in the morning, I'll come and wake you. Go to sleep; you'll need to be fully rested for what lies ahead."

"Two o'clock!" Mother gasped.

"It's the only safe time to cross, Frau Kobsch. I know exactly when the border police run their searchlights and when they change the guard. You must trust me."

"I do," Mother reassured her, steadying herself with a deep breath. "And I'm so grateful for your help."

We climbed into bed fully clothed. Vaguely, I wondered who this woman was, who despite addressing my mother so formally, invited us deep into the sanctum of her home. The heavenly softness of the mattress and comforter and the warmth of my mother's body lulled me into a deep sleep. True to her word, at 2:00 AM, Frau Schönich entered the room noiselessly, shook us awake and led us out into the darkness. Above us, stars glittered in a black and cloudless summer sky. The half-moon gave off just enough light to save us from having to make our way in total darkness. Frau Schönich led us from her house to the edge of a field. Ripe stalks of grain swayed in the breeze, making a gentle, whispering sound. "We have to hurry!" she urged. She grabbed one of my hands and Mother grabbed the other. Together they hoisted me up between them and ran along a narrow path that divided the field. I had the sensation of floating just above the earth, weightless, surrounded by rustling stalks taller than I. Now and then my toes dragged on the rutted path and the women jerked me up higher.

Not until we reached the park-like grounds of a vacant mansion did they set me down. Towering trees and overgrown shrubbery made excellent cover for us. Completely familiar with the territory, Frau Schönich darted from tree to bush to hedge with us close at her heels. Upon reaching the far end of the park, we paused to catch our breath. In the distance, a bright light swept across a wheat field. In its glare, I saw stacks of freshly cut lumber at the field's edge.

"The border patrol is building a fence and placing watchtowers along it," Frau Schönich whispered to Mother. "And see that wheat field just ahead? They're planning to lay it with mines. You came just in time. Soon it will be too late; no one will be able to cross here." Our guide consulted an old pocket watch, holding it up to the moonlight. "In five minutes, the guard will change. When I say 'go,' move forward in a crouching position. If you stand upright, they will see you and shoot. They're armed with rifles and machine guns."

Mother squeezed my hand.

From a newly-constructed watchtower in the distance came another sweeping searchlight beam. Then, silence. A shuffling of boots was heard on the wooden ladders. Muffled voices spoke.

"Now!" the woman hissed, giving us a shove.

Mother took off, bent low. Hugging the satchel, she followed a well-worn path through the wheat. I followed close at her heels.

A shot fired. We stopped, hardly daring to breathe. At last, hearing nothing more, we moved on. Our rustling footsteps sounded unnaturally loud, throbbing in our ears. We stopped just before the wheat field ended at the edge of a road. I huddled close beside my mother. Bits of wheat chaff and dust conspired to tickle my nose and I drew in a sharp breath, ready to sneeze. She seized my head and clapped a firm hand over my nose. My small body convulsed as my sneezes were muffled.

Satisfied that I was finished, she whispered, "Lie down and be silent."

Together we lay hidden in the stalks, waiting for sunrise.

Caught up in the struggle for survival and the intrigue of escape, Elfriede had no way of knowing that the father of the child she led to freedom had been dead since January of that same year. The collapse of Germany and the resulting chaos had dried up the flow of Kurt's financial support. She wondered where he was and how she might find him in order to remind him of his obligation to her and to me now that Lebensborn no longer existed to assume the role of enforcer. Beyond that, did she harbor any tender feelings for the man who had given her, however accidentally, the seven-year-old boy whose hand she gripped as she lay hidden in a field of ripe wheat between East and West?

The Prague of spring, 1945 was not the same whirlwind of gaiety in which Elfriede and Kurt had conducted their affair two and a half years before. War had worked its dark magic on the city. In 1944, Allied air raids destroyed many of its movie houses. Stores sat empty with signs in their windows declaring, *Closed for the Victory of the Reich.* Civil services had broken down to the point that garbage piled up in the streets, exuding a foul stench. Nutritious food was scarce, resulting in weakened immune systems and the spread of disease.

That February, even as Mother and I had sheltered in a basement during the bombing of Dresden, the Allies accidentally bombed Prague.[177] Seven hundred people were killed and over one thousand wounded. The bombs leveled houses and historic buildings in the city center. As a policeman, Kurt Novak bore the responsibility of helping to restore order and supervising the cleanup of rubble.

Upon Hitler's suicide at the end of April, even as the enemy steadily advanced in their direction, Kurt and his fellow SS men took part in Prague's three-day public display of mourning. Almost immediately afterward, Russian tanks rolled into the city. Prague's Czech citizens rejoiced wildly. The Czechoslovak government returned from exile and the remnants of splintered resistance groups rose up, this time united. At long last the tide had turned. Three million Germans in Czechoslovakia now found themselves in grave danger. Czech fury toward the ethnic Germans, who had so enthusiastically identified and collaborated with the Nazi regime, escalated to a fever pitch. All over the city, fierce violence erupted. Kurt Novak's status as SS policeman made him a particular target since men of his ilk had perpetrated most of the crimes toward Czech and Jewish citizens. Along with his 4,000 SS colleagues in the city, my father surely tried to hide any evidence of connection with the hated organization by burning his uniform and any incriminating documents. But how could he hide from the Czech neighbors who had seen him leave for work each morning proudly dressed in the field gray uniform, with black collar patches and silver collar piping, of an SS *Hauptscharführer?*

Vengeful Czechs stormed police headquarters. Using whips and sticks, they beat any SS men they could get their hands on, kicked them to death, hanged them, soaked them with gasoline and set them on fire. They slashed and smashed portraits and photographs of the dead Führer. Men like my father, if they were smart enough to see the writing on the wall, had already stripped off any telltale clothing that connected them to the SS, tossed their guns into ditches and fled for their lives. There was no time to organize the escape of wives and children. Did they realize as they fled that revenge didn't stop at officers; that the families left behind would also be subject to arrest and beatings? Starting on May 5, all Germans in Prague were forbidden to leave their apartments. Thus caged, they were easily rounded up and herded into makeshift internment camps and forced to do heavy labor. They were whipped, starved and beaten. Had Kurt stayed in Prague and survived to be arrested, he would have been tried before a "people's court" and sentenced to death.[178] Maybe he slipped back into his hometown of Komotau at first, hoping to blend in and settle down to resume his prewar career. If so, he was badly mistaken. Small town Sudeten Germans were subject to the Czechs' thirst for revenge, just like the Germans in Prague.

When the initial fires of revenge died down, any remaining ethnic German families in Eastern Europe were expelled from their homelands. Dragged out of urban apartments, chased out of rural farmhouses, they were forced westward, taking with them only what they could carry. Homes and farms that had belonged to their families for generations were looted and confiscated by the Czechs, Poles and Russians. Stripped of their possessions, loaded into boxcars or setting out on foot in long columns, they straggled into Germany proper. They didn't want to be there. Even though they spoke the language, it wasn't home. And the German nationals, trying to pick up the pieces of their own shattered lives, weren't happy to see them. Devastated by the war, Germany was hardly capable of providing sustenance to its own population let alone legions of displaced persons. Among these ethnic Germans herded out of their ancestral homelands were Paul, Helene and Werner Kober and many other of my mother's relatives. Silesia now belonged to Poland.

The fact that my father ended up in Bremerhaven in western Germany and his wife and sons landed in a town called Giesenslage in the Russian zone suggests that he fled Prague to save his own skin, leaving his family behind in hopes they might fare better. Emma and her boys were most likely interned in a camp and then expelled, pushed over the border into Soviet-occupied Germany. Kurt, living alone in Bremerhaven and perhaps hoping to bring his family to the West, died of a heart attack at the young age of 43. His death certificate reads that he was working there as a policeman, and indeed, many former SS policemen were taken back into the ranks of the police in West Germany. Few, if any, questions were asked about their wartime activities.[179]

Well after I'd suffered arterial blockage at age 62 and gone through quadruple bypass surgery, long after my daughter Christina died of a congenital heart condition at age four and my son Joshua had been diagnosed with a hole in his heart that ultimately mended on its own, only after my mother had revealed my father's true name and I found his death certificate in the box she gave me, did I realize that heart disease ran in my family. Elfriede, on the other hand, had learned of my father's heart attack in 1950.

"Why didn't you tell me sooner?" I demanded, deeply frustrated. "It might not have prevented the children's conditions, but it certainly could have prevented mine!"

"I didn't want to hurt your feelings back then," she replied, "by revealing that you were illegitimate."

Suspecting her reluctance to reveal the truth had more to do with protecting her own reputation rather than my feelings, I said, "But if I had known, I could have adjusted my lifestyle sooner, or at least had my heart examined more often."

She merely shrugged. She had preferred a middle-aged me to believe that Rudi was my father, even though I'd never been allowed to take his name. Kurt's diseased or deformed heart, by the way, slipped past the stringent health inspection of the SS. Perhaps the doctors didn't want to see it.

Aryan *Übermenschen* don't have weak hearts.

Somehow, with the sun climbing upward and birds singing, we felt safer, bolder. Mother got to her knees and peered above the stalks. There on the road was a metal crossing guard. We crawled under it and stood up on the other side.

"Are we there yet, Mutti?"

Brushing dirt from her clothing, she pointed to a sign on the pole and read it in a whisper: "Caution: You are now leaving the West German Sector. Yes, Wolf, we're there!"

Our achievement gave us no cause to relax our vigilance. The border was heavily patrolled; if we were caught lingering near it we could be arrested and promptly escorted back into the East. We hurried into the nearest village to try to catch a bus to the nearby city of Hof. The West German *Deutschmark* in Mother's change purse amounted to a mere 2.50, however, and we were stranded. Before long, a Good Samaritan noticed us standing by the roadside and offered us enough coins to make up the rest of the fare.

Once in Hof, we sought out the Displaced Persons camp called Moschendorf. Mother begged the Red Cross personnel there to let me stay while she returned to Görlitz to retrieve Heidi. They refused.

"You should find a relative to take him," they told her. "We're overcrowded as it is, and we have real orphans to deal with. We can't take on a child who has a living parent. But if you return with your daughter, bring both children here and we'll take you as a family."

That very afternoon we caught a bus for West Berlin, which meant heading right back through the Russian zone from which we had just escaped. I've never known how she paid for that particular bus ride—whether the Red Cross station at Moschendorf loaned her some *Deutschmark* or she was allowed to pay in East German currency. At the bus station, before we boarded, she pulled me into a corner and made me change clothes, insisting I change even my underwear. Confused, I complied with her odd request.

When our bus was stopped at the border, we were required to disembark and line up to show our passports. I didn't have one, of course, but was included on my mother's. Again I felt confused as she pulled out a shiny, new-looking passport that I had never before seen. As a seven-year-old, I had no way of understanding that it was forged and that she had tremendous skill at pretending to be from East or West depending on the circumstances. But I had learned to keep quiet when uniforms were present, so I stood there fidgeting. The line was moving so slowly! My bladder was full and growing more uncomfortable by the minute.

Tugging on Mother's hand, I whispered, "I have to pee!"

"Just wait, Wolf."

"No, I can't! I'm going to pee my pants."

She glanced around frantically. At this particular station, passengers bought tickets from a window and weren't allowed inside. If there was a restroom in there, it was off limits. Suddenly her eyes settled on a stand of trees a short distance away. "Run over there," she said.

With desperate urgency, I hurtled toward the trees, fumbling with the buttons on my fly. As I pulled down my underpants, a flurry of what appeared to be scraps of colored paper tumbled out and fluttered down onto the grass. Bewildered at first as to how they had gotten into my underwear, I soon forgot them in the blessed relief of finally emptying my bladder. I finished my business and buttoned my pants. Maybe Heidi had been playing with paper scraps and tossed them into Mother's satchel back in

Görlitz. In any case, they were soaked with urine now and Mother was waiting for me. I hurried back to her, just in time to board a second bus for the ride along the Berlin corridor.

We rode for a few hours then the bus stopped for more *Volkspolizei* to climb aboard and inspect passports. Nonchalantly, Mother pulled hers out and smiled up at the men. They glanced between her and the passport several times. "You live in Bavaria?"

"Yes," she said brightly, admirably disguising her Silesian accent and mimicking the lilt of Bavarian speech. "My son and I are visiting a friend of mine in Berlin."

Whoever had forged the passport had done his work well. The guards nodded and handed it back to her. I felt her body relax and heard her sigh quietly as she returned the passport to her satchel. When the police had exited the bus she turned to me and began to unbutton my pants. Pulling open the elastic waist of my underwear, she slipped her hand inside. Her cold fingers against my warm flesh startled me and I resisted, wiggling out of her grasp.

"Sit still, Wolf!" she hissed. "I'm looking for something." As she fumbled around with no success, her voice rose to a panicky croak. "Where is it?"

"I don't know!" I whined, wishing she would stop. "Where is what?"

"The money!"

A sickening feeling seized my gut. "Some papers fell out when I was peeing but I didn't know what they were."

"Well, where are they? Did you pick them up?" I shook my head.

"Wolfgang! That was all the money I earned from selling our furniture. I need that money! Why didn't you pick it up?"

I could only gaze blankly up at her. Why hadn't she told me I carried such vital cargo in my crotch? Only much later did she explain that she'd pinned it into my underpants secretly, hoping to spare me guilty knowledge and avoid me blurting out the truth if we were questioned by the *Volkspolizei* about money. Although at the time of our crossing, East Germany did not yet officially exist, the Soviet Military Administration had been issuing East German banknotes since the summer of 1948. Mother needed it to return to the eastern zone to get Heidi, perhaps even for a bribe or two. If she, masquerading as a Bavarian, were caught by *Volkspolizei* on her way to West Berlin loaded with money from the Russian zone she would be exposed as a fugitive from the East and arrested.

With that particular danger past, she simply collapsed against the bus window and sobbed. Helplessly I watched, knowing I had made her cry but having no idea how I could have done things differently. The pin holding the money must have worked loose and I hadn't even felt it. Mercifully, she never scolded me again for the loss. For the rest of the trip she had a resigned, fatalistic demeanor about her.

Trotting along beside my mother through the streets of Berlin, my eyes bugged out at the huge piles of rubble and the looming shells of buildings with gaping window holes. Fully half the houses in the city had been destroyed by Allied bombs. All around us the *Trümmerfrauen* were still hard at work. In fact, Berlin appeared to be a city of women. At the end of the war, some fifteen million German men were missing. If the detritus of war was to be cleaned up, it was up to the women they'd left behind. At first, the shell-shocked females had ventured into the streets in search of water and food. Desperate, they cleared away rubble in order to free up water pipes and paths for walking. Before long the Allied military government noticed the German passion for order and cleanliness and ordered the women to continue, offering to pay mere pennies per hour for their labors. The low wages, however, included a bonus of extra food rations. The promise of food was sufficient motivation for the women to work. All over western Germany, females between 15 and 50 sorted through the debris of their fallen cities, carrying off rocks, steel girders, wooden beams and pieces of crumbled wall. They arranged themselves in long lines, passing pails of rubble from one to the next. Wielding hammer and chisel, they scraped mortar off bricks to prepare them for use in rebuilding. Like beasts of burden they pulled heavy-laden carts of rubble along once-fashionable boulevards.

As if grateful to be doing something constructive in the midst of the lingering desolation, the women laughed and chattered as they worked, their scarves and skirts flapping in the summer wind. Their task looked absolutely endless to me, who until my arrival in Berlin had seen little bomb damage.

Mother, consulting a hand-scrawled map, led me to a street where a block of houses remained miraculously intact. Standing at regular intervals along the sidewalk, a row of mature chestnut trees had also survived. They towered over us in full leaf. We stood together for a few moments in a riot of shifting sunlight and shadow beneath the swaying branches. Finally Mother gripped my hand and approached a nearby door to ring the bell. A dour-looking woman peered down at us through an open window before pressing the buzzer to let us inside. We trudged up to the third floor.

"Is it actually you, Elfriede?" She appeared to be around a decade older than my mother, with a severe expression and an unsympathetic look in her eye. She regarded me critically.

"I know this is sudden and unexpected," I heard Mother say. "But do you remember that you owe me a favor? I only need a place for him for a few months until I can bring my daughter out and find a place for us all to live. I can pay you...just not now, not yet."

I could tell by their voices that they harbored little affection for one another. There were no introductions. No one bothered to explain to me who the woman was or how my mother knew her. As I peered around, a strange feeling gripped the pit of my stomach. The apartment had a slightly musty smell despite being clean and neat. Furniture made of heavy, dark-stained woods like oak and walnut lined the walls. It felt like a place where only old people had lived; there was nothing there to suggest a child had ever set foot inside or would be welcome to do so.

"Mutti, let's go now," I whispered, tugging on her hand.

"Hush, Wolf. That wouldn't be polite."

Yet she remained standing near the door, making no move to sit down and drink coffee or eat cake as she might have done if she were making a polite social visit. Eventually we made a brief walk-through of the whole apartment.

"It's so big," marveled my mother, wide-eyed.

"I'm lucky," the woman replied curtly. "Many families are crammed into temporary quarters, forced to share space with strangers. I have a formal dining room, a kitchen, a living room and two bedrooms. This building suffered absolutely no bomb damage."

I gazed up at the high ceilings with their ornate plaster moldings and the tall windows overlooking the chestnuts' brilliant green foliage. In one of the rooms, a spare bed looked particularly heavenly, all lumpy and soft. I hoped I might sleep there that night curled up beside my mother.

Suddenly Mother spun me around to face her and dropped to one knee. "Good-bye, Wolf. I'll come back soon. Behave yourself, and do what you are told."

No amount of tears and shrieking could hold her back. She was gone in a flash, and I was left standing beside a woman who looked as horrified as I was by the prospect of our living together.

Walter and Elisabeth Kobsch

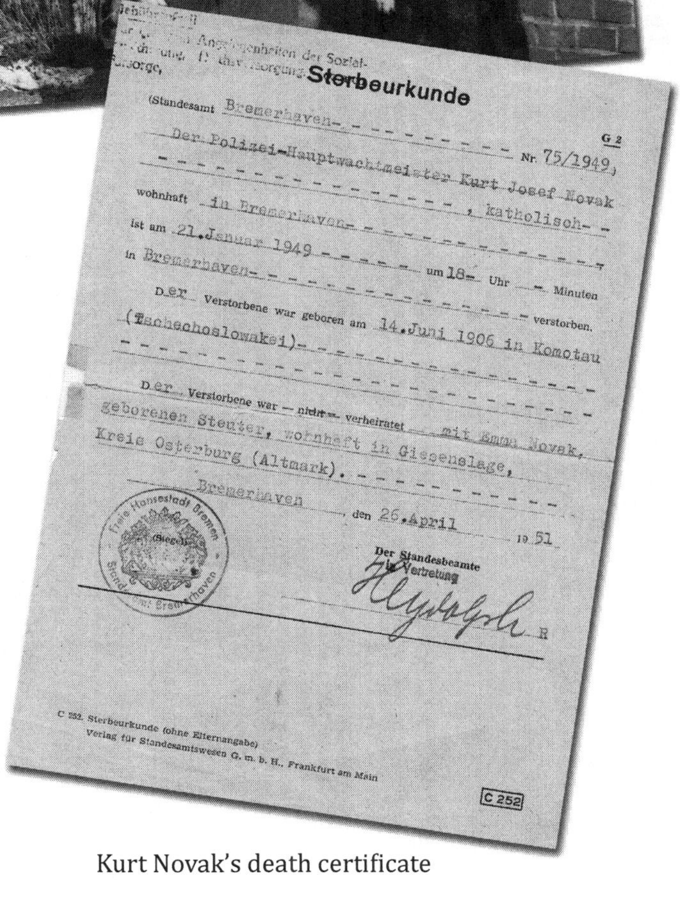

Sterbeurkunde

(Standesamt Bremerhaven- G 2 Nr. 75/1949)

Der Polizei-Hauptwachtmeister Kurt Josef Novak, katholisch-

wohnhaft in Bremerhaven-

ist am 21. Januar 1949

in Bremerhaven- um 18- Uhr - Minuten verstorben.

Der Verstorbene war geboren am 14. Juni 1906 in Komotau (Tschechoslowakei)-

Der Verstorbene war — ~~nicht~~ — verheiratet mit Emma Novak, geborenen Steuter, wohnhaft in Giesenslage, Kreis Osterburg (Altmark).

Bremerhaven, den 26. April 1951

(Siegel) Freie Hansestadt Bremen Standesamt Bremerhaven

Der Standesbeamte
In Vertretung

C 252. Sterbeurkunde (ohne Elternangabe)
Verlag für Standesamtswesen G. m. b. H., Frankfurt am Main

C 252

Kurt Novak's death certificate

The border transit and refugee camp Moschendorf
was the gateway to freedom for hundreds of thousands of
German prisoners of war, civilian detainees
and displaced persons of the Second World War,
who came from the far reaches of the East.

—Moschendorf Memorial

CHAPTER 13

I don't remember ever knowing her name. She lives on in my memory as simply, "Frau." Every morning, she put on a dress and hat and heels and marched with a prim cadence off to work in an office somewhere, leaving me to fend for myself. As long as the weather was mild, she locked me out of the apartment until she arrived home in the evening. On days of bleak weather, especially as autumn approached, she reluctantly allowed me my own key, instructing me to disturb nothing in the place. Barred from the building on dry-weather days, I spent my time playing in the street with neighborhood children. Mountains of rubble surrounded our block, enticing us to climb and explore, though none of us dared. We had been strictly warned against it, told that unexploded bombs, grenades, mortar shells and machine gun rounds lay buried in the debris and could be set off by careless, curious boys.

If at first I looked forward to Frau coming home and relieving my loneliness, I quickly learned that I was better off without her. She never smiled at me. Not once did she hug me or touch me or show me any warmth. There was no conversation between us. She merely returned home each evening, banged around in the kitchen, plopped the most minimal amount of food possible in front of me and ordered me to bed.

One day in September, she instructed me to scrub myself extra clean at the wash basin. She was taking me down the street to the neighborhood kindergarten, she explained. At seven years of age, I towered above the other children and barely fit into their little chairs and riding toys. I felt oafish and clumsy next to my tiny classmates, but since I could neither read nor write it was impossible for me to join my own peers, who would be just beginning second grade. To guide a late bloomer through academic catch-up would require much more commitment and dedication than Frau was prepared to give. Putting me in kindergarten was a way of getting me out of the apartment, keeping me occupied and out of trouble. So I sat in a circle with my little kindergarten mates playing games, learning to share toys, singing and clapping along to babyish songs about butterflies and bumble bees.

The children were fascinated by me. "You talk funny," they remarked, not unkindly. "Why?"

At a loss to explain the Silesian accent I had no doubt picked up from my mother, unable myself to grasp where exactly I belonged or came from, I merely shrugged and made the best of my circumstances by smiling and being friendly.

Kindergarten was a haven of sorts. It relieved my crushing loneliness. Back home at Frau's apartment, that loneliness drove me outside to seek playmates no matter how wet or chilly the weather. The boys I played with in the street during the afternoons were closer to my own age. If their mothers kept them inside because of foul weather, I still had my faithful companions, the horse chestnut trees. Over time I became intimately familiar with every inch of them—the leaves, so like hands with fingers, reaching out to me from their stiff, green stem "arms," the rough bark that split into small sections curling up around the edges. The conkers the trees yielded were a special prize. Magically they appeared in September, hanging high above me until the wind shook the branches and they fell at my feet. When I had peeled off the spiky green husk, I held a smooth mahogany-colored treasure.

All through the autumn as the leaves turned yellow and brown, the neighborhood boys and I collected chestnuts. For lack of real toys we improvised, boring holes into the outer shell and inserting small sticks to turn them into cars and trucks or animals. We impaled them on taller sticks to build towers. We flipped them, tossed them and kicked them like balls. The prettiest ones I carried up to the apartment and stashed away to be taken out and handled during the long evenings alone in my room. By November most of them had fallen, but I could still see a few stubborn ones clinging to impossibly high branches.

"I have an idea!" I told my playmates one drizzly day when Frau had left me a key. "There are lots of canes and umbrellas upstairs. I'll go on the balcony and throw them into the tree. They'll knock the chestnuts loose and you can catch them when they fall."

"All right, Wolf," they said, positioning themselves below in anticipation.

Frau did indeed have an impressive collection of canes, walking sticks and umbrellas. Since she herself needed no help in walking, they must have belonged to her late parents. One by one I launched them into the tree, taking careful aim at the desired conkers. One or two chestnuts fell. Most of the missiles remained firmly lodged in the tree. Panicked, I rushed downstairs and tossed the fallen canes and umbrellas up to try to knock down those that were stuck. They stuck fast as well. My friends and I threw chestnuts up but they merely fell back again to bounce playfully around our feet. Not one cane or umbrella remained in the container near Frau's front door. It didn't help that the trees had lost most of their leaves. By the time Frau entered the apartment that evening, she had seen all too clearly the fruits of my mischief.

Her taut lips went white. From somewhere in a cabinet she retrieved an old leather whip from the days when Berliners rode around in horse and buggy. She thrashed it against my legs and buttocks until I lost control of my bladder. Urine ran down my legs into my shoes and soaked through the front of my pants.

This enraged her even more. "Take off your pants!"

With no clue where my mother was or if she was ever truly coming back for me, I had no choice but to obey. Frau kept me alive. She fed me, gave me a bed to sleep in and a roof over my head. No other adult existed in Berlin to whom I might turn for comfort or sustenance. If I lost her, how would I survive? If I tried to find the home of one of my kindergarten teachers and by some miracle she let me live with her, how would my mother know where to find me if she ever did return? Resigned, I unbuttoned my pants and let them drop. Frau swooped down, grabbed me under the arms and slung me up onto the dining room table.

"Stand up straight!"

In this position, I was just the right height for her to achieve perfect aim with the whip. It whistled through the air and snapped on my bare flesh until I screamed for mercy. Tears streaked my face and dripped down onto the polished surface of the table. With a disgusted scowl she finally turned and walked away, taking the whip with her. "Go and wash yourself."

Sobbing, feeling large throbbing welts rise on my skin, I slid off the table, picked up my wet pants and went to fill the wash basin with cold water. That night, even lying in the soft bed was painful; there was no position in which I could lie that didn't irritate the welts and the scabs forming on the worst of them. Far worse was the damage deep inside. For the first time, I felt truly abandoned, as if the severe whipping were a sign that my mother had forgotten me completely. I had gotten used to Frau slapping and hitting me for the slightest infractions: spilling my food, knocking over a cup, making too much noise when she was trying to read the newspaper. But never before had she used the whip. By that vicious act she seemed to be saying, "You are completely at my mercy. See? I'm not even afraid anymore of what your mother might say."

Still sniffling, I retrieved the collection of chestnuts I kept hidden beneath the bed. They felt smooth against the skin of my hands and their warm, cheerful color comforted me.

In mid-November, I began to cough. My relentless hacking irritated Frau, but she never felt my forehead for fever or asked me whether I was feeling ill. She continued to send me to kindergarten each morning with a slice of bread and butter for snack time. My teachers were alarmed one day to see me slumped against the wall, listless and disinterested in playing games with my classmates. My cough had already caused them some concern, but they assumed my guardian was seeing to it. One of them called in a doctor who carried me away to a nearby clinic. Surrounded by white-clad grownups, I lay staring up at the stark white ceiling while they hovered over me, poking at my ribs with a cold object, shining lights into my eyes and throat.

One of them brandished a long needle attached to a cylinder and tube. "Hold still, Wolfgang."

I began to shake with terror. It took all of their combined strength to hold me down as I writhed and screamed, determined not to let the needle stick my flesh. Redoubling their efforts, they succeeded at last and left me lying there sobbing. They conferred with one another in urgent whispers. Phone calls were made. I could hear them speaking my name as if I were a mere object or an intangible theme to be discussed. Someone scribbled markings onto a cardboard placard and suspended it with string around my neck. They loaded me into a car and whisked me off to a bus station where, for the first time, a nurse bent down to my eye level and explained things to me.

"Wolfgang, you have an illness called tuberculosis. You caught it because you're weak and haven't been eating enough. It can be cured but we must send you away where you'll be better fed. Do you understand?"

I nodded solemnly, remembering all the nights I'd gone to bed still hungry after devouring what Frau put on my plate. Part of me felt terrified at the thought of leaving the only home I'd known for the past five months; the rest of me felt elated at the prospect of leaving Frau. To my horror she materialized before me once again, showing up at the bus station and speaking to the nurse. For an instant I feared she had come to take me home with her. Then without so much as a good-bye, she turned and left. The nurse helped me board a bus for a mysterious destination and waved farewell to me as it pulled out of the station.

During an interminable ride along the Berlin corridor I hacked incessantly, fogging the window with each puff of expelled breath. The rolling East German landscape blurred before my tired, bloodshot eyes. Finally I disembarked at Hof in Bavaria, still sporting the handwritten sign around my neck. A tall man in a green jacket with shiny brass buttons approached. He bent down to my eye level and extended a hand. "You must be Wolfgang Kober."

I nodded, placing my feverish hand in his.

"Come with me," he said with a conspiratorial wink. "I'll buy you a coke."

We climbed into a vehicle and drove through town until we arrived at a place I felt sure I had seen before.

"This is Camp Moschendorf," he said as we entered, driving past neat rows of no-frills wooden barracks.

Yes, I've been here, I thought, before Mother took me to Frau in Berlin.

I spent the afternoon in an office playing checkers with a succession of young men in uniform. Despite being sick and exhausted, I wanted to laugh when they spoke amongst themselves. Their strange language sounded garbled, as if their mouths couldn't form words correctly, and no wonder! Their jaws moved comically from side to side when they spoke, turning each word into jibberish. One of them gave me a chocolate bar. Another brought me a fizzy drink of some kind. It tickled my tongue but tasted heavenly. By evening, I could barely keep my eyes open. Suddenly I heard the most beautiful sound in the world.

"Wolf!" Mother hurried to me and wrapped me in her arms.

"They've reserved a bed for him in the hospital barracks," a soldier informed her. "You'll need to check him in yourself."

Later, sitting beside my bed as the nurses tended to me, my mother explained where she had been since leaving me in Berlin. "I went back to Görlitz for Heidi and I brought her here to Bavaria. But she didn't crawl through a wheat field like you, Wolf. We traveled to East Berlin and took the underground train to the western side of the city. Imagine that! No one was watching, and it was so much easier that way. Then we took a bus here, the same one that brought you just now."

Berlin? She had passed through Berlin on her way to Hof and instead of taking me with her, had left me with Frau? Just how long had she been living here without me?

As if intuiting my sense of betrayal, she hurriedly explained, "I wanted to find a place for us to live before I brought you here, Wolfi. A refugee camp is no place for a family. I knew I had to find a job and an apartment. You were big enough to live without me, but Heidi needed me with her. I also knew you were going to kindergarten and it was good for you to have routine."

So, she had communicated with Frau. Had the woman deceived her into thinking I was perfectly fine and happy? Or had it merely been convenient for Mother to believe so, with or without any convincing from my erstwhile caregiver?

"Where is Heidi?" I asked.

Mother looked suddenly weary. "Heidi has been very sick with diphtheria and scarlet fever. She's been in a special hospital for months now, and is getting the best possible care. They say she might be able to come home in a few weeks."

"Come home to where? Camp Moschendorf?"

"Let's hope not, Wolf. I might have found a job today. If they hire me, I'll be working at a big department store, called Kaufhaus Saale. While you're in here getting well, I'm going to look very hard for a place for the three of us to live."

My tuberculosis had been caught early and the treatment proved effective. Within days, I was discharged from the hospital barracks and, keeping to a strict regimen of medication, joined my mother in the family quarters. We bedded down in a corner of one of the long barracks. Blankets suspended from ropes provided us and the thousands of other displaced families at Moschendorf with the illusion of privacy. During the nights I heard the coughing, snoring and whisperings of hundreds of other people, but it comforted rather than disturbed me. It felt good to sleep next to my mother after longing for her so desperately in Berlin.

Camp Moschendorf had been built by the Nazis as a subcamp for the infamous concentration camp, Flossenburg. Five thousand people left homeless by the war were sheltered there. Like us, many were refugees from the Soviet occupation zone; some were ethnic Germans who had been driven out of Poland and Czechoslovakia. Others were German POWs returning from the Soviet Union. The latter group cycled through the camp faster, using it merely as a stopover on the way home. I felt sorry for the POWs and tried not to stare, but it was hard. They had a haunted look in their eyes; they were emaciated with bones protruding awkwardly at elbow and wrist joints. Some of them shook uncontrollably as they lit cigarettes and raised them to trembling lips.

During the days, when my mother was visiting Heidi or searching for an apartment, I joined the other camp children in lining up for thick, steaming pea soup and a slice of bread with butter. We used the same tin can cups for soup and for the daily treat of hot chocolate. That delicious drink, combined with the compassionate smiles of the Red Cross workers, convinced me I had landed in heaven. Every day I happily skipped off to the camp kindergarten, once again a seven-year-old boy playing with children barely out of toddlerhood. The overburdened first and second grade teachers in the camp simply had no extra time to help me catch up in order to join their classes. So I played my days away with the little ones, blissful in my perpetually uneducated state. Besides, my growth had been stunted by hunger. Despite being larger than the kindergarteners I was puny for my age, with stick-like limbs and a head that seemed too big for my body.

One day I eagerly took my place in line to wait for hot chocolate. A bigger boy, who always seemed to elbow his way into line ahead of me, received his ration and then began to show off a skill he'd honed to perfection: spinning his tin cup around and around his head at warp speed without losing a drop of the precious liquid. He'd completely mastered the trick of using centrifugal force, making it look easy. This stunt intrigued me. Convinced I could do it too, I began to mimic his actions, swinging my full mug furiously, enjoying what I imagined were the other children's admiring eyes on me. Unlike the bigger boy, however, I had no idea how to bring the swinging mug to a successful stop so that I could drink the delicious treat. I grew desperate and dizzy. When I stopped my arm abruptly, the hot chocolate sloshed out of the cup and all down my arm. The children's laughter stung more than the scalding liquid. Shame-faced and with eyes smarting, I quickly swallowed the tiny bit of chocolate left in the bottom of the cup and ran away to hide.

The population of our barracks fluctuated constantly. Families on the other side of the blankets, whose voices and rhythms we had become accustomed to, would pack up and leave one day and before nightfall, new ones took their places. Soon it was our turn. Kaufhaus Saale had agreed to hire Mother. Always neatly presented despite her extreme poverty, not a hair out of place and with a fetching, dimpled smile, she'd managed to convince the store owners that she belonged behind the cash register. Her promised salary was minimal, however. Apartments were in high demand and owners reserved them for the highest bidders. Nevertheless she found a cold-water flat by agreeing to take on the job as janitor for the whole building.

Our flat was on the second floor of a large subdivided house that stood behind another house, with the effect that it was hidden from the view of people on the street. We entered it by walking through a tall gate and crossing a courtyard. The sun had trouble finding it as well, blocked as it was by the larger house and other buildings surrounding it. Yet Elfriede Kober Kobsch felt proud to once again be mistress of her own dwelling. She'd managed to assemble a couch, a rickety table, an armoire for our clothing and a handful of dishes. Once the furniture was in place, it dominated most of the floor space. We fetched cold water from a tap in the hall which we shared with the other tenants. Selecting wood from a pile in the courtyard and starting a fire in our little stove became my daily responsibility. It made me feel grown up and useful.

When at last we were able to bring Heidi home from the hospital, the three of us squished onto the couch together to sleep at night. Heidi and I were restless sleepers, tossing and turning all night long. Mother soon found this intolerable. Tired of dragging herself to work each day with dark circles under her eyes, she left the couch to Heidi and me, choosing instead to sleep on the floor. Even so, one of us children invariably tumbled off the narrow couch before morning, dragging the covers with us. If I woke in the night, lucky enough to have maintained my place on the couch but shivering for lack of covering, I could hear the scritch-scratch of mice scrambling across the wooden floor. Lying there, I felt guilty for possessing the couch and silently willed the rodents to stay off my mother and sister.

Mother's nightly plight evoked pity in the kindhearted owners of the department store where she worked. As far as they could tell, she was one of thousands of young war widows who had been happily married to the father of her children before he fell in battle while serving his country. They gave us a small evergreen tree equipped with the candles and clip-on holders so essential to German Christmas celebrations. The three of us decorated the tree with tiny paper stars and angels Mother cut with a knife for lack of scissors.

On Christmas Day, Mother took us to the Lutheran church half a block from our new home. It is the first time I remember ever entering a church. Something about the candles, the organ music and the warmth of all the people packed inside the building comforted her and gave her strength to face the new year with its grim anniversary of Rudi's departure and death. Attending church on Christmas was to become Elfriede's pattern for the rest of her life.

Later at home, we enjoyed a dinner of pork and potatoes painstakingly prepared by Mother with our minimal selection of pots and utensils on the wood-burning stove. Meat was still carefully rationed in the American zone but she had saved the roast to make a special holiday meal that would have been unthinkable in East Germany. Later that day, her employers stopped by with *Stollen,* a sweet raisin bread topped with powdered sugar and filled with almond paste. When they saw our cramped space and guessed that Mother was sleeping on the floor, they exchanged concerned looks. Soon a metal bed frame was delivered to our house along with a mattress. Now our one-room apartment was even more cramped, but Mother had the luxury of a bed to sleep in.

No longer eligible to attend kindergarten at Camp Moschendorf where I'd just begun to feel at home, I was now enrolled in the local kindergarten in our new neighborhood. My four-year-old sister and I walked there together every morning, she turning into one classroom and I into another. If Mother was hoping that one of the kindergarten teachers would graciously volunteer to spend extra hours with me, teaching me to read, spell, add and subtract so that I could rejoin my seven-year-old peers, she was sadly mistaken. The teachers in the Hof kindergarten showed me little kindness and no pity. This time, the younger children avoided me. Heidi, younger and more adaptable, blended in well, but I stood out as an obvious refugee; they heard it in my Eastern accent, saw it in my shabby, inadequate clothing and could undoubtedly smell it when I approached them.

Mother, rushing off to work each morning, had no time to supervise my grooming. She merely instructed me to wash and dress myself while she busied herself getting Heidi dressed and fed. We had no bathtub or sink of our own. The freezing water from the tap felt so unpleasant on my skin that I did only the bare minimum by splashing a little of it on my face and drying it off quickly. For a toilet we had only a shared outhouse-like room on our floor. It contained a board with a hole in it. Somehow the waste made its way down to the sewer system. We wiped our bottoms with scraps of old paper and it felt luxurious when that paper happened to be smooth, like newspaper or magazine pages. There was no sink near the "toilet" to remind a busy seven-year-old boy to wash his hands.

Though Mother boiled water on our stove and bathed us in a metal washtub every Saturday, toward the end of the school week my abysmal efforts at self-grooming left me smelling ripe. Every day I wore the same pair of *Lederhosen.* The thick, unwashable leather absorbed dirt and sweat and food spills and became pungent in its own right. They were my only pants and every day I wore them over the same thin shirt.

Our kindergarten had a collection of wooden wagons in the play yard, big enough to hold several children. Laughing and jostling, my classmates would pile into the wagons and the teachers pulled them around in circles. Any time I approached a wagon hoping for a ride, the children would push me away. The teachers allowed it. They even looked on approvingly. Theirs was the prevailing attitude in Hof. We newcomers might be fellow Germans but we were still filthy refugees from the East and didn't belong there. West Germans were struggling to rebuild their own postwar lives and communities. Why should they have to take care of us as well? Food supply was still well below its prewar level. Allied bombings had made decent lodgings hard to find, so why didn't my family and others like us go back to where we'd come from or keep within the confines of Camp Moschendorf and let the Red Cross feed and house us?

Children excluding those whom they perceive to be different is common and perhaps understandable, but this cruelty on the part of the teachers stung me then and still baffles me today. It seems the hunger and poverty resulting from the war either brought out the worst or the best in people depending on their deeper natures. How fickle is the human heart! Had the Nazis triumphed and the school been presented with the SS-issued certificate of my elite Aryan status, might not these same teachers have fawned over me, making sure I was included and treated with respect?

I dreamt about those wagons at night and fantasized about them during the day. *One day I'll have my very own wagon,* I promised myself. *I'll take it to the kindergarten and proudly pull it around the yard. Then everyone will feel sorry for how they treated me.*

In the fall of 1950 came a long-awaited gift. I was allowed to enter the first grade. I felt so much older walking into that classroom, but my attire hadn't changed. The other pupils wore new, clean *Lederhosen* and when the weather turned cold they supplemented the short leather pants with sweaters and long wool socks. Some even switched to wearing long pants.

Our classrooms were located in a former convent situated behind the *Rathaus*. The building was dank and cave-like. Local children wore jackets to school; they wore shoes and boots in the snow. I had no jacket. My feet were covered with threadbare socks and sandals, even in deepest winter. My *Lederhosen* turned icy to the touch so I taught myself to walk with a strange, stiff gait in order to avoid my bare legs coming into contact with their outer edges. None of this escaped my classmates' notice. Snickering at me under their breath, they excluded me just as the kindergartners had, shooting me looks of disdain as they formed cliques and organized ball games on the playground.

Lacking friends, I played with Heidi at home in our courtyard after school. We hopscotched together or made up our own games. We had no ball and no toys. Ingenuity was vital if I was to have the playthings so coveted by small boys everywhere. I learned to wedge pieces of wood together in such a way that they resembled cars or trucks. Once I found a rusty, discarded wind-up car in a corner of the yard but the winding mechanism was broken and it rolled along in a lopsided fashion. Heidi couldn't muster up much enthusiasm to join me in playing with it, so I kept it squirreled away as a treasure to occupy myself when I was truly alone.

If it rained, my sister and I played in the attic among the clotheslines where the only light streamed down from a tiny window in the roof. Our apartment was a mere ten by eight feet, large enough only for eating and sleeping. If the weather cooperated, we stayed outside, running around town unsupervised, keeping track of time by the chiming of the town hall tower clock. In our building, the only people who ever said hello to us were a mother and her adult son who were also refugees from the East. They lived in the room next door to ours and occasionally bumped into us at the water spout and funnel sink in the hallway. Otherwise, they kept to themselves.

As fall turned to winter, I sensed a growing excitement among my classmates. December 6 was fast approaching, the day Saint Nicholas came to leave treats in the shoes of well-behaved children. If the generous saint had ever visited me before, I couldn't remember it. No one had spoken of him. To my childish mind, it seemed completely plausible that he would have passed over East Germany where the idea of "treats" was superfluous to people aspiring only to scrounge together enough nutrients to keep themselves alive. But in the Hof grammar school, much was made of the saint's impending visit and the fact that his assistant, Schwarze Peter, so called because he was covered with coal dust, would drop a lump of coal into the shoes of children who had misbehaved while Nicholas himself would bestow nuts, candy or gingerbread cookies on those who had comported themselves admirably. This worried me. Admittedly, I'd sunk to unparalleled depths of delinquency during the past year and a half, carelessly losing hundreds of marks while peeing in the woods and tossing Frau's umbrellas and canes into a tree. To hope for gingerbread or candy seemed almost ludicrous under the circumstances. Still, I hoped. I spoke to no one of my fears. On the morning in question, I raced to the freezing hallway where I had left my shoes so as to make it easier for St. Nicholas to find them. Stuffed into my little shoes were an apple, a pear, a few walnuts, and a new pair of socks from Kaufhaus Saale. I felt vindicated! Someone somewhere understood that a young boy might make mistakes but still mean well.

Elfriede, early 1950s

David and Heidi (in center)

David and Heidi modeling in a fashion show at Kaufhaus Saale

Here where once Aryanism ruled supreme,
Negroes are finding more friendship, more respect,
and more equality than they would back home.

—Ebony magazine, 1946

CHAPTER 14

During the winter, our school's classrooms were moved out of the freezing convent and into wooden barracks-like structures situated on a soccer field. My elderly teacher's name was Herr Gulden. A balding, muscular ex-Army sergeant still military in his bearing, he remained aloof except when meting out the strict discipline he believed young pupils needed in order to become responsible citizens. Herr Gulden had a handful of favorites in the class. I was not one of them. The children he favored sat docilely with hands folded on their desks; they were deferential and soft-spoken.

"I like you," he would say as he paused at their desks, beaming down a doting smile.

Not only was I woefully behind in the basics, but I struck Herr Gulden as a rude upstart. I had too much energy and wiggled in my seat. Bursting with curiosity, starving for the knowledge I'd been denied for so long, I would shoot my hand in the air and blurt out, "That can't be true!" or "Are you sure about that?" whenever something sounded outrageous to my eight-year-old ears. The other children, more familiar with classroom etiquette, stared open-mouthed at me. I was so eager to learn, to engage, and so excited to finally be a big boy sitting at a school desk. But my artless, clumsy manner offended Herr Gulden and disrupted his well-ordered classroom.

"Wolfgang," he would say with a world-weary sigh. "Step forward."

I learned to obey promptly. As I walked forward, crest-fallen, I prepared myself mentally for the punishment he seemed to reserve only for me and a pair of other delinquents. The boys occupying the front desk, familiar with the routine, popped up from their bench and prepared to hold me down by the wrists and ankles. Resignedly I laid myself down across the length of the desk. Herr Gulden fetched the bamboo cane. He adjusted his grip. It whistled through the air and smacked my backside, the stiff, almost petrified *Lederhosen* doing nothing to cushion its blows.

As spring rolled around, the boys in my class began to organize soccer games at recess and after school. I lined up with the others, eager to play. Finally when everyone but me had been chosen, one of the team captains would feel obligated to include me. Once I was on the field, however, no one passed me the ball. Despite being puny for my age and bearing the lingering effects of malnourishment, I longed for the skills my classmates seemed to possess in abundance. I imagined myself deftly dribbling, powerfully kicking, scoring goals and blocking shots. But my foot never touched the ball. Much to my disgrace, my soccer skills remained undeveloped.

I couldn't believe my good fortune when at last I met a couple of boys at school who showed interest in befriending me. Like me, they were outsiders in Hof. Their clothing and accents, like mine, gave them away as poor and from the East. Kurt, Günther and I never entered each other's homes. Instead we played in the streets, drawing hopscotch courses with the odd bit of chalk or charcoal on sidewalks or in my courtyard. Sometimes we traipsed along the banks of the Saale River, or made our way to the remnant of the medieval wall that had once surrounded Hof. The underground caverns beneath the wall enticed us. They were blocked off but we sneaked through, pretending we were explorers in deep caves. With no toys to occupy us, our imaginations took over and entertained us for hours on end.

One day, while running the streets of Hof in my filthy *Lederhosen*, I spied an American boy whose father must have been an officer at one of the nearby military installations. On the grass of his front yard he was playing with a miniature metal fire truck, painted bright red with a white ladder. I gazed at the object with ravenous eyes. Every detail of that exquisite truck imprinted itself onto my brain as I stood there watching him. Even though Germany had a long and rich history of designing and manufacturing top-notch toys for children, my war-time slice of life had never exposed me to such luxuries. Indeed, I'd never imagined such toys even existed.

The boy glanced up at me. He said something in the weird language of the soldiers at Camp Moschendorf. Was he telling me to get lost or that I smelled funny and looked ragged and dirty? No, he was smiling! He held out the fire truck to me. In a flash, I was through the gate and by his side. We played happily together despite our inability to communicate verbally. That he actually let me touch the precious toy seemed nothing short of miraculous. Even more astonishing was when he ran inside and returned with more cars and trucks, a whole arm full of them. If my pungent odor bothered him, he gave no indication as we sat there in the grass making motor noises through protruding lips.

I returned to his house again and again, never daring to knock on his door but always hopeful of finding him outside. Whenever he was in the yard he invited me to play, sharing his possessions with the ease of a child who had plenty to go around. My encounter with him taught me something useful. I made a point of learning in which houses other American families lived on the economy and stood watch whenever I could, waiting for those children to come outside. Like the first boy, they readily shared their toys with me—amazing, breathtaking toys like a *Dick Tracy* mechanical motorcycle and a slinky. My favorites, however, were the vast array of enameled steel vehicles: tractors, buses, dump trucks and cars. Most of the toys had a military theme: an army truck with antiaircraft gun, jeeps, miniature planes shaped like *Mustangs, Thunderbolts, Spitfires, Flying Fortresses* and a red, green and yellow tin army plane with real spinning propeller and wheels. We giggled happily together as we played with these miniature implements of war, oblivious of the horrifying extent of the world conflict that had brought our young lives together.

I didn't learn much in the classroom that year or during any other school year in Hof. No one took the trouble to try to help me catch up with the other students. Mother, on the other hand, tried to teach us things she thought were useful, like how to recognize edible mushrooms. On weekends, she led Heidi and me on forest walks, pausing to pluck *Steinpilze, Pfifferlinge* and *Champignons* to supplement our diet.

"Look closely," she instructed, snapping a *Steinpilz* in half. "If you touch the sponge in the cap and it turns blue, that means it's old. It won't taste good."

She taught us to look for the orange striations in *Pfifferlinge*, the nutty, rich-flavored fungi that were so chewy and satisfying, almost like meat.

In the forest we came across American tanks, positioned near the border, their barrels pointing eastward. At the sight of them, Mother would grow quiet and pensive then take us by the hand and lead us quickly away.

My mind was always spinning, trying to fit the pieces of life's puzzle together. Anything mechanical fascinated me. I could stand mesmerized for what seemed like hours, staring at kites, airplanes and cars and wondering how they worked. The Gründig radio in our apartment beckoned to me, almost begging me to dismantle it to see what was inside, to discover how the classical music Mother loved passed through it on its way to our ears. Only the knowledge that I would receive a whack with the broom kept me from giving in to that temptation. Sometimes I came to awkward, false conclusions about the nature of things for I had no basic mathematical or scientific foundation from which to begin and no one to explain them to me.

Smart enough to sense I was fighting a losing battle in the classroom, I began to dread school. Instead, I daydreamed about rowing down the Saale River in one of the rental boats I saw other boys enjoying. On sunny days after school or on weekends, I would go and sit on the riverbank, watching the local boys line up and hand the boat owner 50 *Pfenning*. This entitled them to jump in a boat and row away to what I perceived as high adventure. Repeatedly I begged the owner to let me take a boat out "just this once," for free. Not surprisingly, he refused.

Whenever my mother gave me a penny or if I found one in the gutter, I stashed it away in a little cardboard, can-shaped "piggy" bank kept on a shelf above our stove. After months of this, my savings finally totaled fifty cents. I emptied the bank, carried the money down to the river and paid for a boat. Oh, how glorious was that day! The Saale swelled with the runoff of a long winter's snow. Blossoms floated down, carried on the breeze, settling on the water's surface and giving off a faint sweet scent. I rowed and rowed until my skinny arms ached. Caught up in the rapture of the experience, I stayed on the water far longer than my allotted time and when I returned the boat owner gave me a tongue lashing. I hung my head, knowing I had overstepped my bounds. But as I gazed downward, I spied on the ground a large silver coin reflecting the sun as if trying to get my attention. A coin worth two *Deutschmark*! Immediately I scooped it up and handed it to the red-faced man. He took the extra fifty cents I owed and gave me the change, which I promptly took home and deposited in my little bank to use for another boat ride one day. I never told Mother about finding the coin. Had she known, she would have made me save it and spend it on something less frivolous than an hour on the river. She hadn't wanted me to go on the first boat ride; in fact, she'd fretted and sighed impatiently the entire time I was on the water, worried that, not knowing how to swim, I would fall in and drown.

Mother worked long hours to make ends meet. When school let out for the day, Heidi and I occupied ourselves on the streets or in the courtyard until she dragged home in the evening. If it was cold and rainy, we let ourselves in to the apartment and waited for her there. Any extra energy she had, she used to try to educate herself about current events and political developments in our volatile border region. She made an effort to train Heidi from a young age in the skills she'd been taught were vital to a woman's survival and fulfillment, such as sewing, baking, and how to pound a *Schnitzel* flat before breading and frying it to perfection. It grieved her that she had no garden in which to instruct us how to grow vegetables, a skill she believed every child should learn in case war came again and starvation threatened. Mother made every effort to pass down to us her inherited German reverence for hard work. While making everyday tasks look easy, she answered our endless questions and endured our clumsy attempts to mimic her actions.

Mother always kept our Gründig radio tuned to a classical music station. She adored Wagner and German folk music. Mozart, Strauss, Bach and Beethoven elevated us and brought dignity to our low-status lives. To this day, hearing *Die Fledermaus* or a Strauss waltz transports me back to that tiny room and my industrious mother, and I feel the strong, comforting presence of the woman she used to be.

In those postwar years, Germans were actively distancing themselves from all things Nazi, and a cloud of shame hovered over anyone perceived to have obvious ties to the embarrassing era of National Socialism. No one in Hof knew that I was a Lebensborn child, but rumors about that Nazi "breeding" organization and its ties to the now-scorned SS were still circulating, even growing and taking on a life of their own. Elfriede was already getting prying questions as to why my last name was Kober and not Kobsch. How long, she wondered, could she keep the secret?

Ex-Nazis were not hounded by the occupying powers in the West as they were in the East. Food and jobs were more plentiful. Still, Elfriede wanted more for her little family. Punching keys on the cash register all day long, watching better-off women walk away with purchases she could only fantasize about, she dreamed of the kind of life she'd seen in American films in Prague theaters, at least before December 1941 when the United States joined the conflict against the Axis powers and Hollywood films were banned. No advocate of women's liberation and the product of a National Socialist upbringing that emphasized marriage and motherhood, Elfriede dreamed of a husband to provide for her. She wanted to stay at home, minding her children, wearing frilly aprons and cooking delicious meals for her man when he came home at night. But in war-ravaged Germany, marriageable men were scarce. Thousands of women had to labor and toil to earn money for food before they cooked it, after which they tucked their children in bed and slept alone on cold nights. Despite being far superior to East Germany, postwar West Germany would never fulfill Elfriede's dreams. So she set about making them come true in the best way she knew how.

Hof, situated on the borders with communist Czechoslovakia and East Germany, became a strategic location for the U.S. Armed Forces. Military installations along the sensitive frontier area, as well as a nearby radar site, intelligence operations and a radio and television transmitting station for Berlin brought an endless supply of American men who were lonely, homesick and eager for female company. This was fortuitous for Elfriede had a way with men. Just walking down the street she turned heads. She knew how to catch a soldier's eye and smile with just the right combination of aloof respectability and flirtatiousness. In the spring and summer of 1950, she had begun to apply these skills assiduously with successful results.

Once Heidi and I were tucked up on the couch to sleep at night, Mother quietly arranged her newly permed hair, applied lipstick, pulled on a fresh dress and stockings and slipped out to the pubs frequented by Americans, whom the Germans called "*Amis*." Soon a number of *Ami* men were knocking on our door, dropping by for a chat and a drink and bringing gifts of canned milk, nylon stockings and chocolate. Their eyes followed Mother hungrily. Only now and then did they glance at Heidi and me and smile with vague disinterest. So easily did Elfriede attract these U.S. soldiers that she felt no pressure to make a hasty decision. She could afford to wait until just the right man came along.

One soldier in particular stands out in my memory. He was like no one Heidi and I had ever seen. Leo's dark brown skin, fuzzy, close-shaved hair and brilliant white smile mesmerized me. None of Mom's other suitors paid so much friendly attention to me and Heidi. He would arrive at the entrance to our courtyard dressed in khaki shirt, pants, tie and cap and open the door to the back seat of a military jeep, inviting Heidi and me to climb inside. Mother sat in front with him. She washed and dressed us up for these occasions in spanking new clothing from Kaufhaus Saale which she'd managed to purchase by making small payments. By this time, Heidi had a new smocked wool dress and white stockings and I sported a wool jacket with shorts and thigh-high socks to keep my legs warm, a welcome change from the stiff, smelly *Lederhosen*. As Leo drove us through Hof on our way out to the Bavarian countryside, I sat proudly gazing out the jeep window and imagined myself a prince surveying his kingdom while being chauffeured around in a fancy carriage. Heidi and I would smile at one another over the picnic basket stashed between us on the back seat, anticipating the special treats Leo always thought to include.

He spoke not one word of German. Heidi and I spoke no English, and our mother had learned only a handful of English phrases by that time. But when Leo spread out the picnic blanket and opened the basket, we communicated with the most universal of gestures—wide eyes and delighted grins. Out came American white bread, its taste and texture so like cake to us who lived on a steady diet of coarse, sour rye. Cheese and sandwich meats he produced in miraculous abundance. We draped ourselves over Leo's broad shoulders, watching his every move as he opened a tin of Vienna sausages and proffered its contents to our eager, grasping fingers. Last of all, as if we needed a reward for having devoured our lunch, he brought forth Hershey bars, a whole one for each of us. Leo laughed in genuine delight as he watched Heidi and me swoon with ecstasy as the chocolate melted in our hot little mouths and dribble down our chins when we giggled.

These picnics were the closest thing we knew to "eating out." In the center of Hof stood a palatial building surrounded by a scrolled iron fence, its gate set between two stone pillars. It was a restaurant called "Theresienstein." The tables on its terrace were covered in white linen and set with real silverware. I used to press my face between the iron railings, watching summer patrons at outdoor tables sipping coffee and eating *Apfelstrudel* topped with a delicate sprinkling of powdered sugar. "Oh please can we go there?" I would repeatedly beg, tugging on my mother's hand as we passed by. She merely rolled her eyes and pulled me along, saying, *"Es kommt gar nicht in Frage!"* (Absolutely out of the question!)

Maybe that's why she seemed especially content on these outings with Leo, during which she came as close to treating her children to a restaurant as she was ever going to get on her limited means. In the mellow afternoon sunlight she radiated a youthful joy. Leo treated her with respect and genuinely enjoyed her children's company. This was what she was looking for in a man. He made her happy. How strange to feel this way after all the Nazi rhetoric she'd absorbed about "inferior" races! Life had indeed turned upside down; nothing was as before and perhaps never would be again. Life with this man could be good, she mused. She couldn't help but imagine how shocked and scandalized her father and siblings would be if she were to marry a black man, and she actually enjoyed picturing the look of horror on Paul Kober's face. However, though she was no expert on American society, Elfriede sensed deep down that if she married Leo and moved to America she would be trading one kind of stigmatization for another. In trying to rid herself and her children of the clinging stain of Nazism, was she prepared to drag them instead into a compromised position in 1950s America—life in a bi-racial home? Somehow she intuited that that sort of thing just wasn't done, or at least, wasn't accepted by a broader American society. Her practical nature warned her away from such an arrangement despite her warm feelings for this kind, handsome soldier.

Technically, the occupying U.S. Army discouraged its soldiers from fraternizing with German women. But no one really enforced the rules and white American men proceeded to date whomever they pleased, figuring that if they fell in love and got engaged, the imposed three-month waiting period and careful screening of the German fiancée wasn't much of an obstacle. The repercussions for black soldiers, however, were more severe. For many of them, especially those who hailed from the Deep South, postwar Germany offered a taste of freedom such as they had never known. Nazi rule had been defined by racism, but that was all over now. Southern black American servicemen found much more acceptance among Germans than back home among their white countrymen. The only women around happened to be white, and black soldiers could date them without fear of getting beat up by an angry mob. They'd left Jim Crow laws far behind, across the Atlantic Ocean. In Germany they could enter pubs, nightclubs and cinemas at will. The only objections they ran into were those of their commanding officers, who disapproved not really because of the rules against fraternization but because of the racial bias they had brought with them from back home. They simply could not lay to rest their view that blacks and whites had no business dating each other.[180]

Yet with their gentlemanly behavior and their unflagging generosity, black American soldiers captured the hearts of several thousand German women. The phenomenon resulted in thousands of what came to be known as "brown babies." Sadly, those black men who fathered children with German women were forbidden to marry the mothers of those children. As far as the Army was concerned, it was doing the men a favor since interracial marriage was illegal in half of all American states. The potential difficulties of such marriages were too obvious to ignore. In order to break up the ill-fated liaisons, superior officers transferred black soldiers they believed had become too involved with German women away to other Army bases. Any babies resulting from those relationships were either kept by their mothers to be raised under great stigma in German society, or given up for adoption to black American couples.[181]

Leo's commanding officer likely noticed him spending more and more time with Elfriede and decided to preemptively order a transfer before things could get out of hand. And Leo, understanding the racial nuances and potential difficulties far better than my mother, probably viewed his relationship with her as a passing fancy. Our beloved weekend picnics ended when he was transferred away after a few short months. No other of Mom's American suitors treated Heidi and me as well as Leo did. Still, we sensed she was waiting for someone to come along who lived up to the high standard he had set.

If Elfriede was disheartened over Leo's departure, she concealed it well as she resumed the business of pub-hopping and meeting men. She moved forward in the confident assurance that there were plenty more where Leo had come from—an endless supply, in fact, as the Cold War escalated. With a stubborn optimism, she continued to date American soldiers over the next year and a half, as many as she could squeeze into her busy schedule of cashiering and caring for two young children.

Then something happened to bring her search for a man to an unexpected and abrupt halt.

My first clue was gleaned from a neighbor's offhand comment. Our only real friends in Hof were other refugees from the East. Most of them lived nearby in tiny cold-water flats. Like us, they dressed in inferior clothing. Many were gaunt, struggling to replace the weight they had lost while living hand to mouth on the run westward or on scant food rations under Russian occupation. West Germany was heaven compared to communist Poland or the newly created German Democratic Republic, but they were far from home, having lost everything familiar. Most were cut off from relatives by the iron curtain. An ever-present cloud of gloom and hopelessness seemed to hover above their heads.

"She'll never make it, you know," remarked one such woman to me as I played "roll the tin can" with another boy on the sidewalk just outside her apartment building. Her prematurely gray hair was bound up in a scarf, exposing a deep worry crease in the middle of her forehead.

Puzzled, I stopped hitting the can with my stick and squinted up at her.

"To America," she clarified, crossing bony arms over the bodice of her threadbare housedress. "They won't let her in with two little kids. How will she support herself? She doesn't even know anybody over there."

I shrugged and ran off to play elsewhere, completely confused. What was she talking about? Mother wasn't planning to go anywhere; if she had been she would have told Heidi and me. But the pooh-poohing went on, and from an ever-increasing chorus of friends and acquaintances. They weren't shy about speaking their minds when they dropped by for coffee or ran into us on the streets: "Who do you think you are, Elfriede? You're pushing your luck. A single mother with no husband! Look at us. We're grateful to be here in West Germany. You should be satisfied with what you have. Do you really believe the USA will roll out the red carpet for the three of you? America isn't letting many Germans in these days; the emigration list is miles long. You might as well give up!"

Now that I came to think of it, my mother had seemed somewhat preoccupied lately. In the privacy of our home I approached her, seeking answers. "Mutti, are we going to America?"

"What? Wolf, why do you ask me such a thing? I have a good job here in Hof. We have this nice apartment!"

Her denials confused me. Surely I hadn't imagined all the nay-saying comments; they'd been spoken right in front of me. Yet her stubborn insistence that I was mistaken made me feel foolish. I backed off. Maybe our "friends" were just jealous that Mother had more than her share of American suitors who supplied her with treats from the commissary. Could that be why they were coming to wrong conclusions or making up crazy stories about her intentions?

But on September 19, 1952, two large wicker basket trunks suddenly appeared in our cramped apartment, taking up valuable space. Frantically, Mother began filling them with household items like feather pillows, bedding, pots and pans. This, with her uncharacteristically buoyant demeanor, confirmed to me that she was indeed up to something, but sensing she would only rebuff my curiosity, I kept silent. A cold fear began to gnaw at me. Would she leave Heidi and me behind? Was it true what the neighbor woman had said, that America didn't want her dragging two young children with her?

When she had packed all she could get her hands on, she sat down on her bed with me and Heidi and pulled out a telegram. "This piece of paper," she explained, "says that there is room for us on a ship. We have only three days until it sails!"

"But Mutti," I protested, "you told me we weren't going anywhere!"

"Oh Wolf, I didn't want to get your hopes up, in case it fell through. Way back when we were living at Camp Moschendorf, I applied to the Lutheran World Federation for help in getting a sponsorship. There are so many Germans wanting to move to America and there were so many papers to fill out. Many times along the way I thought they wouldn't take us because we're so low on the waiting list, but now we finally have a sponsor!" Her eyes sparkled as she gushed on, "Your birth certificate was the hardest part. I didn't have one for you; it took ages to get a substitute. They kept telling me it would take years to receive permission to go. But in the telegram, it says that another mother and two children had to cancel their voyage because of illness. That made room for us; we're taking their place on the *SS America!*"

Elfriede , Heidi and David.
Photo taken by Leo.

Heidi and David

Elfriede

David in the first grade with a new jacket, at last

Elfriede, Early 1950s

At long last, the principle is recognized that displaced persons should be admitted to the United States. Two hundred thousand displaced persons may be admitted in the next two years.

—U.S. President Harry S. Truman

CHAPTER 15

The days that followed brought a frenzy of activity. Mother had discovered her Aunt Liesbeth, her mother's sister, living in Bavaria. My great aunt arrived ready to help. Together the women crammed more household items into the wicker baskets, items they had no idea were unnecessary. Hauling bedding and pots and pans to the New World might have been vital a century earlier, but Mother and Great-Aunt Liesbeth were, at heart, simple Silesian farm folk who couldn't imagine not needing to drag such implements along on the journey.

While my mother was clearly ecstatic about our future, I sat aloof, moping and watching the preparations. Were we really going to haul these bulky baskets to Bremerhaven and halfway across the world? Why did we have to leave Germany at all? At the age of 10 and only in the third grade, I'd finally managed to make a friend or two, albeit from the ranks of despised refugees like myself. These days, I was feeling less like a refugee and more like a native Bavarian, having learned to mimic the speech inflections of the locals. Was I to be the "new kid" yet again? Inwardly I shrank from the prospect of entering another culture. My future American schoolmates were sure to pick on me. If experience had taught me anything, it was that kids could spot a misfit a mile away, and I could never hope to masquerade as anything but a misfit when I couldn't even speak their language.

Sulking dejectedly, I kept my misgivings to myself. Mother was too harried to suffer patiently my doubts. If I voiced them, she would surely grab the broom and swing it at me like she always did when I got on her nerves or sassed her. Or she would quote to me for the hundredth time the trite saying engraved on a wooden plaque on our wall:

Nicht mekern, besser machen.
(Stop complaining and improve things.)

On September 22, Heidi's birthday, Liesbeth accompanied us to the station and we boarded the train to Bremerhaven. Under normal circumstances, a train journey would have excited me. On this day, I sat glumly watching the flat northern German landscape roll by, contemplating a future for which I couldn't work up any enthusiasm. All too soon the train rolled to a stop right near the harbor and we alighted with our two behemoth trunks. Porters took them in hand and soon we were walking up the gangway of a former troop transport, the *SS America.*

Mother had learned of Kurt Novak's demise two years before in 1950 when she'd traced him through the Bavarian Red Cross in order to try to re-establish his financial support of me. Informed that he was living in Bremerhaven, she wrote to the registry office there trying to locate him. Promptly came the reply that Kurt had died on January 21, 1949. This development rendered me eligible to receive orphan benefits if Elfriede could only prove that Kurt was my father, which was no small feat when all record of his paternity had been sworn to secrecy and buried somewhere in the Lebensborn Central Administration. Six months later on February 24, unaware that most of the Lebensborn documents had gone up in flames, Mother wrote to police headquarters in Münich:

To the directorship of the Münich Police...

I request that you please inform me of where I might find the documents pertaining to former Lebensborn children that were kept in the Lebensborn Central Administration in Münich. Records of the Lebensborn organization assuming guardianship of my son were sent to Münich, and now, in order to receive orphan benefits, I urgently need documents proving his father's identity. Please answer as soon as possible.

She received a prompt and succinct reply, written on March 1, 1951 from someone named Hofmaier:

To Frau Elfriede Kobsch...

Unfortunately the whereabouts of documents pertaining

to Lebensborn children is unknown to us. We recommend that you contact the former head of Lebensborn, Mr. Max Sollmann, who lives in Münich on Widenmayer Strasse...and direct your inquiry to him.

Was there just the slightest hint of sarcasm in that reply? In July of 1947 Max Sollmann, along with his deputy Inge Viermetz, Dr. Gregor Ebner and Günther Tesch had been tried in Nuremberg for crimes against humanity, since Lebensborn had kidnapped and attempted to Germanize eastern European children and forced abortions on women judged to be carrying racially impure babies. In March of 1948, Sollmann was acquitted of those particular crimes but pronounced guilty of membership in a criminal organization—the SS. His prison sentence of two years and eight months plus thirty days' labor was declared already served, and his fine reduced to 50 *Deutschmark,* a mere slap on the wrist. He left Nuremberg a free man. Sollmann's notoriety and high-profile connection with the SS made him a reviled figure in postwar Germany where everyone was doing his best to distance himself from all things Nazi.

Whether or not Elfriede contacted Sollmann is unknown to me. But somehow she obtained a new birth certificate, or a copy of the original dated March 30, 1951. This new document declared my birthplace to be Pernitz, Austria and made no mention of Heim Wienerwald.

What thoughts occupied Elfreide's mind as she led her young son aboard ship in the very city where his father lay buried? Did a shadow of mourning fall over her heart for her erstwhile lover? Or did she view Kurt's death at the young age of 43 as advantageous, cementing her decision to never reveal his identity to that son, promising a burial of inconvenient truths as well as a dead body?

Rudi was the one Mother mourned, the one whose legacy she wanted to be associated with. All throughout my life she deliberately gave me the impression, without coming out and saying it in so many words, that Rudi was my father as well as Heidi's. The strange fact of my last name being different was just one of many mysteries I accepted without question, such as why Opa Kobsch hated me so intensely and why my mother had left me for so long-with a cruel stranger in Berlin.

Upon entering the gigantic ocean liner, my spirits lifted. Our third class cabin was uncomfortable and we had to share it with other passengers, but the vessel held many wonders for a boy of 10. Between bouts of seasickness, I spent the voyage bouncing between the ship's three movie theaters, watching cowboy westerns. When the screens went blank, I hurried off to inspect every accessible inch of the ship. I was relentlessly curious. How were those lifeboats suspended in a neat row over my head and by what intricate process might they be lowered should we need them? How did the captain steer the ship when I couldn't see him standing on the bow, turning a wheel? Why did he have to stay hidden in the bridge where I couldn't watch his every heroic move?

Mother gave up trying to keep track of me. Stricken as she was with nausea and needing to care for Heidi, whose temperature had spiked in what threatened to be a relapse of scarlet fever, she had no choice but to let me run free and hope I possessed enough common sense to stay on the right side of the deck railing.

The voyage, during which we encountered massive waves that tilted the ship to a 45-degree angle, lasted eight days. By the time we arrived in New York, Heidi's condition had significantly worsened. That meant quarantine. Heidi remained on the ship, tended to by medical personnel, while Mother and I were required to disembark in a city of strangers. Fortunately Mom had charmed a ship's steward—a young Puerto Rican man whose grandparents lived in a Brooklyn high rise. This elderly couple welcomed us into their tenth floor apartment even though it was already crowded with various children and grandchildren. A delicious, exotic smell pervaded the place. The grandmother was always busy at the stove and she fed us spicy beans and rice, so absolutely foreign to our palates but delightful just the same.

In that apartment sat the first television set I had ever seen. It was an old Dumont model. The reception was terrible with scratchy white lines blurring the picture, but seeing human figures move around inside that tiny box and hearing them speak absolutely mesmerized me. I shook my head, trying to wake myself up from dreaming. What kind of world had I entered that people even had miniature movie screens in their own homes?

The large extended family of our Puerto Rican hosts lived nearby in other apartment buildings. After school, a whole network of siblings and cousins met on the sidewalk below, the older ones supposedly supervising the younger as they gossiped with school friends. Amongst themselves, they chattered away in Spanish but tried to communicate with me in English.

My inability to speak or understand either Spanish or English hardly interfered as I joined in their fun. They taught me how to make a scooter out of an orange crate by nailing to its bottom wheels stripped from old roller skates. Hooting and cheering, we flew down Brooklyn sidewalks, wheels grinding loudly on the pavement. Several times, the children pooled their change and treated me to one of their many neighborhood movie theaters. Their generous gesture thrilled me for I had come to adore the big screen on the *SS America.* Before the voyage, I had visited a theater only once before, in Germany. That had been a serious, somber affair in which the theater was pitch-dark. After a gong sounded and the curtains parted, the audience watched the film in utter silence, remaining perfectly still, holding their bladders until the very end. When the film was over, the curtains closed, the lights came up, and the German viewers filed out in deep contemplation as if from a funeral. To my amazement, American theaters were absolutely raucous in comparison. People walked in and out during the films, meeting friends, visiting the restroom at will, munching on popcorn and sipping soda through colorful straws. A top-billed film was stopped at its most suspenseful point whereupon a "B" movie flashed up on the screen. Only when the "B" movie had finished did the main attraction continue, a master ploy to keep the audience hooked and hanging around to buy more popcorn and sodas. I fell for the ploy and tumbled headlong in love with the movies, a love that has lasted my entire life. My first few halting English phrases were picked up in those Brooklyn matinees, watching reruns of *Dick Tracy* serials—useful expressions such as, "I ain't yella," "Holy smokes!" and "What's the dope?"

On the ocean liner, Heidi and I had seen the word "Chicago" printed somewhere. We'd giggled together about how silly and nonsensical the word looked, just like gibberish. We tried to sound it out, saying it in all kinds of crazy ways, puzzling over what it meant. Now, in a Brooklyn theater, I sat gazing up at a James Cagney gangster film and heard the strange word spoken in its proper context, at last grasping its meaning.

In a flash, one week had passed and Heidi's quarantine was lifted. In true German fashion Mother and I took leave of our Puerto Rican hosts by giving them firm handshakes, oblivious of the fact that they would have happily hugged us good-bye if we had given them the chance. The three of us boarded a Union Pacific *Zephyr* bound for that crazy-sounding place, Chicago.

During our long overland journey, the laxness of the American train system shocked us. We were used to precise punctuality. The disruption of war aside, if a German train was scheduled to pull out at 10:23 AM, it did so, while the American train appeared to keep only to an approximation of its printed schedule. We entered Chicago later than anticipated, but still in time to catch our Seattle-bound connection.

On a dark October night, two days after leaving Chicago, the *Zephyr* slowed its rhythmic chugging and screeched to a gradual halt. Mother jumped up, taking both Heidi and me by the hand and leading us to the exit. Groggy with sleep, we climbed down the steep steps with the conductor's help, jumping onto the stool he'd placed outside for our convenience. He unloaded our suitcases and trunks. Then he tossed the stool back inside, leaned far out and waved his lantern to signal the conductor to drive on.

We three stood not at a station but at the intersection of a road and the railroad tracks. The moon was concealed behind clouds. All around us stretched a vast expanse of nothing and our only light, that of the train, was slowly disappearing westward. A chill wind rustled the corn stubble in the flat fields around us.

"Where are we?" I asked.

"He said this was Brookings, South Dakota." Mother's voice sounded small and frightened. I wasn't used to that and it sent a shock-wave of fear through me. She was the strong one; she knew the answers to all our childish questions. What could this mean?

Suddenly she broke into a wailing sob. "Oh, what have I gotten you children into?" She sank onto one of the wicker trunks.

I felt for her in the dark and grabbed hold of her arm. "Mutti, you're here with us, aren't you?" I awkwardly tried to console her. "We'll be okay; I'm sure we will...." I went on babbling, wishing I could believe my own words. Heidi drew closer to her. Mother's shoulders shook under our hands as she wept.

"But Heidi has been so sick, and it's cold. No one is coming to get us…why did I bring her here?"

"Don't cry, Mutti," we urged over and over again, perhaps more for our own sakes than for hers. She was all we had in the world. Seeing her display such weakness shook us to the core.

After a while, a pair of headlights appeared on the horizon then just as quickly disappeared. There they were again! Now they progressed steadily toward us until we could hear the car's motor growing louder. A black 1949 Chevrolet pulled to a stop just yards from us. Like a growling monster, it sat idling in the road. In my young life I had seen neither an automobile so massive nor one so elegant and smoothly curved, adorned with chrome and stainless steel trim. Its large, round headlights glared at us over a wide grill mouth.

A door opened. Out stepped a rotund, short figure. He hurried to Mother and with his big paws pumped her hand up and down. "It's me, Klaveter!" he announced in a booming voice. "Welcome!"

A sigh of relief escaped me when I realized he was speaking German.

"Children, this is our sponsor," explained Mother, her relief audible.

Klaveter loaded our luggage into the Chevy's cavernous trunk. All three of us squeezed into the front seat beside him because the back seat was filled with car tires. As he drove into the black night he sang, in English at the top of his voice, "You are my sunshine, my only sunshine."

He drove straight to his chicken farm and led us into a flimsy wooden house. By now a fierce autumn wind was sweeping over the prairie. It howled and whistled around the house shaking the wood siding, sounding as if it would invade the dwelling at any moment and break it to pieces, hurtling us across the endless flat landscape. There was no electricity. Klaveter lit kerosene lamps and used one to guide us to a room containing a huge lumpy bed with brass headboard. A stack of tires made up the footboard. I glanced around me. The bedroom walls were made of grayish, weathered wood and the room smelt of greasy rubber. I felt cold air blowing on me as if the wind had followed us right inside.

In the morning, we awoke to Klaveter's boisterous singing. We pulled on our clothes and joined him in the kitchen. The fiftyish, pot-bellied bachelor stood there in saggy blue jeans, stained gray sweatshirt and a cap with a visor, skillfully juggling pots and pans.

"I made boiled, fried, scrambled and poached!" he announced.

"Eggs?" asked Mother, peering around at her grubby, untidy surroundings. The house had an air of decrepitude about it, as if Klaveter cared far more about housing his chickens properly than himself.

"Yes! I didn't know what kind you'd like, and if there's one thing I don't run out of, it's eggs. I can afford to waste a few here and there."

In fact, eggs had brought this perpetually jovial farmer and my mother together. He'd signed up as a sponsor with the Lutheran World Federation, eager to help a fellow German and hoping for someone, possibly a wife, to help him run his chicken enterprise. When he learned that Elfriede had grown up on a chicken farm collecting, cleaning, candling and sorting eggs, it seemed to him a match made in heaven.

But there was no chemistry. Quickly he realized that this attractive young woman, no matter how chicken-literate, would not be interested in a life on his drab prairie spread. His farm was of an impressive size and he had outfitted it with modern equipment, but Elfriede had a certain elegance about her, incongruous with tramping in and out of his huge coops in boots covered with chicken crap. They talked things over. Klaveter, being a deeply kind and generous soul, agreed to help her find work elsewhere. A little wistfully he promised to put in a word for her at the local egg processing plant where he felt sure she could put her expertise to good use. We continued to live in his house, where by daylight we could see outside through cracks in the walls. Our host sometimes left us there alone overnight.

Mother, who couldn't help noticing the unappetizing build-up of dust and grime in our sponsor's kitchen, finished a bite of scrambled egg one morning and said sweetly, "Mr. Klaveter, where do you stay when you don't come home at night?"

"In Brookings. I have a little house in the middle of town, and when it gets too late to come home, I just spend the night there."

"Does anyone else live in it?"

"Nope."

Mother smiled. Her random stab had struck gold. "I wonder then," she continued, with well-honed tact, "if we might not get in your way out here. My children need to go to school and that would mean a lot of driving back and forth for you. What if I were to clean this house from top to bottom for you as a sort of down payment on rent for the house in Brookings? Afterwards, I'll clean that house too. Wolf, Heidi and I could move there and leave you in peace."

The thought of a woman's expert touch in scrubbing out the grime of umpteen years of bachelor farming tempted Klaveter. He quickly agreed. He reckoned rightly that Elfriede would keep his town house spic and span. In a matter of days he'd moved us into the turn of the century clapboard home on a pleasant tree-lined street in Brookings. Despite smelling musty, it felt downright civilized compared to his rickety prairie house. Mother unpacked our trunks. Only now, after receiving linens and blankets and a full kitchen's worth of dishes and utensils and cooking implements, all donated to us by local Lutheran church members, did she recognize how needless it had been to haul bedding and pots and pans across the Atlantic.

Sighing deeply, she took stock of our surroundings. The neglected town house was a huge improvement over the farm, but still rough around the edges. "I'll have to get busy sewing curtains and finding a picture or two to hang on the walls." On top of all this, she began work at the egg processing plant. All day long she fetched heavy crates of eggs, carrying them to her candling station, sitting in a darkened room holding each egg up before a light. Her expert eyes easily detected bloody whites, blood spots, and meat spots as well as evaluating the germ development. When she finished her grading and sorting, she hauled the eggs away and picked up a new crate to begin the process all over again. Before long, she had set aside enough of her earnings to repay Klaveter for our passage to America.

While our mother toiled in an atmosphere she once thought she had left behind forever, Heidi and I attended school. Heidi was just the right age to start with her peers in first grade, and she fit seamlessly into her new environment. I, however, felt utterly lost. But it wasn't long before I began to pick up on English, and to my surprise, I progressed quickly. The Brookings teachers sympathized with me and devoted extra time to help me fill in my educational gaps. After one week spent in first grade, I was moved up to the second grade, where I stayed for the rest of the school year. Despite being two years older than my classmates, I was scrawny for my age and fit in nicely. The students displayed a friendliness I'd never before encountered, except for the U.S. military children in Hof. "What's your name again?" they would ask out of genuine curiosity, screwing up their faces in bewilderment when I replied for the umpteenth time, "Wolfgang."

"I heard your sister call you Wolf," said one, "just like the animal!"

"It's not like the animal," I objected. "It's just a name. Wolf is short for Wolfgang." How could they not get it? It was so elementary to me. I'd known a dozen other Wolfgangs in my German schools. What exactly was the problem here? Many of the American kids in Brookings had German last names, but it was their grandparents or great-grandparents who had emigrated. The few who possessed any passed-down knowledge of how to pronounce German stepped in to try to help.

"You mean, Wolf—gang, like a gang of crooks?" one kid would say.

"No," another tried to explain. "Gang sounds like gong."

"Like a Chinese gong?"

The whole thing was exhausting.

I adored my new school. In Brookings, no refugee stigma clung to Heidi and me. Our house contained a real clawfoot bathtub and, regularly washed, I no longer repulsed my schoolmates with my body odor. Though at first I attracted a few curious looks, no one teased me for being a foreigner and no one held a grudge at my hailing from America's all-too-recent arch enemy, Nazi Germany. The teachers were kind and treated all of their students equally, making sure our coats were zipped up, our mittens securely on, and that we made it home safely in a snowstorm. One day we filed into the school auditorium and watched the film, *Great Expectations*. Remembering Herr Gulden's austere classroom, I thought I had entered Seventh Heaven. Never in postwar Germany would schoolchildren experience such a treat.

I joined the Boy Scouts, relishing the chance to spend time with other curious, active youths. Their fathers were our leaders. Watching these men with their sons, I began to feel twinges of sadness over my fatherless state. Overhearing innocent comments like, "Joey, you're the spitting image of your dad!" or "That kid's going to be a fast runner just like his old man," began to elicit new and painful emotions. Alone in my room, I held one-sided conversations with the deceased Rudi. "I'm so sorry you were killed by the Russians," I would tell him. "It makes me sad that I'll never get to know you. You're gone now, so I have no father. But there's nothing we can do about it, is there?" It still didn't occur to me to question why, if Rudi Kobsch had fathered me, I went by the name Kober. Stubbornly I clung to the belief that he was my father because no one had ever told me otherwise.

Alone with Mother, out of my hearing, Heidi sometimes inquired why my last name was different from hers. Mother always shut her down by replying, "Because that's just the way it is." Fearful of society's disapproval, Elfriede undoubtedly led our new American friends to believe that she had been married twice and that I was the child of her first marriage. None suspected otherwise. Only those who had reason to inspect her official documents would have known that Kober was her maiden name.

On our first Thanksgiving in America, a neighbor family invited us to dinner. When handed a slice of pumpkin pie by our smiling hostess, I anticipated a heavenly treat and quickly took a bite. It tasted like mud. Eager to show gratitude and not offend, I forced myself to gobble down the rest, faster than lightning in order to get the disgusting ordeal over with. I'd already finished by the time the other children were just nibbling tentatively at their first forkfuls. When our hostess finally sat down to eat her slice, she made a horrible face and pushed her plate away.

"Oh, I'm so sorry!" she exclaimed. "I completely forgot to add sugar!"

Everyone laughed and pointed at my plate, but I didn't mind being the butt of the joke for having devoured the tasteless mush. The laughter came from genuine amusement rather than cruelty, and it felt wonderful.

Snow fell on Christmas that year, a day of rare respite from the howling prairie wind. I went outside to watch huge flakes slide out of the sky and hit the ground with a wet plopping sound. How like Germany it felt, and so different from South Dakota's usual small biting flakes that swirled in the wind. A twinge of homesickness tugged at me that day. Real candles burning on freshly cut evergreens, half-timbered houses with steep, snowy roofs, soaring church towers, rolling, forested landscapes—these had become the mere stuff of Christmas card pictures. Yet I was growing fond of Brookings and its friendly people. This was now home, for keeps.

Or so I thought.

The hard physical labor in the poultry plant began to take a toll on my petite mother. The strain was beginning to show both in her face and body. Her sympathetic supervisor praised her candling skills, but encouraged her to seek less taxing work elsewhere. Although we weren't churchgoers, the local Lutheran church had bent over backward to help our little family, providing us with clothing and household items we needed. Mother's boss contacted the pastor, who made inquiries of a Baptist pastor in Madison, Wisconsin. This pastor had a friend in the rural town of Tomahawk who had recently been widowed and needed temporary domestic help. He agreed to let Mom, Heidi and me live with him on his farm for the entire summer of 1953 in exchange for Mom cooking and cleaning. In her spare time, she planned to search for employment.

Once again I said good-bye to a place in which I'd come to feel at home. Each time it happened, I learned to shut down the painful emotions of leave-taking just a little bit more effectively.

In Brookings, South Dakota, 1952

Elfriede's attempt to locate Kurt Novak for child support

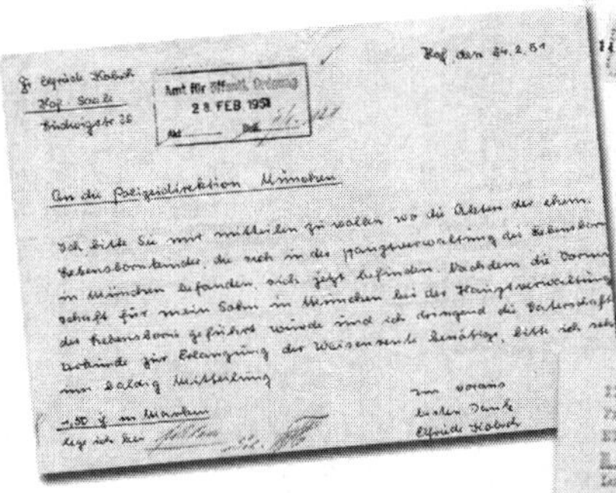

Elfriede's letter seeking proof of Kurt Novak's paternity from Lebensborn

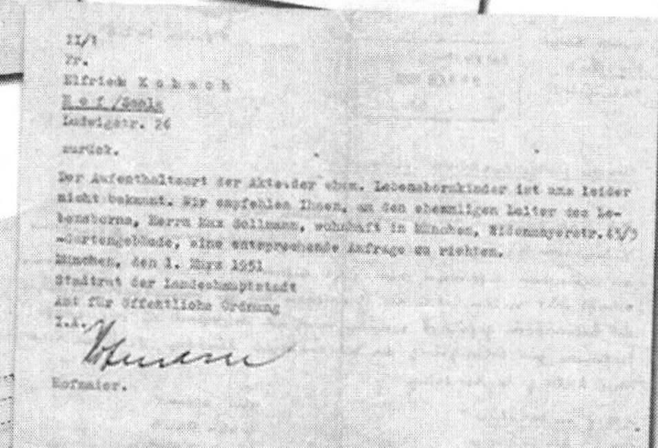

II/1
Fr.
Elfriede K o b s c h
H o f /Saale
Ludwigstr. 26
zurück.

Der Aufenthaltsort der Akten der ehem. Lebensbornkinder ist uns leider nicht bekannt. Wir empfehlen Ihnen, an den ehemaligen Leiter des Lebensborns, Herrn Max Sollmann, wohnhaft in München, [illegible] -Gartengebäude, eine entsprechende Anfrage zu richten.
München, den 1. März 1951
Stadtrat der Landeshauptstadt
Amt für öffentliche Ordnung
I.A.

Hofmaier.

The reply from Münich police suggesting Elfriede contact Max Sollman

The birth certificate Elfriede obtained for David

Names and attributes must be accommodated to the essence of things, and not the essence to the names, since things come first and names afterward.

—Galileo Galilei

CHAPTER 16

Living with the farmer in Tomahawk, Heidi and I ate three square meals a day, had the run of his farm and fell into bed exhausted each night only to wake again the next morning refreshed and ready to explore. Neither Heidi nor I remember his name because we never called him by it. We called him simply, "Opa." By nature easygoing, he was fit and slender with silver hair and lively gray eyes. He made the daily rounds of his farm wearing what looked to me like an oversized train engineer's cap. Sometimes we rode about with him on a tractor or followed his hunting hound around the farm, watching him nip at the milk cows to drive them into their stalls. Opa gave Heidi and me each a calf to take care of all summer. We relished the role of nurturers. He brought fresh milk to the breakfast table every morning and taught us to fish. The only time that patient man ever scolded me was when, trying to be helpful, I set the cows' salt lick in the water trough, thinking it would be easier for them to reach. Of course it dissolved and rendered their water undrinkable. But Opa's displeasure was brief and soon forgotten, as if he understood little boys and their penchant for mischief.

By summer's end, Mother's sewing skills had landed her a job as a wedding dress maker at a Madison bridal boutique. In a fit of determination, she used her meager resources to buy several yards of white satin and thread. Borrowing a sewing machine from the Baptist pastor's wife in Madison, she constructed an elegant bridal gown, donned it herself and hurried straight to the shop.

"I make. Do you like?" she inquired with a hopeful smile.

The boutique owner approached her with a skeptical look.

But after examining the French seams and nearly invisible hemming stitches, the woman nodded approval and hired her.

Our temporary lodgings at the Tomahawk farmhouse had been more than adequate, but now that Mother had a job she needed to live in Madison. Summer was coming to an end, and although Opa's commitment to keep Heidi and me was also drawing to a close, she still had found no housing she could afford. Once again, the kindhearted pastor stepped in by offering her a small temporary room in his home and telephoning another Baptist pastor who lived just outside Madison between Lakes Monona and Mendota. Arrangements were made for Heidi and me to transfer there while mother continued her search.

Our new host, unlike Opa, was sickly and cranky with a stern, critical demeanor. He had a sallow face and a skeletal frame. He must have desperately needed the money our mother paid him because it seemed contrary to his nature to suffer the presence of two noisy children in his stiflingly quiet, spotless home. Two women lived with him. His wife and spinster sister kept their distance from us as if to say to the pastor, "You agreed to bring these children here so you deal with them."

To our great relief, Mother came to fetch us just around the time school was to start. At last she had found a place large enough for the three of us. Our new apartment stood just one block off Capital Square. What luxury! It was massive compared to anything we'd ever resided in before, with three bedrooms, a full kitchen, dining room and living room. Since it was the full ground floor of a large Victorian house, it had two roomy porches both front and back. Thrilled to begin sixth grade at Washington Elementary, I was nevertheless irked at having to explain and re-explain my odd German name to amused but friendly classmates.

Our lives couldn't have changed any more completely from what they had been back in Germany. Shortly after being hired by the bridal shop, Mother's prowess at cooking had secured her an even higher paying job as assistant chef at the Madison Club, a congregating place for wealthy old men. She continued to supplement her income by part-time sewing, but her job as cook took priority. We never went hungry now. Mother endeared herself to the old cronies of the Madison Club by cooking traditional German and Silesian dishes such as pork roasts, beef roulade, *Schnit-*

zel, potato dumplings and lentil stew with tender chunks of ham. She brought home the leftovers and we feasted on the rich, salty fare. This was a side of our mother we had never before seen. Her skill as a cook astounded me, almost as if she had miraculously acquired it upon arrival in America, but of course she had never had the opportunity to show off cooking skills to us in Germany because food was so scarce. This new development was heavenly! For the first time in our lives, Heidi and I approached plumpness as we devoured the gleanings of desserts our mother baked for the members of the Club—streusel cakes, apple and plum cakes and sky-high tortes layered with whipped cream.

I made friends easily in Madison. My new buddies helped me build a fort out of scrap wood in my backyard, where we sat around together reading comic books and discussing what we would do if we had superhero powers. Those comic books worked a kind of therapy on me. For so much of my life I'd been a puny, helpless boy buffeted about by the whims of circumstance. Now, through the ministrations of Superman, The Flash, Captain Marvel and Captain America, I imagined myself in the role of potent avenger and mighty rescuer, and it felt good. Identifying with and losing myself in the adventures of Batman and Captain Comet allowed me to release my feelings of inferiority and summon an inner me that I admired and respected.

If comic books were my therapists, movies became my tutor in the English language and in American ways. For a quarter each, my friends and I could see a film at the Orpheum Theater, just one block away from my house. I thrilled to the sappy singing of Howard Keel and Ann Blythe in *Rosemarie,* imagining myself decked out in the uniform of a Canadian Mountie and riding a tall horse. The Orpheum cultivated in me a love of musical theater and film that lingers to this day.

In Madison, my English improved by leaps and bounds. Heidi and I became Mother's tutors in the language as she constantly pestered us to teach her various words and phrases and help her pronounce them correctly. It was so much harder for her as an adult to learn to speak with fluidity, but she was absolutely determined to learn to communicate.

Mother didn't mingle socially with the men she cooked for at the Madison Club. They were mostly well past retirement, sitting around smoking pipes and cigars, reading newspapers over their pot bellies and passing the time of day with each other. Instead, she joined the German-American Club. Made up of a mixture of military and business people as well as new immigrants from Germany, it was a veritable wellspring of potential boyfriends for someone as pretty as she. Its members met together one evening a week to dine, play cards and dance. Ever skillful at reeling in suitors, Mom brought home date after date and introduced them to Heidi and me. Once she had done so, she stood back and watched. Did he take an interest in her children? Did he bend down and look us in the eye, asking us questions? Or did he mumble a terse, "Hi, kid," and look longingly at the door. Resolved to marry a family man as well as a good provider, our mother soon dropped those who failed the test. She could afford to be picky, to make her children a priority in her choosing of a lifetime partner. Unlike Germany, America seemed to have plenty of men to go around, and seldom did one of them fail to show interest in the petite European emigrée with the charming accent, big brown eyes and dimpled smile. Neither did it hurt that she cooked like a dream.

One day in 1955, I straggled up to the house upon returning from a Boy Scout camping trip. A stranger was sitting on a chair on our front porch. Hauling my backpack and sleeping bag up the steps, I tossed them down and stood there giving the newcomer the once-over. Mom quickly appeared at the front door.

"Wolf, this is Clem Bugno."

Clem stood up. He had dark, curly hair and a gentle expression. Not exceptionally tall but taller than Mother, he had a studious look about him as he peered down at me through horn rimmed glasses. I mumbled a muffled hello and remained guarded. If, as so often happened with my mother's suitors, he was here today and gone tomorrow, I hesitated to expend the mental energy of getting to know him. Clem wasn't put off by my hesitation. In place of a stiff handshake, he laid an arm about my shoulders. "It's so nice to meet you, Wolf. I've already had a chance to get acquainted with your sister, and now I look forward to knowing you better. I want to hear all about that camping trip."

This made a change! Nearly all of Mom's other dates gave the distinct impression of gritting their teeth and merely putting up with Heidi and me so as to claim the true prize—a night out with our mother.

"I've never heard the name Bugno," I blurted. "What the heck kind of name is that?"

"Don't be rude, Wolf!" chided Mother.

Clem laughed. "It's all right Elfriede. Bugno is an Italian name, but I only have it because of an adoption somewhere back in my family line. My family is 100 percent Polish. After my father died, my Mom remarried and her last name became Niedzielski."

"He has a huge family," added Heidi, who'd been eavesdropping quietly from behind the screen door.

"Yep," he admitted. "Six full siblings, four step-siblings and two half-brothers."

Clem had only just joined the Air Force and was stationed at Truix Air Field near Madison. Lately, it had been strongly hinted at that he might be sent to Germany. So when one of Mother's friends who worked at the airbase library offered to set him up on a blind date with an attractive German widow, the idea intrigued him. Very quickly he became a regular fixture around our house. He loved spending time with us in the evenings and on weekends, laughing un-self-consciously as we tried in vain to coach his pronunciation of German words, relishing sharing the hearty leftovers Mom brought home from the Madison Club.

Clem and Elfriede married just three months after meeting. That was okay with me, but the dizzying events that followed left me reeling.

"Wolf, come here for a few minutes," called Mother. "I want to talk to you."

Reluctantly I tore myself away from Batman's latest adventure and emerged from my bedroom to sit beside her on the couch. Mom and Clem had been married for a little over one month. His overcoat and hat on the coat rack, his newspaper on the coffee table with half-empty packages of Chesterfield cigarettes lying atop it gave our home a completeness that felt right.

"Clem has received his orders to report to Ramstein Air Force Base in Germany."

"What? He's leaving us?"

"Of course not! We're going with him."

"To Germany? Mutti, no! We can't go back there." I gaped at her, dumbfounded. We were so happy now, living so well. Why would Clem drag us back to a place where we'd lived in a cramped cold-water flat and scrounged for food? A place where I'd been picked on so mercilessly by my peers? "But everyone is so nice to us here," I objected, more feebly this time.

"Things are different now, Wolf. We're returning to Germany as Americans, not Germans. I've applied for citizenship, and it won't be long now until I receive it. Clem intends to adopt you and Heidi, so you'll both have your citizenship too."

I stared blankly, straining to grasp all the implications of this. Before I could form a word in reply, she continued, "There's one more thing. When someone is adopted, that person's name can be legally changed. Of course, you'll take Clem's last name, but I'm wondering if you might like to change your first name too. You can pick one you like, any name at all. Think about it."

Dazed, I wandered back to my room. The comic book story lying open on my bed seemed dull compared to the changes sweeping through my 13-year-old life. Did I want to change my name from Wolfgang to something else? You bet I did, but what? I lay on my back, arms folded behind my head and staring up at the ceiling. Through my mind ran all the names of my friends: Fred, Jimmy, Bobby, John, Richard and David.

David was my favorite friend out of the whole bunch. From the first day I'd met him at Washington Elementary, the sandy-haired kid with the friendly grin and infectious laugh had become my closest, most trusted companion. We trekked through the woods together building forts with fallen cottonwood, birch and ash branches. We sat for hours side by side, reading comic books in his bedroom or the fort in my backyard and rode our bicycles together all over Madison. Since we shared the same sense of humor, it seemed we were always laughing.

I'd spent so many happy hours in his company that I wanted to be called David. Not only was I thrilled to rid myself of the name Wolfgang, but I also decided to jettison the ultra-Aryan Rüdiger. As far as I was concerned, I had no need of a middle name.

When I asked David if he'd mind my taking his name, he voiced no objection. In fact, he was honored and pleased. Rightly sensing that we weren't likely to meet again after my overseas move, my friend understood that this was my way of taking him with me as I entered an unknown future. And indeed, sharing his name has kept the memories of those happy childhood days in Wisconsin alive in me, all the way to the present.

Clem flew away to Europe in September. Meanwhile, Mom, Heidi and I packed up, said our good-byes to Madison and traveled by train to stay with Clem's family in Scranton, Pennsylvania until he signaled the okay to join him in Germany. His parents' noisy, boisterous household absorbed us easily. There were so many extended family members living close by that I couldn't quite get their names straight, but they all treated Heidi and me with warmth and kindness. Not only had we gained a father, but into the bargain was thrown a whole pack of cousins with which to play. It pleased me especially to see how the entire Bugno family embraced our mother, welcoming her into their midst with joy. I'd never seen her so happy. Living in the bosom of this close-knit family for one month anchored me and eased my fears about returning to Germany.

In October, a *Super Constellation*, the kind of airplane I'd seen so many times in movies, carried us back to Germany. The pretty flight attendants treated us like royalty. Us! I couldn't stop grinning at the realization that we had left Germany penniless and were now returning in high style.

At Ramstein we resumed our happy family life. Clem was a busy man, responsible for the flight operations of the base, but whenever he had free time on weekends he spent it with us, taking long Sunday drives into the German countryside, enjoying lazy picnics, stopping at cafés for coffee and cake afterward. This congenial man had little in common with me—he was bookish and enjoyed indoor activities, while I lived for the outdoors—but time and time again he set aside his preferences to insure that I enjoyed myself. Although he would have preferred a hotel, he spent one hard-earned, precious week of vacation camping in tents along the French Riviera merely because I loved outdoor living. Every morning when he emerged from his cramped tent, he smacked his head on a gnarled, low-hanging tree branch, eliciting amused giggles from us kids. Patiently he endured the misery for my sake.

Clem had come into my life a little too late to influence my personality development or my interests, and to erase the pain of my fatherless youth. It was impossible for him to stand in the gap for the father I'd missed during my most vulnerable years. Yet both he and I were at peace with that. He accepted me for who I was and never tried to change me. I treasured his presence in our family, recognizing it as a great blessing. Perhaps the most valuable gift he gave me was his tender and respectful treatment of my mother. Secure in the knowledge that he would take care of her, I rested more easily and gave myself permission to separate from her emotionally.

I looked for comic books in Germany but never found any. It was just as well; I didn't really need them anymore. My fascination with superheroes had served its purpose and helped guide a frightened child out of his shell. Now it was time to lay them aside and proceed with growing up. My love affair with German trains, however, was rekindled at Ramstein. Every day after school, I hopped on my bicycle and pedaled down to the military train depot. Leaving the bike on a grassy bank, I'd sit near the tracks whiling the afternoon away by watching the trains coming and going. Prewar steam locomotives chugged past, lifting my hair with the wind they generated. Like old friends from early childhood, I recognized them as they hurtled by, grinning with the sheer joy of reunion. The engineers would hang out of the window, watching the track. Often they waved at me, calling out *"Guten tag!"* or *"Hallo!"*

The train watching ritual was as therapeutic as comic books had been in Madison; it bridged the chasm between my early years in Görlitz and my teen years at Ramstein—between a resented, illegitimate boy and a full-fledged member of a happy family. My life had changed at warp speed but the trains rolled on as they always had. Watching them for hours on end had a healing effect. Through a tumultuous time of transition, the unceasing, predictable arrival and departure of the locomotives kept me grounded.

One Saturday morning I awoke early to Mother clattering around in our apartment's kitchen. Not even Clem was awake yet.

"What's going on?" I inquired through a sleepy yawn.

Startled, she glanced up at me then dropped her forehead dejectedly into one palm. "It's your grandfather, Wolf…no, I mean David. Your Kober Opa is coming today for a week-long visit."

"Kober Opa? Doesn't he live in East Germany?"

"Yes, he does. Apparently the communist government

doesn't consider him a flight risk so they've let him out for a while. Besides, he's in his seventies now, and no loss to East Germany if he defects. He wrote me last month, asking if he could come. I don't want him here, but what can I do? He's my father."

Mother had always been tight-lipped about her father. She'd gone to great lengths to keep me and Heidi away from him, even right after the war when she learned that he and several other family members were living in Görlitz. She'd reconnected with her brother Werner, who, after spending time in a British POW camp, had worked in a bakery in Görlitz for a time before making his way to Bavaria. Despite friendly feelings toward Werner and her sister Helene and a continuing closeness with her sister Lisbeth, Elfriede's relationship with Paul Kober seemed fractured beyond repair.

When my grandfather entered our apartment at Ramstein, it was as if a cold wind blew in with him. Mom kept to the opposite side of the room from wherever he was. She looked utterly miserable, as if she were counting the seconds until he departed. Yet driven by a latent need to impress him and win his approval, she labored hard over complicated meals and desserts for which he offered no praise. Not once did he ask any of us questions about ourselves or show the slightest interest in us as individuals. From a safe distance, I scrutinized the man whose name I had carried before my adoption. He had a broad forehead topped with thinning, silver hair. Stocky of build, he exuded fitness and seemed unusually well-toned for a man his age. I found out why when Clem took us all out driving one day.

"You Americans and your fancy cars," Kober scoffed. "I don't have a car in East Germany, and I don't need one. I walk everywhere or ride my bicycle. Just look at me! I'm in great shape. I haven't suffered one bit from not riding around everywhere on my butt, letting some motor do all the work."

As we drove on, whenever we noticed and remarked upon a tall, modern building or a bridge under construction, Kober Opa snorted derisively.

"It's fake! All these things are staged in order to fool visitors and make us think the West is so advanced. East Germans are far better educated and have a better standard of living than anyone in the world, and that includes Americans and West Germans!"

His constant political diatribes irritated us all. Mom hadn't realized just how fully her father, after being forced out of Silesia, had embraced his new life in East Germany. Ever the opportunist and perhaps mostly to save his own skin, he'd become an ardent devotee of communism, subscribing to an "If you can't beat 'em, join 'em" philosophy.

Living in the center of an escalating Cold War, Clem grew nervous at Kober's outspoken praise of communism. Out of the old man's earshot, Clem hissed, "Elfriede! Do you know what could happen to me if I'm discovered to be hosting a card-carrying communist? We live on an American Air Force Base for crying out loud!"

"Shh!" she warned. "I had no idea! When it comes to politics, my father drifts whichever way the wind blows. When I was a teenager he was a full-fledged Nazi. He used to patrol our village wearing a swastika on his Block Assistant uniform. How could I have known he'd turn into a devoted Stalinist?"

Kober Opa wandered outside one sunny afternoon to find me throwing a baseball with my buddies. Seeing the hard sphere whiz through the air and land in my glove with a loud smack, he shook his head in bewilderment. "Why are you doing that, David?"

"It's baseball. That's how it's played. Haven't you ever heard of baseball?"

"For God's sake, no!"

"Watch," I said. I turned and threw the ball against the wall of our apartment building. It bounced back into my glove. "It's made of cork, rubber and yarn inside. See those bats over there? We use them to swing at the ball, and if we hit it, we run bases."

Thoroughly bemused, still shaking his head, he dismissed me with a sweep of his hand as if I'd been talking gibberish. Then he turned and walked away.

"If they know so much in East Germany," I asked Mother later that day, "Why hasn't Kober Opa even heard of baseball?"

That evening at the dinner table, my grandfather turned suddenly to my mother. "Elfriede, you owe me 10 *Deutschmark*."

"What?"

"Remember that time you asked me for money to spend in Bunzlau on something or other? No doubt it was only a frivolous trinket. Well, you never paid me back. I want that money now."

We searched his face for a sign he was joking, but found none.

"I was 14 years old when that happened!" she exclaimed.

"It's never too late to pay one's debts, and you owe me," he groused, returning to his meal.

Clem glanced at his wife with genuine pity, as if a piece of the puzzle had just dropped into place for him. In his adoring eyes, any faults Elfriede possessed could be explained away by this miserly brute of a father's effect on her young life.

For the remainder of the visit, Mom dutifully served her father three meals a day along with afternoon coffee and cake. She bit her tongue to keep from lashing out at him. When he finally left, there were no hugs good-bye, no tender sentiments expressed. With a relief shared by the whole family, I watched him leave, thankful to no longer bear the name of Kober.

Like Kober Opa, the elderly Walter and Elisabeth Kobsch were allowed to leave the DDR in order to visit us at Ramstein. To my intense relief, Walter had mellowed during our years apart and no longer displayed any loathing toward me. Neither did he exude warmth and affection. Yet the visit was pleasant for us all. Opa and Oma expressed pride in my mother for achieving her dreams, and gratitude to Clem for providing a happy home in which their beloved Heidi could grow up. Naturally they were both overjoyed to see their granddaughter again, but as before, Oma also treated me as a precious grandson. For the first time in my memory, her tenderness was not overshadowed by Walter's abhorrence of me.

After an eight-month stint at Ramstein, Clem was promoted to Non-Commissioned Officer In Charge of Erding Air Force Base in Bavaria. No sooner had we moved into the military housing community called Williamsville than we received a joyous visit from Aunt Lisbeth and her husband Hans. With them were their two children, Peter and Rosel, and Lisbeth's daughter Inge.

"Wolf Rüdiger!" Peter shouted upon seeing me. All throughout the visit, when not calling me "Bub" he continued to call me by my former given name until one day Clem laid a firm hand on his shoulder and corrected him, saying, "Please remember that his name is David now. Don't call him by his German name anymore."

Once she had settled in, Mother embarked upon something she had obviously been planning for months—a visit to our former neighborhood in Hof. This was to be no ordinary jaunt. It was a triumphal return, a deliberate, well thought out flaunting of her success before the eyes of the naysayers who had insisted she'd never make it to America. Familiar with the gossip grapevine in Hof, Mom knew that once certain key people laid eyes on her, news would travel fast. Soon all of them would realize how wrong they'd been.

On the day of our visit, she saw to it that Heidi and I were impeccably dressed. My sister donned a pale pink frock and black patent leather shoes. I suited up in herringbone pants, a freshly starched and ironed shirt, well-cut jacket and leather shoes. Gone forever was the ragged boy in pungent Lederhosen and worn-out sandals. Mother attired herself with special care that day, wearing a springy pastel yellow dress with pinched waist and flared skirt, and a hat embellished with lace and a delicate spray of artificial berries, the likes of which the still-struggling Eastern refugees of Hof could never afford. I felt proud of her beauty as I sat in the backseat of our car during the three-hour drive, gazing back and forth between the passing countryside and my mother up front beside her handsome American husband. Naturally, she intended to show Clem off too. Eagerly she anticipated looks of envy on the faces of the war widows she'd left behind.

Mom directed Clem to park our green 1955 Pontiac Chieftain conspicuously on the Ludwigstrasse. We might just as easily have taken the train, but arriving in this ostentatious boat was part of her shock and awe strategy. The Pontiac was polished to a brilliant sheen. None of the people we'd known there could even remotely dream of owning such a vehicle. Germany was still limping forward, struggling to recover from the devastation of war, and the few cars on the streets were a homely black or white.

Mother slammed her car door hard for maximum effect. Slipping her arm through Clem's, she led him around town, pointing out our old haunts. A handful of our former neighbors on Ludwigstrasse, leaning out their windows to watch the world go by, caught sight of her and called out greetings. Gleefully she marched right up to them, chirping, "Hello! It's so nice to pop back here for a visit!"

Our former neighbors' faces looked careworn but hopeful. They still seemed subdued, painfully aware of having been knocked down a peg from prewar life. Mom's overblown confidence and self-assurance only highlighted their lack of such. They were a proud people in survival mode. In their drab and utilitarian, if no longer ragged clothing, they gaped unabashedly at our fancy duds. Their open astonishment pleased Mother to no end.

Standing there in the street with my family, I glanced around at my former neighborhood. Some of the buildings had been repaired and repainted but most still bore the marks of neglect in a society where day to day survival and recovery from the trauma of war took priority over the beautification of dwellings.

"I'm an American citizen now," Mother informed everyone she met. "I'm living with the other Americans at Erding Air Force Base." This wasn't mere boasting of having reached her goal of emigration, but also a statement to the effect of, *I identify with the conquerors, your occupiers. Not with you, the vanquished.*

Elfriede left Hof that day a satisfied woman. The fact that she'd endeared herself to no one by bragging and sowing envy among her still-smarting countrymen seemed not to bother her one bit.

As we drove away that evening, I regretted not bumping into any of my former schoolmates, the ones who'd laughed at me and excluded me because of my shabby appearance, as well as the few who had befriended me toward the end. I wanted the former to see how well dressed I had become, and the latter to know I had not forgotten them and still thought of them fondly. When I expressed this to Mother, she said, "Don't worry, David. By noon tomorrow, every one of them will have heard about your visit. They'll know every detail about what you were wearing and they'll realize that you won in the end."

Clem and Elfriede's wedding day

Clem and David with Kobsch Oma at Ramstein

David at Ramstein

David as an American
Boy Scout at Ramstein

Kobsch Oma and Opa visiting Ramstein

Thus if you have really handed yourself over to God,
it must follow that you are trying to obey Him.
But trying in a new way, a less worried way.
Not doing these things in order to be saved, but because
He has begun to save you already.

—C.S. Lewis

CHAPTER 17

While we were stationed at Erding, another Air Force wife invited Mom to attend a Mormon church in Münich. Aside from her yearly Christmas church visit, never before had I seen her show the slightest interest in anything religious. Her sister Lisbeth had become a Jehovah's Witness by this time, and perhaps Mother was grasping for some kind of anchor, something to give meaning to her life, or at least explain it. Clem, a Catholic, had no intention of joining her, so Mom took Heidi and me with her on Sundays. I soon came to dread the weekly pilgrimage. A postwar pall seemed to hover over the place as if Germany's sins rested on the congregants' weary shoulders. The building's interior was gloomy, and to my youthful eyes the people there seemed sad, as if weighed down with the burden of striving to be impossibly good. I had no concept of God whatsoever. No one in my family had ever mentioned him except to curse. Even back in Rauschwalde when violent thunderstorms passed overhead and I hid under my bed, it had never occurred to me to pray for I'd never seen anyone do it or talk about it. Although before eating we often uttered the ubiquitous German table prayer, "*Komm Herr Jesus, sei unser Gast und segne was du uns beschertest hast,*" I thought of it more as a ritualistic poem than anything having to do with belief in an actual God. Hence, nothing about that church in Münich piqued my interest.

However in 1959, when Clem was transferred to McGuire Air Force Base near Philadelphia, Mom continued her involvement with the Mormons. In our new community of Levittown, I found them to be a friendly, hardy bunch. Several men in the church took me under their wing. They were kind and encouraging, and the youth activities kept me occupied and out of trouble.

Before long, without thinking too deeply about spiritual things, I was baptized into the Mormon Church. For me, it was a gesture indicating that I wanted to be part of this great group of people. With their commitment to upright living, they were a good influence on me, something I desperately needed at the time. Although I later came to take a different path in my understanding of God and my relationship with him, I remember the Levittown Mormons fondly and with gratitude for how they reached out to me.

In any case, Mom's sojourn with the Mormons turned out to be brief, lasting only two years. The Mormon emphasis on clean living and good works had been a concept she could easily grasp and measure, a way for her to fight the persistent feelings of guilt she carried around, to battle the accumulated shame that dogged her relentlessly. In the end it proved ineffective. She abandoned her brief flirtation with Mormonism, instead seeking other ways to suppress painful memories.

Soon she had something else to occupy her. Mother was pregnant. This time around, she proudly displayed her growing belly. For the first time ever, she was carrying the child of a man to whom she was legally wedded, and would give birth with a gold band on her finger. Clem was delighted. Our brother Bruce was born in May of 1961, when Heidi was 15 and I 18. Mother and Clem adored him and so did we; there was something deeply satisfying about his arrival, as if his appearance was the bright bow on the gift of the family we had become. Nevertheless, as Mother and Clem settled into a happy domestic routine with their new baby, I began to push at boundaries.

Despite the good Mormon influence in my life, I was a teen getting too big for his britches. I became restless and argumentative. Mother, so doting on little Bruce, displayed increasing disappointment in me. More and more she insisted that I behave impeccably and achieve greatly, as if to compensate for my dubious beginnings.

"You must strive to be a doctor or a lawyer, David," she insisted. "I brought you all the way here to America so you could make something of yourself. I want to feel proud of you." Her demand for perfect grades and that I aim for a high-profile career seemed to have nothing to do with my particular talents and gifts and everything to do with her own craving for acceptance and prestige. My teenage employment flipping burgers at McDonald's and changing tires at a local truck stop weren't good enough for her. I was a kinesthetic learner who needed plenty of physical, hands-on activity to stimulate my brain. Unable to understand or accept that I was more interested in figuring out how things worked than in sitting at a school desk poring over books, Mom badgered me relentlessly to achieve academic heights and make her proud. It seemed as if I single-handedly bore the responsibility of making up for her perceived lacks. Her unrealistic and self-focused demands finally caused something to snap inside of me.

"I'll be what I want to be, not what you want me to be!" I shouted at her on more than one occasion before storming off, slamming the front door behind me.

I began to skip school. In the same green Pontiac Chieftain we'd flaunted in Hof, which I'd purchased from Clem for three hundred dollars, I drove south into Philadelphia and spent whole school days at the cinema. I stayed out late into the evenings, ballroom dancing on roller skates rather than doing homework. Other days, I'd cut school early in order to get downtown to the junction of 46th and Market Streets in time to dance on *American Bandstand*. In those days, the show aired every afternoon from Monday to Friday and was filmed in a cramped space called "Studio B." We local teens poured into the city center, lining up around the block in hopes of being let in to show off our dance moves. My skills at performing such hip stunts as the Twist, the Bop and the Stroll on national television failed to impress my mother, however, and things only grew tenser at home.

One day while downtown I received a parking ticket. Since the car was still registered under Clem's name, he soon found out about it and confronted me.

Defiant, I admitted, "Yeah, I was in Philly. What are you going to do about it?"

Calmly Clem informed me that he knew exactly what he was going to do about it. "You'll be joining the Air Force, David. In fact, I've already made the necessary inquiries and gotten the ball rolling."

Stunned, I gaped at him with open mouth.

"David, you know that I'm being sent to Vietnam. You realize as well that you and your mother haven't been getting along lately. She has little Bruce to care for and leaving you here with her while I'm gone would be like throwing a lit match on a gasoline-soaked rag. The Air Force will be the best thing for you, you'll see."

He was right, of course.

As soon as I received my high school diploma, I was whisked off to Lackland Air Force Base for testing then sent to Keesler AFB in Biloxi, Mississippi. As a teenager at Erding, I'd already begun to indulge my childhood curiosity by tinkering with electronics. By scavenging, buying and begging various parts such as crystal diodes, earphones, resistors, batteries and capacitors, I built a miniature radio from scratch. The employees at the base hobby shop offered me welcome advice as I pursued my passion. I had also experimented with woodworking, channeling my restless energy into building an 18-foot Hiawatha canoe in the base woodshop, which I could take out on the Sempt River any time I wanted. Feeling an intense pride in my accomplishment, I enjoyed my canoe until the day I carelessly left it unguarded at the river's edge. When I returned, it was gone. One year later, my hunch that it had been carried off by envious German boys who had seen me using it was confirmed when I spied a group of them paddling it happily along the Sempt.

In Levittown, I had continued to experiment with electronics. My friends and I cobbled together ham radios out of spare parts. One day I tore apart an old Dumont television set, extracted the high voltage anode, and wrapped a towel around it. Holding it with heavy work gloves, I proceeded to wield all 26,000 volts of it, zapping bugs in our garage. All over the house, plug receptacles began to arc with fire shooting out one hole and circling back to the next. They began to turn black. Enraged and screaming, my terrified mother burst into the garage and ordered me to stop. "You could have killed yourself and burnt our house down!" she gasped.

Now I finally had an opportunity to legitimately and safely indulge my passion for taking things apart and putting them back together as I studied electronics and was trained in the Strategic Air Command Communication System. Once this training was complete, the Air Force sent me to Offutt Air Force Base in Omaha, Nebraska.

While stationed at Offutt, I filled my spare time by managing a local roller rink, where I enjoyed meeting every pretty girl who came in and showing off my skate-dancing abilities. As I grew out of my awkward teenage years and into my twenties, I was an odd mix of Old World and modern American tastes. When attending dances in Omaha, I couldn't always relate to my peers' choice of music for the disc jockeys to play. Deep down, I still preferred the classical music that had defined my European childhood, but there was little place for that in 1960s Midwestern America, at least, not among those of my age group. So I danced to new favorites like "Chantilly Lace" and "Melodie d'Amour," honing my skills and using up the excess energy that I always seemed to have in abundance.

One evening at a dance, I approached a group of GSO girls I knew from the roller rink. "Oh, there's David!" called out one of them, giving a friendly wave. Standing among them was a girl I'd never seen before. She wore a summery pink satin dress with lace over the skirt and her dark brown hair was arranged in a fashionable beehive. When I smiled at her, she flashed big brown eyes in my direction, then looked shyly away. Little did I know that when she caught sight of me approaching, she'd heard a small voice in her head saying, "This is the man you'll marry." Immediately she rejected the idea. He's way too confident, she thought. Look at how he swaggers when he walks! He's even a little bowlegged.

I ignored her the rest of that first night, spending my time talking to and dancing with the other girls. But Jaclyn showed up at other dances. Gradually I began to notice how many of the other guys swarmed around her, asking for dances, trying to sit close and slip their arms around her shoulders. There was an air of fragility about her that brought out my protective instincts.

"She needs me to look out for her," I thought, "because she's so naïve and innocent." Gradually I worked my way into her orbit and without asking whether she needed it or not, took on the role of her personal chaperone and chauffeur. Wherever she needed to go, whether to a dance or on an ordinary daily errand, I offered to drive her. To my chagrin, however, she maintained a stubborn attachment to another airman named Stuart. And maddeningly, he continued to ask her out, ignoring my sour looks and jealous stares. Resolved to win her for myself, I knew it was time to do a little wheeling and dealing.

One day I carried a television set out to my car, an old 20-inch Emerson black and white model that I had fixed up. I drove it to the dance hall. During the event, while the others were whirling and jitterbugging, I lured the airman outside and opened the trunk.

"Hey Stuart," I said. "Five bucks and it's yours. But only on one condition."

"Yeah, what's that?"

"Stop dating Jaclyn."

He blinked at me through the dusky evening light, astonished. I stared back without flinching to show that I wasn't kidding.

"Well?"

Stuart ran one hand along the edge of the appliance. "You like her that much?"

"Yeah. Do you?"

He shrugged. "Sure, sure, she's nice and pretty and all that. But there are plenty of other girls I like too." His eyes wandered down to the sweet deal in my car trunk. "Okay, I'll take it." He pulled out his wallet, paid me off then transferred the prize to his own car.

Jaclyn was mine. Before long, we were married.

It was a bit of a shock to learn that her father, Jack, had been one of the *B17* pilots who had dropped incendiary bombs on Dresden. He had died when his plane crashed in France toward the end of the war. His death still saddened Jaclyn, who never knew him, and it sobered both of us to think that while following orders, he came within mere miles of killing his future son-in-law. But Jaclyn's mother, Bernice, merely winked at us newlyweds and said, "You're sleeping with the enemy."

Her family accepted me with warmth and a generous spirit. A devout Christian, Jaclyn's mother seemed so at ease with herself and at peace. This puzzled me. Somehow, through films, books and general societal opinion, I'd absorbed the notion that the Christian religion was a burdensome taskmaster requiring its adherents to follow strict rules and strive for perfection. But Bernice explained to me that her faith was in a loving, gracious God, whose son Jesus had died so that she could be forgiven. She didn't have to earn salvation through good deeds and perfect living. The ease with which she lived out this faith—doing good to others because she was thankful for God's love rather than because she hoped to earn his love, admitting her faults and trying to grow out of them, accepting God's forgiveness with thankfulness—really caught my attention. It was a beautiful message to me after living with my mother's constant disappointment in my inability to live up to her unrealistically elevated standards. Deep down, I wrestled with this new and powerful witness in my life. During those early years of our marriage, privately and unbeknownst to Jaclyn, I still considered myself a Mormon, and didn't want to be disloyal to the only church I had ever known and into which I had been baptized. Not that I was attending any church at all at the time. I simply felt that I was living a decent life and any need for right standing with God had been taken care of by virtue of the fact that I'd undergone baptism into a church filled with good, solid, right-living people. Yet my mother-in-law continued to speak to me every chance she got about having a relationship with God based on grace as opposed to striving to earn his favor through good works. Jaclyn, who had already come to understand and embrace the simplicity of the gospel message, waited eagerly for me to finally grasp it.

At last, while sitting one day at Bernice's kitchen table, a light bulb finally switched on inside my head. Finally I understood that I could not earn my way into God's kingdom, but had only to acknowledge my need of a savior and accept the salvation provided for me through Christ's sacrifice of his life for me on the cross. This gracious, undeserved salvation extends to all who call on his name, and I am so thankful for Bernice's long-ago persistence in explaining that to me.

My mother never understood my choice to become a Christ-follower. She always seemed to view my, or anyone's, claims of being a Christian as a personal affront to her—a challenge, as if they were declaring they were better than she. I now understand this to be partly an insidious result of the pain of an abused childhood and experiencing two illegitimate pregnancies in a conservative, traditional society, the lingering shame of which she refused to release. The taint of Nazism, so despised by the whole world, clung to her like a stench that only she could smell and seemed to make her sicker as her life went on. How I longed for her to see herself as God saw her, to know she was loved by him, to grasp hold of the divine grace that could have freed her!

Elfriede's devoted husband, baby son and new life in America where few cared to pry into her past, merely served to bury that sickness and were unable to ultimately conquer it as long as she refused to confront it within herself. It sprang up again and again in her demands of perfection from me and in her caustic criticisms of my wife. Jaclyn, who had worked hard all her life to overcome a speech impediment caused by a tongue deformity that required childhood surgery, was overflowing with people skills. Warm and engaging, a good listener, she valued interpersonal relationships. Quality time spent with our six children was far more desirable to Jaclyn than keeping a spotless house and cooking fancy dinners. At first guilty of expecting Jaclyn to perform just like my mother, I came to realize how unimportant such things were to me and to prize my wife's unique qualities.

One day Mother remarked, "Jaclyn isn't good for you. She doesn't push you to achieve."

Thinking this was exactly why Jaclyn *was* good for me, I ignored Mom's critical appraisal. Jaclyn accepted me for who I was, encouraging me at every turn. I felt blessed beyond measure to have her in my life.

Because both Jaclyn and I love children, we chose to have a large family. With great excitement, we looked forward to each new baby, but whenever Jaclyn was pregnant, Mom would say bitingly, "Oh, not again! We don't need more of that kind in the world."

Crushed, we puzzled over her vicious words. What could she mean? Mom didn't say such things to Heidi and Bruce and their spouses when they were expecting. Did she believe that Jaclyn would produce inferior specimens of human beings merely because she didn't have a college degree or wasn't an obsessive, fastidious homemaker? That made no sense; Mom herself had only been educated through the ninth grade. Was I producing inferior human beings because I'd failed to achieve her desired outcome of becoming a doctor or a lawyer? At that time, I still thought Rudi Kobsch was my father. Now that I know my true parentage, I believe her cutting remarks came from three possible sources.

First was the subconscious influence of the racial indoctrination she'd absorbed during 12 years of Nazi rule in school, in the Reich Labor Service and in the Lebensborn home, where that indoctrination grew in intensity. Over and over she had learned that her calling as a German woman was to produce racially pure, genetically perfect children and raise them in an immaculate household. By marrying a woman with a congenital defect, I ran the risk of producing "inferior" children. Had she pushed me so hard to achieve because she truly believed deep down that I was what Lebensborn promised her I would be—genetically superior? Her sojourn among the racially elite was supposed to have produced a *Wunderkind*.

Or did her dismay at our growing family come from something else entirely—lingering shame over her Nazi past? I was conceived and born during a time in my mother's life when she had surrendered herself, heart and soul, to National Socialism. Whether or not, deep inside, she regretted this association with Nazism, the fact remained that Hitler's genocidal regime was and is almost universally reviled. Mother craved respect and prestige. She craved belonging and full acceptance in her adopted homeland. My existence was her "fly in the ointment," her one unbreakable tie with an inconvenient past. In repeatedly saying, "We don't need more of your kind," she may have been saying in essence, "David, you were born at a time in my life I'd just as soon wipe from memory. Now here you are, resurrecting the past with each new child you produce."

There is a third possible reason for her cruel words and that is continued shame over my illegitimacy. Heidi, conceived out of wedlock but legitimized by a posthumous marriage, had since infancy borne her father's name. Bruce entered the world within a loving marriage. Only I remained as a bastard child. Himmler's new morality aside, my mother had likely never reconciled herself to having stepped outside the bounds of social convention. My very existence was a constant reminder of this misstep. Any children I produced might potentially bear Kurt Novak's features or personality traits, compounding the memory and insuring its refusal to die.

Mom's verbal attacks cut Jaclyn and me so deeply that we recoiled and never asked her why, perhaps fearing the answer.

When Heidi and I were small, our mother was stoic and not overly demonstrative or affectionate, but she had been patient and tender in overall demeanor towards us, making allowances for our childish mistakes. Many times over the years I wondered where that woman had gone. During the hungry years in Germany,

Elfriede had to be strong and suppress her fears. Now it was as if all the stress of that long ago time bubbled up to the surface, at times boiling over at the slightest provocation. Hunger had marked her and she bore the scars to the end of her life. My mother showed love through food, and it was an aggressive love indeed. She found it nearly impossible to relax and enjoy visitors' company without first feeding them and it mattered little to her if they were hungry or not. If Bruce and his family, who lived nearby, promised to arrive at 6:30 PM for dinner, Mom would call them at 5:30 PM to their utter confusion, demanding to know where they were and insisting, "Dinner is ready!"

For me, her obsession with finishing every scrap of food on the plate was her only easily explainable quirk. I've since learned it is an obsession she shared with many others of her generation of Germans. Those who have gone hungry see waste as the ultimate sin, an incredibly foolhardy act. Once Jaclyn and I returned to Mom's home from a day trip with our children.

"I've cooked you some dinner," she announced, even though we'd been careful to tell her we would be eating elsewhere.

"But Mom, we ate at a restaurant. Remember?"

"Sit down," she insisted. "I've cooked it and you will all eat every bite of it."

To please her, we tried to simulate hunger but in the end could not accommodate her wishes. She was simply unable to view her demand as unnecessary force feeding. In her mind, it was 1946 again and my family, a family she'd strongly hinted she didn't even want, must store up every bit of nutrition, every scrap of fat, because lean times lurked just around the corner.

Still very much in love, she and Clem grew old together and enjoyed gardening, fishing at Woodland Park and visiting casinos all across America in their succession of ever larger motor homes. Her insistence on protecting her husband from the disgrace of her past ended only with his passing. Only when she felt she had nothing more to lose did she find her way clear to admit the truth to me.

In some ways, advancing age mellowed my mother. In the late 1980s after decades of refusing to communicate with her father, she broke down and tried to bridge the chasm between them by mailing him a letter containing a photograph of Bruce's newborn son. Once the ice was broken, Paul and Elfriede reconciled and corresponded a handful of times.

Toward the end of her life, Elfriede seemed more and more to retreat mentally to the world of her childhood. She regaled Bruce's wife, Janine, with stories of the chicken farm that had been the pride of lower Silesia, attracting university students with its modern technology. The place she had longed to escape now took up residence in her mind.

She spoke over and over again of her mother, saying, "Janine, she was so beautiful and sweet. I loved her so, and was brokenhearted when she died. My father used her accident to his advantage; he never got her adequate medical care. You see, he wanted to marry that witch, Schönfelder Grete."

Sometimes she spoke of Rudi. When she did, her eyes took on a faraway look and a wistful smile crossed her lips. Clem had been an excellent husband and a good man, but Rudi was her deepest, truest love and his memory had not faded through the passing of decades. Kurt Novak existed as a mere pile of papers in a box in a closet, but Rudi lived on in Elfriede's soul.

David and Jaclyn

David in high school

David and Bruce

All the Germans marched with Hitler,
all of them, believe me.
But we are the outcasts, we of the SS.
It makes things so much simpler.

—Max Sollman

CHAPTER 18

One day in the summer of 2010, Bruce, alarmed at being unable to reach Mom by phone, stopped by the house where she had lived alone since Clem's death one and one half years before. Mom lay on her bedroom floor unconscious. She had suffered a stroke. As quickly as possible we rushed to her hospital bedside, Heidi from California and Jaclyn and me from Texas. Together we three siblings made the painful decision to take her off of life support.

During that last year of her life, a pleasant, gentle quality had returned to Elfriede's personality that had not been in evidence for decades. It was as if the weight of pretense had lifted with Clem's passing and she could finally relax and be honest about who and what she was, no longer needing to protect him from painful truths. The irony is that being the gracious sort of fellow Clem was and loving Elfriede as deeply as he did, he wouldn't have cared one bit whether she'd been raped or willingly entered into that long-ago affair with Kurt Novak. It would not have mattered to him that she'd given birth to me in an SS-affiliated Lebensborn home. The onus to hide these facts was entirely of Elfriede's own making and added an unnecessary burden to her life.

Sitting there, at her funeral, I battled the emotions of regret and anger that threatened to squash my tender memories and sense of gratitude. If ever a woman was complex, it was Elfriede. I thought of what she had chosen to divulge and couldn't help wondering what all she had kept hidden. What secrets had she taken with her to the grave, never to be uncovered?

Small questions gnawed at me. Why hadn't my mother had a birth certificate for me? Heim Wienerwald should have issued her one either at my birth or when she came to remove me from the home. Unable to prove that she could support me adequately and thus secure official permission to remove me, had she sneaked me out and spirited me away without going through the proper channels? Or had she lost my birth certificate when she fled the oncoming Russians so urgently in January of 1945? Was it, along with other personal documents, left at Lisbeth's house, to which neither sister was allowed to return, and swallowed up with the Russian take-over of the eastern half of Görlitz? If that were the case, why did the copies of Kurt Novak's ancestral lineage survive to travel all the way to Colorado with her? Could she have willingly left my birth certificate behind or even destroyed it in order to hide evidence of connection with the SS?

Why hadn't she trusted me enough to tell me more? Why hadn't I tried harder to win that trust, assuring her that there was nothing she could reveal about herself that would make me love her less? Perhaps the answer lies in what historian Dorothée Schmitz-Köster identifies as common among Lebensborn children who grew up in an atmosphere of murky half-truths: fear of rejection. Fear of being abandoned, if only emotionally.[182]

I am far from unique. Like me, the majority of the estimated 6,000 Lebensborn children born in Germany proper have lived lives based on lies. Also like me, some of them, fortunate enough to have been kept and raised by their mothers, were never forgiven by their grandparents for being illegitimate and ruining the family's good name. A tiny fraction of this group had the opportunity to know their fathers, but many were absorbed into a new marriage and took on their stepfather's last name, even as I did. Yet they sensed that something wasn't quite right. Intuitively they knew they didn't fit in without ever being told why. Others, raised by single mothers who never married, were simply told their fathers had died in battle and grew up believing they'd been born into a marriage torn apart by war. Not until well into their 50s and 60s, when parents began to pass away, did they discover the truth in documents kept squirreled away or from distant relatives who finally felt free to share the truth about their origins.[183]

The old-fashioned values so maligned by Heinrich Himmler died hard, and single mothers who couldn't claim legitimate widowhood were looked askance at in postwar Germany, just as they had been in earlier decades. Their children often suffered teasing and social ostracism without comprehending why. Had their German neighbors, so eager to distance themselves from Nazism, known about a Lebensborn birth, the taunts would have been crueler still. For Lebensborn, to which persistent rumors of a top-secret Nazi breeding program stubbornly clung, became a scapegoat of sorts in postwar Germany. Its close association with the reviled SS, coupled with sensationalized novels and films throughout the 1950s and 1960s and beyond, made Lebensborn a convenient whipping post[184] to which the average German, living in a society burdened with the collective shame of National Socialism, could point as an extreme example of Nazi ideology and say, "That was Hitler and his crazy followers—I had nothing to do with any of that."

No wonder our mothers hid the truth. Still, it doesn't lessen the pain. I have never so much as even glimpsed a photograph of my father. Repeated attempts to locate my half-brothers have led only to dead ends. I have so little information to go on in my search. Do they know I exist? Would they even want to meet me if they knew? The knowledge that my father, as a man closely connected with the SS, undoubtedly committed heinous and barbaric acts repels me, yet I cannot suppress my natural curiosity about him. Did he look like me? Would he be proud of what I have become? Did he ever regret his wartime actions and repent of them in his heart before he died? I hope so.

Historian Dorothée Schmitz-Köster interviewed 67 Lebensborn children for her 2010 book, *"Deutsche Mutter, bist du bereit...,"* in which she so eloquently chronicles our common experience. In it she relates that some Lebensborn children were absorbed into adoptive or step-families, grew up well loved, and were never told the truth. They never suspected anything, never asked questions, and to this day do not know they were born in a Lebensborn home. Many of those who were adopted or placed in foster care and sensed something amiss, discovered the truth through persistent questioning, starting at square one: Who was my mother? Who was my father? Heartbreakingly, Schmitz-Köster tells of adopted Lebensborn children who after diligent searching, found their birth mothers only to be rejected by them. These women had turned to Lebensborn because of its promise of absolute secrecy, and now, 60 years later, here were the dreaded secrets themselves, resurrected and standing on their doorsteps. After all their efforts at concealment, the embarrassing truth had caught up with them. Fear of a husband or other children finding out caused such women to close the door on their Lebensborn children, both literally and figuratively.[185]

The few Lebensborn children able to locate their fathers were also often rebuffed. The men had built lives and families with other women, and their Nazi-era offspring were not welcome to share in those lives. It made all too perfect sense. The last thing a German man would want, even decades after the end of the war, was to be outed as a former member of the SS. Those like myself, fortunate enough to have been raised by our own mothers, often approached their mothers with questions during childhood only to be shut down by dismissive, perfunctory answers that closed the discussion.[186] Elfriede's demeanor would change whenever I attempted, in my youth, to ask her questions about our family history in Germany. Her anger at my innocent probings confused me. I did not understand that she was hiding things from Clem, and fearful of such conversations leading to exposure. As a result, I remained incredibly naïve about my origins and background, continuing on in a perpetual twilight of ignorance despite obvious discrepancies in my own life story.

We Lebensborn children, whether aware of our origins or not, understood all too well that our mothers' emotions were fragile.[187] They had experienced war traumas and deprivations. We proceeded cautiously, walking on eggshells, bending over backward to not bring up subjects that so obviously caused them distress, and in the process denied our own humanity and our right to know the truth.

Dorothée Schmitz-Köster believes that only two percent of the German Lebensborn children have declared their origins publicly, preferring instead to keep the truth hidden once they discovered it. All too aware of the persistent "stud farm" and "breeding" rumors, they chose silence rather than having to constantly ward off society's false impressions of their origins. Given that our fathers were mostly SS men guilty of heinous brutality while committing war crimes, this instinct to bury the shameful truth is completely understandable. Others, who have gone public with their stories, have found value in meeting together with other Lebensborn children, seeking mutual support and understanding.[188]

In my youth, I put up an invisible wall to keep others from getting too close to the inner me. Those who knew me would have described me as a social butterfly, but that was a defense mechanism; flitting from one person to another was a way of ensuring none of them got too close. Only after meeting Jaclyn and entering into relationship with my Savior, Jesus Christ, did I allow that wall to start coming down piece by piece. The Holy Spirit's refining work in my life has persisted and prevailed, yet that invisible wall is still not fully dismantled and perhaps won't be until I reach heaven. Knowing I am loved and accepted by God has nevertheless been tremendously healing for me. Looking back over my life and recognizing his hand at work, guiding and protecting, even before I was aware of his existence, convinces me that my birth was no accident, at least in his eyes. In that pitch-dark wheat field, crisscrossed with searchlights, between East and West Germany, in a nameless border jail from which my mother was inexplicably released, in the emigration bureaucracy that allowed our little family to replace another of exactly the same size—I see divine intervention and mercy in abundance.

I was fortunate in that when I began my investigation into the past, several of my German relatives were still alive and willing to talk. Many other Lebensborn children found out too late. No relatives remained who could fill in the gaping holes in their histories and they are doomed to live the rest of their lives with no answers. Unlike my mother, who for some unknown reason kept my father's family documents, many single Lebensborn mothers kept no such records.[189] If they died early, or even into old age steadfastly refused to divulge a father's name, there is no way for a Lebensborn child to find it thanks to the organization's strict secrecy policy and the burning of files by the SS in Münich during the war's last days.

Sadly reminiscent of my mother's refusal to approve of my life choices and her derisive words to Jaclyn and me, a good many Lebensborn mothers who kept their children were unable to let go and fully express love and acceptance of the children who embodied their shame and besmirched their reputations. So many Lebensborn children still live with the pain of being shunted here and there, the unfulfilled longing to know their real parents, or at least have a name or a face to gaze at in a faded, wrinkled photograph. Only late in life have they begun to make sense of their past—why they never felt fully loved or accepted—and to deal with feelings of abandonment and rejection.[190]

To comprehend at last why a grandfather, so doting and affectionate with a little granddaughter, might glare at a small boy and hiss, "I hate you!"

After the war, Red Cross and other aid workers did their best to repatriate the Polish and other Eastern European children who were so brutally torn from their homes and subjected to Lebensborn's harsh regime of brainwashing. But by that time, many of them could no longer understand or speak their native languages. If their parents were dead they were distributed around to distant relatives who were struggling under communist rule and didn't welcome another mouth to feed.[191]

The thousands of babies born to German fathers and Norwegian mothers in Norway have suffered their own brand of pain, as have those Lebensborn children born in other Western European countries. Their vital documents detailing parentage and origins were destroyed as the Third Reich crumbled and the SS's promise of support and guardianship vanished into thin air. Especially in Norway, these children of German fathers grew up with discrimination, viewed as the despised offspring of the enemy and stark reminders of the Nazi occupation. They felt rejected or at best merely tolerated by both family and society, not understanding what they had done to deserve the cold treatment they received, even as I never understood why Kobsch Opa hated me so. As they grew and tried to take their place in society as adults, an invisible current of discrimination prevented them from achieving dreams. A group of Norwegian Lebensborn children has in recent years pursued filing lawsuits against the Norwegian government, seeking compensation for the discrimination and harassment they suffered.

Some Norwegian Lebensborn babies, who had been relinquished by their mothers and transported to Germany in hopes that SS families would adopt them, ended up in Sweden after well-meaning aid workers attempted to return them to Norway. The Norwegian government rebuffed these efforts. The babies' documents were changed to obliterate the Lebensborn records of their parentage. They remained in Sweden, advertised as orphans found in concentration camps and offered up for adoption.[192]

Schmitz-Köster noticed during her interviews that the Lebensborn children she met seldom looked like Aryan supermen and women, but were rather of average height with a wide range of eye color. Most of them had blond hair in youth that darkened with age. They were subject to, and passed on, various inherited illnesses, giving the lie to Nazi theories of genetic selection.[193] Himmler's efforts simply did not produce the desired results. Neither did the Lebensborn program, the awarding of the Mother Cross, marriage loans or any other reward or incentive to produce children succeed in raising the birthrate in Germany. Most Germans continued to prefer small families, especially during wartime with its food scarcity and bombings.[194]

I used to attribute my mother's lack of demonstrative affection and overly high expectations to her being Old World German, as well as to her own harsh upbringing. But learning of Schmitz-Köster's assessment of what she gleaned from her interviews dropped my jaw. The German author was told by most of the Lebensborn children she spoke with that their mothers were distant, keeping them at arms' length emotionally.[195] Though Lebensborn officially encouraged mothers to keep and raise their babies, the whole Lebensborn experience did not foster closeness between mother and child. Hiding the pregnancy, weaving a web of absolute secrecy around the birth, burying the father's identity, living in a separate wing of the home and seeing the babies only to feed and change them, then leaving them behind for months and years at a time—these things produced disconnection rather than bonding.

My mother did not treat me coldly in my early childhood but she gradually became cool and disapproving as I grew older. The majority of Lebensborn children Schmitz-Köster interviewed revealed that their mothers had extremely high and unrealistic expectations of them. Some of the children were physically abused by their mothers, a good many of who never married. How could they? Men their age were scarce, having been consumed by the war. The Lebensborn children tried hard to earn their mothers' love by performing well and not making waves. But this kind of pressure often resulted in fractured relationships later on as the children realized they could never quite be good enough.[196]

As far as the Air Force was concerned, I excelled at my job. At the height of the Cold War, I was entrusted to help implement the SACS communication system, the iconic red phone at the underground Strategic Air Command headquarters at Offutt Air Force Base in Nebraska. First cleared as "Confidential," I rose steadily to "Secret," "Top Secret," "Top Secret Cryptographic," then "ESI" (Extra Sensitive Information). Finally, I reached the level of "Battle Staff." Later, I was offered a lucrative job with Texas Instruments and traveled around the world establishing new plants for the company, including one in Freising, Bavaria. Yet none of these achievements satisfied my mother. She continued to bemoan the fact that I had not succeeded in making something of myself, nor had I "made her proud."

There exists the possibility that deep down, Elfriede still believed herself to be elite and that she'd absorbed Nazi racial ideology so thoroughly that it still influenced her view of people. Of course, she never would have admitted to that and may not even have been consciously aware of the continuing influence of National Socialism on her thinking. I tend more toward the belief that her inability to overcome the persistent feelings of shame from her close association with Hitler's regime kept her from growing into a person who could extend grace to herself and to others. I believe that my mother, perhaps without even realizing it, wanted me to compensate for my dubious beginnings, to prove that I was not merely the spawn of an evil regime but a bright and shining light that reflected favorably upon her. She hoped to bask in that light as a way of removing her own unremitting shame.

But life is full of paradoxes. It is possible that both these things, delusions of eliteness and crippling shame, existed side by side within her to the end of her days, constantly warring, never leaving her in peace.

Elfriede came of age under a system of dizzying contradictions and double standards. The Nazi regime claimed to promote traditional family values and vowed to strengthen the under-pinnings of society by supporting marriage and families. Yet National Socialism undermined marriages by encouraging married men to have affairs and father children out of wedlock and to divorce women who suffered from infertility. Men who did so were considered, at least by Himmler and his ilk, to have served their country well. If a married woman, however, became pregnant by a man who wasn't her husband and applied to give birth in a Lebensborn home, she was rejected outright.[197] Her disloyalty to her husband was considered a disgrace, even to proponents of the "new morality."

The Wehrmacht, while stubbornly clinging to traditional and time-honored moral values, fought a war for a Nazi government that endorsed illegitimate births. Yet, incongruously, a Wehrmacht officer was not allowed to marry a woman who gave birth to such a child, even when he himself had fathered the child in question.

In 1933 it became legal to forcibly sterilize, along with genetically "inferior" people, beggars, homosexuals, prostitutes and women who had given birth to several children out of wedlock. The latter two were considered to be degenerate—of weak mind and inferior character.[198] However the same Nazi authorities who promoted the forced sterilization of such women encouraged the SS "elite" to father children with prostitutes in Norway so long as they embodied the correct racial criteria.

Despite National Socialism touting a new morality, many Nazi organizations such as the Reich Labor Service and the League of German Girls dismissed female employees from their jobs if they were found to be single and pregnant. Yet these very organizations had exposed young women to the idea that such a pregnancy was honorable in the first place.

The Nazis strongly discouraged and enacted strict laws against abortion. But their pro-life stance rings hollow in light of the fact that the SS was busily murdering Jewish babies, both in and outside the womb, as well as forcing abortion on women whose babies were not expected to meet rigid racial requirements.

In today's world, some of the avant-garde ideas of Hitler, Himmler and their cohorts have become commonplace. But I find myself wanting to say to those who embrace euthanasia, who advocate aborting fetuses who test positive for genetic abnormalities, who approve of would-be parents selecting anonymous sperm donors on the basis of physical or mental attributes: do you know what kind of company you keep? You are aligning yourself with some of the ideology of the most prolific murderers of the twentieth century.

Some of the mothers of Schmitz-Köster's interviewees, feeling less threatened with the passage of time, tended to relax their guard in extreme old age. Parents, husbands, former neighbors, even siblings had died off and could no longer judge or criticize. These women, like my mother, eventually spilled their secrets.[199]

I recognize how blessed I am to have had a mother who chose to return and extract me from Heim Wienerwald and raise me herself. Whether that was her intention all along or a last minute decision matters little in the end. She never said, "I love you," to me, but she kept me close to her, protected me, scrounged for food to feed me, and brought me and my sister safely out of communist East Germany. All these things were her practical way of showing love. I was doubly blessed to have an adoptive father chosen specifically by her for his fatherly qualities, who truly cared for my well-being and did his best to bring me up in an atmosphere of kindness and understanding.

My dear wife Jaclyn and our precious children have grounded me over the years, loving me unconditionally through all of life's ups and downs. They are my pride and joy. But most of all I find joy in God, who has been a faithful, loving and gracious Heavenly Father to this once-fatherless child.

Elfriede Bugno

Jaclyn, 1980s

David and Jaclyn, 2014

EPILOGUE

In the late 1950s, while stationed at Erding Air Force Base in Bavaria, Clem and Mother took Heidi and me to Münich for a short holiday. We shared lunch in a restaurant downtown, then strolled along the streets near the *Rathaus*, browsing in store windows. As I stood beside my mother, admiring the fashionably dressed mannequins in a department store display, a tall, statuesque figure drew up beside her. In the window's reflection I watched him remove his hat and give a genteel bow. Though only in his early forties, his hair was gray and thinning. He possessed a military bearing, but wore a civilian suit and tie.

"Oh, hello, Kurt!" she exclaimed in surprise. A smile of genuine delight spread across her face.

"Elfriede, how nice to see you again," he said, "and how lovely you look!"

I had no trouble believing he meant what he said. Mom did cut an elegant figure in her full length herringbone coat and wide-brimmed hat trimmed with glossy feathers. I paid only scant attention to the man. For the most part, my eyes remained fixed on the mannequins and the clothes they modeled. He and Mother exchanged pleasantries and caught each other up on the progress of their lives since the war. She smiled and laughed in genuine joy at seeing him again. After a while, I glanced up in time to see him kiss her gloved hand in parting. She took me by the arm and together we strolled back down the street toward where Clem and Heidi inspected another shop window.

"Who was that, Mutti?"

"Kurt Huebler, from Aschitzau-Thommendorf," she replied. "I knew him a long, long time ago, back in my childhood."

Many years later, after Clem's death, I learned through the not-so-veiled innuendoes of family members that Kurt was the Wehrmacht officer my mother claimed had fathered me in order to gain admittance into Heim Wienerwald. At last, I understood that that chance encounter during which I observed his wavy reflection in the shop window, was as close as I had ever come in my youth to viewing even a murky, shadowbox tableau of the true events surrounding my birth.

Both Herr Huebler and I left that long-ago encounter none the wiser, but my mother must have smiled secretively to herself.

Heim Wienerwald, the once luxurious and world famous lung sanitarium, has since 1945 served a variety of purposes. It has been, in turn, a home for undernourished children, a hotel for mine workers and their families and a youth hostel. In 2007, a woman was caught hoarding dogs and cats in the building and forcibly removed. It now stands completely empty.

David and Jaclyn

LIST OF LEBENSBORN HOMES

Germany
Heim Hochland at Steinhöring (1936)
Heim Harz at Wernigerode (1937)
Heim Hohehorst at Bremen (1937)
Heim Kurmark at Klosterheide near Berlin (1937)
Heim Pommern at Bad Polzin near Stettin (1938)
Heim Friesland (1938)
Heim Taunus at Wiesbaden (1939)
Heim Sonnenwiese at Kohren-Sahlis near Leipzig (1942—a children's home)
Heim Schwarzwald near Offenburg in Baden (1942)
Heim Franken 1 and 2 in Schalkhausen near Ansbach (1944—transit children's homes)

Austria
Heim Wienerwald at Pernitz (1938)
Heim Alpenland at Oberweis am Traunsee (1943)

Norway
Eleven homes divided up between Oslo, Bergen, Trondheim, Geilo and the province of Hedmark

Belgium
Lüttich

Luxembourg
Heim Moselland near city of Luxembourg

France
Lamorlaye near Paris

Acknowlegments

Ephesians 2:8–10 says, *For it is by grace you have been saved, through faith—and this is not from yourselves, it is the gift of God—not by works, so that no one can boast. For we are God's handiwork, created in Christ Jesus to do good works, which God prepared in advance for us to do.* Therefore I have dedicated this book to my Lord and Savior; it is through his grace alone that I have eternal life, not because of anything I have done.

I also thank my mother, Elfriede, who brought my sister, Heidi, and myself out of East Germany and ultimately to America.

Much love and gratitude goes to my wife, Jaclyn, who, through all of this, has remained steadfastly by my side. She has been my cheerleader and my encouragement, and I thank God for her.

I appreciate all of my children and how they have supported me and stood by me as I traveled this road. I'm grateful for the gift of love, peace and comfort that God gave me when two of our daughters, Tina and Dawn, went home to be with him.

Much gratitude goes to Jenny who has done so much research and has brought my ramblings into a cohesive flow.

Another important person in my journey has been Jaclyn's mother, Bernice, who helped me understand why I needed Christ in my life and how important it was to tell this story.

Moreover, thank you to all of my friends who influenced and encouraged me to share this story as a great treasure, a gift that God had prepared in advance. My family and friends remind me that this is not only my walk through life but it is the Lord's, for Romans 8:28 says: *In all things God works for the good of those who love him, who have been called according to his purpose.*

My prayer is that all those who read this sequence of events come to the knowledge that God is ultimately in control, but he allows us to make life choices. His desire is that all people accept his saving grace and enjoy eternal life with him.

SOURCES

This book is based on extensive interviews with David and Jaclyn Bugno and Bugno family interviews with Elfriede Kober Kobsch Bugno and extended family members in Germany, as well as family documents. For help in understanding the relevant historical and political aspects of Elfriede's and David's stories, the following were consulted:

Thomas Bryant, *Himmlers Kinder* (Wiesbaden: marixverlag, 2011).

Peter Demetz, *Prague in Danger* (New York: Farrar, Straus and Giroux, 2008).

Heide Fehrenbach, *Race after Hitler: Black Occupation Children in Postwar Germany and America* (Princeton and Oxford: Princeton University Press, 2005).

Daniel Jonah Goldhagen, *Hitler's Willing Executioners: Ordinary Germans and the Holocaust* (New York: Alfred A. Knopf, 1996).

Marc Hillel and Clarissa Henry, *Of Pure Blood* (New York: McGraw-Hill, 1976).

Peter Longerich, *Heinrich Himmler* (Oxford: Oxford University Press, 2012).

Wolfram Mallebrein, *Der Reichsarbeitsdienst: Geschichte und Entwicklung* (Coburg: Nation Europa Verlag, 2000).

Agnes Moosman, *Die Bagatelle* (Stuttgart: Jan Thorbeke Verlag, 2001).

Michelle Mouton, *From Nurturing the Nation to Purifying the Volk: Weimar and Nazi Family Policy 1918–1945* (Cambridge: Cambridge University Press, 2009).

Norman M Naimark, *The Russians in Germany: A History of the Soviet Zone of Occupation, 1945–1949* (Cambridge: Harvard University Press, 1997).

John Pimlott, *The Historical Atlas of World War II* (New York: Henry Holt and Co., 1995).

Cornelia Rabitz, "Berlin Exhibition Reveals Role Police Played in Holocaust," Deutsche Welle, April 10, 2011, Http://www.dw-world.de/dw/article/0..14973508.00html.

Dorothée Schmitz-Köster, *"Deutsche Mutter, bist du bereit…."* (Berlin: Aufbau Verlag, 2010).

SOURCES FOR CHAPTER HEADING QUOTES

CHAPTER 1

Paul Fulde, "Die Jungehe als Lebensborn jeder Rasse und jeden Volkes," Monatshefte Mecklenburg-Lübeck 13. Jg. 145 (1937): 24, quoted in Thomas Bryant, *Himmlers Kinder* (Wiesbaden: Marix-verlag GmbH, 2011), 175.

Pamphlet issued by SS headquarters: "Sieg der Waffen - Sieg des Kindes," Nordland Verlag (1941): 29, quoted in Bryant, *Himmlers Kinder*, 127.

CHAPTER 2

Franz Kade, Die Wende in der Mädchenerziehung: Ein Beitrag aus der Praxis der dorf-eigenen Schule (Breslau/Dortmund (1937): 6, quoted in Bryant, *Himmlers Kinder*, 210.

CHAPTER 3

Pamphlet issued by SS headquarters: "Sieg der Waffen - Sieg des Kindes," Nordland Verlag (1941): 5, quoted in Bryant, *Himmlers Kinder*, 125.

CHAPTER 4

Heinrich Himmler, speech to SS officers, Münich (1937), quoted in Peter Longerich, *Heinrich Himmler* (Oxford: Oxford University Press, 2012), 352.

CHAPTER 5

"Heilig ist uns jede Mutter guten Blutes," Das Schwarze Korps, Zeitung der Schutzstaffeln der NSDAP—Organ der Reichsführung SS, 3. Jg.,52. F., Berlin (1937): 9, quoted in Bryant, *Himmlers Kinder*, 122.

CHAPTER 6

Rudolf Hess, "Sieg der Frauen," Das Schwarze Korps, Zeitung der Schutzstaffeln der NSDAP—Organ der Reichsführung SS, 6. Jg. 1. F., Berlin (1940): 6, quoted in Bryant, *Himmlers Kinder*, 142–43.

CHAPTER 7

Rudolf Hess, "Sieg der Frauen," Das Schwarze Korps, Zeitung der Schutzstaffeln der NSDAP—Organ der Reichsführung SS, 6. Jg. 1. F., Berlin (1940): 6, quoted in Bryant, *Himmlers Kinder*, 142–43.

CHAPTER 8

Heinrich Himmler, speech to SS officers, Posen, Oct. 1943, quoted in Longerich, *Heinrich Himmler*, 596.

CHAPTER 9

Heinrich Himmler, speech to SS officers, Posen, Oct. 1943, quoted in Longerich, *Heinrich Himmler*, 660–61.

CHAPTER 10

Adolf Hitler to Albert Speer, March 1945, quoted in Albert Speer, *Inside the Third Reich* (New York: Simon and Schuster, 1970), 440.

CHAPTER 11

Norman M. Naimark, *The Russians in Germany: A History of the Soviet Zone of Occupation*, 1945–1949 (Cambridge: The Belknap Press of Harvard University Press, 1995), 384.

CHAPTER 12

Naimark, *The Russians in Germany: A History of the Soviet Zone of Occupation*, 1945–1949, 181.

CHAPTER 13

Inscription on the base of the memorial statue to Camp Moschendorf, Hof, Germany.

CHAPTER 14

Ebony Magazine (Oct. 1946): 5–10, quoted in Heide Fehrenbach, *Race After Hitler* (Princeton: Princeton University Press, 2005), 34.

CHAPTER 15

Harry S. Truman, "Statement by the President Upon Signing the Displaced Persons Act," June 25, 1948. *Public Papers of the Presidents, The American Presidency Project*, accessed August 9, 2015, www.presidency.ucsb.edu/ws/index.php?pid=12942&st=displaced+persons+act&st1=

CHAPTER 16

Galileo Galilei, *Discoveries and Opinions of Galileo* (Harpswell, Maine: Anchor Publishing, 1957) quoted on *goodreads.com*, accessed August 9, 2015,
http://www.goodreads.com/quotes/644431-names-and-attributes-must-be-accommodated-to-the-essence-of

CHAPTER 17

C.S. Lewis, *Mere Christianity*, (New York: Macmillan Publishing Co., 1952), 129.

CHAPTER 18

Max Sollman to Marc Hillel and Clarissa Henry, quoted in Marc Hillel and Clarissa Henry, *Of Pure Blood* (New York: McGraw-Hill Book Co., 1976), 16.

NOTES

CHAPTER 2

1. Michelle Mouton, *From Nurturing the Nation to Purifying the Volk: Weimar and Nazi Family Policy, 1918–1945* (Cambridge: Cambridge University Press, 2007), 4–15.
2. Ibid., 37.
3. Ibid., 15–19.
4. Ibid., 56–62.
5. Ibid., 48–68.
6. Agnes Moosmann, *Die Bagatelle: als Arbeitsmaid im Reichsarbeitsdienst* (Stuttgart: Jan Thorbecke Verlag, 2001), 67.
7. Mouton, *From Nurturing the Nation to Purifying the Volk,* 124–136.
8. Rudolf Hess, "Der Sieg der Frauen," *Das Schwarze Korps* 6 (Berlin, 1940): 6, quoted in Thomas Bryant, *Himmlers Kinder: Zur Geschichte der SS-Organisation "Lebensborn e.V." 1935–1945* (Wiesbaden: Marixverlag, 2011), 142–143.
9. Dorothee Schmitz-Köster, *"Deutsche Mutter, bist du bereit...", Der Lebesborn und Seine KInder (*Berlin: Aufbau Verlag GmbH & Co. , 2010) 59.
10. Bryant, *Himmler's Kinder,* 156-157
11. Marc Hillel and Clarissa Henry, *Of Pure Blood,* (New York: McGraw-Hill, 1976), 41–42.

CHAPTER 3

12. Agnes Moosmann, *Die Bagatelle: als Arbeitsmaid im Reichsarbeitsdienst* (Stuttgart: Jan Thorbecke Verlag, 2001), 29
13. Wolfram Mallebrein, *Der Reichsarbeitsdienst: Geschichte und Entwicklung,* (Coburg: Nation Europa Verlag), 154–155.
14. Moosmann, *Die Bagatelle,* 34, 47.
15. Ibid., 47–48.
16. Peter Longerich, *Heinrich Himmler* (Oxford: Oxford University Press, 2012), 412–13.
17. Ibid., 202–209, 249–251.

CHAPTER 4

18. Peter Longerich, *Heinrich Himmler* (Oxford: Oxford University Press, 2012), 122.
19. Ibid., 126.
20. Ibid., 126–27, 315–16, 352–382.

21. Ibid., 255–261, 286–88, 305, 312–14, 629–30.
22. Ibid., 286-88, 312-14, 352-382.
23. Ibid., 462.
24. Michelle Mouton, *From Nurturing the Nation to Purifying the Volk: Weimar and Nazi Family Policy, 1918–1945* (Cambridge: Cambridge University Press, 2007), 224.
25. "Heilig is uns jede Mutter guten Blutes," quoted in Thomas Bryant, *Himmlers Kinder: Zur Geschichte der SS-Organisation "Lebensborn e.V." 1935–1945* (Wiesbaden: Marixverlag, 2011), 122.
26. Rudolf Hess, "Der Sieg der Frauen," quoted in Bryant, *Himmlers Kinder*, 142–143.
27. Longerich, *Heinrich Himmler* (Oxford: Oxford University Press, 2012), 232.
28. Ibid., 462–464.
29. Bryant, *Himmlers Kinder,* 148–149.
30. Dorothee Schmitz-Köster, *"Deutsche Mutter, bist du bereit..." Der Lebensborn und seine Kinder* (Berlin: Aufbau Verlag GmbH & Co., 2010), 60.
31. Mouton, *From Nurturing the Nation to Purifying the Volk,* 86–90.

CHAPTER 5

32. Dorothee Schmitz-Köster, *"Deutsche Mutter, bist du bereit..." Der Lebensborn und seine Kinder* (Berlin: Aufbau Verlag GmbH & Co., 2010), 15–30.
33. Thomas Bryant, *Himmlers Kinder: Zur Geschichte der SS-Organisation "Lebensborn e.V." 1935–1945* (Wiesbaden: Marixverlag, 2011), 158–61.
34. Schmitz-Köster, *"Deutsche Mutter, bist du bereit...",* 46–47.
35. Bryant, *Himmlers Kinder*, 92–93.
36. Ibid., 80–84.
37. Ibid., 102, 137.
38. Peter Longerich, *Heinrich Himmler* (Oxford: Oxford University Press,
39. Ibid., 12–15, 39–41, 47–48, 54–55, 138.
40. Ibid., 42, 59.
41. Ibid., 21–26, 40, 717.
42. Ibid., 64–69, 79.
43. Ibid., 125.
44. Ibid., 89–116.
45. Ibid.
46. Ibid., 31–34.
47. Ibid., 59–66, 77-81.
48. Ibid., 275–76.

49. Ibid., 599–600.
50. Ibid., 279–81.
51. Ibid., 281–86.
52. Ibid., 285–86.
53. Ibid., 282–85, 519–20.
54. Ibid., 265–66, 218, 220, 251, 262–63.
55. Ibid., 293, 516, 519–20.
56. Ibid., 218–225, 274.
57. Ibid., 218–20, 266.
58. Ibid., 270.
59. Ibid., 288–94.
60. Ibid., 255–74, 599–600.
61. Ibid., 466.
62. Ibid., 731.

CHAPTER 6

63. Dorothee Schmitz-Köster, *"Deutsche Mutter, bist du bereit..." Der Lebensborn und seine Kinder* (Berlin: Aufbau Verlag GmbH & Co., 2010), 95–104.
    Thomas Bryant, *Himmlers Kinder: Zur Geschichte der SS-Organisation "Lebensborn e.V." 1935–1945* (Wiesbaden: Marixverlag, 2011), 247–52.
64. Bryant, *Himmlers Kinder,* 298.
65. Schmitz-Köster, *"Deutsche Mutter, bist du bereit...",* 23, 208.
66. Heinrich Himmler, undated letter to General Wilhelm Keitel, quoted in Bryant, *Himmlers Kinder,* 145.
67. Adolf Hitler, *Mein Kampf* (Münich, Eher Verlag): 446, quoted in Bryant, *Himmlers Kinder,* 130–131.
68. Lebensborn brochure, Sept. 30, 1937, quoted in Bryant, *Himmlers Kinder,* 137.
69. Schmitz-Köster, *"Deutsche Mutter, bist du bereit...",* 159–60.
70. Bryant, *Himmlers Kinder*, 78, 161.
71. Schmitz-Köster, *"Deutsche Mutter, bist du bereit...",* 152–58.
72. Bryant, *Himmlers Kinder*, 298.
73. Schmitz-Köster, *"Deutsche Mutter, bist du bereit...",* 158–60.
74. Ibid., 158–59.
75. Ibid., 150.
76. Bryant, *Himmlers Kinder*, 231–32.
77. Martin Staemmler, *Die Frauen und die Rassenpflege* (Münich, 1934), 128, quoted in Bryant, *Himmlers Kinder,* 54.
78. Bryant, *Himmlers Kinder,* 152–54.
79. Felix Kersten, *Totenkopf und Treue.* Heinrich Himmler ohne Uniform (Hamburg, 1955), 225, quoted in Bryant, *Himmlers Kinder,* 153–154.

80. Ibid.
81. Ibid., 155.
82. Martin Bormann's notes recording Hitler's thoughts on the subject, "Securing the Future of the German People," (1944), quoted in Bryant, *Himmlers Kinder,* 180.
83. Bryant, *Himmlers Kinder,* 156.
84. Schmitz-Köster, *"Deutsche Mutter, bist du bereit...",* 278–79.
85. Letter from Dr. Leonardo Ambrogio Giorgio Giovanni Conti to Heinrich Himmler (1942), quoted in Bryant, *Himmlers Kinder,* 171–72.
86. Schmitz-Köster, *"Deutsche Mutter, bist du bereit...",* 275 79. Bryant, *Himmlers Kinder,* 173–74.
87. Schmitz-Köster, *"Deutsche Mutter, bist du bereit...",* 151.
88. Michelle Mouton, *From Nurturing the Nation to Purifying the Volk: Weimar and Nazi Family Policy, 1918-1945* (Cambridge: Cambridge University Press, 2007), 226-35.
    Schmitz-Köster, *"Deutsche Mutter, bist du bereit...",* 61, 186–87.
89. Bryant, *Himmlers Kinder,* 158.
    Heinrich Himmler's *Zeugungsbefehl* of Oct. 28, 1939, quoted in Peter Longerich, *Heinrich Himmler* (Oxford Univ. Press, 2012), 462–463.
90. Schmitz-Köster, *"Deutsche Mutter, bist du bereit...",* 161–65.
91. Bryant, *Himmlers Kinder,* 210–18.
92. Schmitz-Köster, *"Deutsche Mutter, bist du bereit...",* 148, 208–12.
93. Bryant, *Himmlers Kinder,* 201-3.
    Schmitz-Köster, *"Deutsche Mutter, bist du bereit...",* 131.
94. Schmitz-Köster, *"Deutsche Mutter, bist du bereit...",* 192–194.

CHAPTER 7

95. Peter Demetz, *Prague in Danger* (New York: Farrar, Strauss and Giroux, 2008), 69–73.
96. Ibid., 165–70.
97. Peter Longerich, *Heinrich Himmler* (Oxford: Oxford University Press, 2012), 568–71.
98. Demetz, *Prague in Danger,* 170.
99. Ibid., 170.
100. Longerich, *Heinrich Himmler,* 569–70.
101. Ibid., 511, 534, 547, 564.
102. Ibid., 571–74.
103. Ibid., 573.
104. Ibid., 575–81.
105. Ibid., 620, 628.
106. Dorothee Schmitz-Köster, *"Deutsche Mutter, bist du bereit..." Der Lebensborn und seine Kinder* (Berlin: Aufbau Verlag GmbH & Co., 2010), 58–59.

107. Longerich, *Heinrich Himmler*, 620.
108. Ibid., 620–21.
109. Johanna Scholz, *Mutterpflichten*, quoted in Thomas Bryant, *Himmlers Kinder: Zur Geschichte der SS-Organisation "Lebens born e.V." 1935–1945* (Wiesbaden: Marixverlag, 2011), 118.
110. Bryant, *Himmlers Kinder*, 218.
111. Schmitz-Köster, *"Deutsche Mutter, bist du bereit..."*, 139–42.
112. Bryant, *Himmlers Kinder*, 254–55.
113. Ibid., 131-32.
114. Schmitz-Köster, *"Deutsche Mutter, bist du bereit..."*,191–92.
115. Ibid., 192–96.
116. Michelle Mouton, *From Nurturing the Nation to Purifying the Volk: Weimar and Nazi Family Policy, 1918–1945* (Cambridge: Cambridge University Press, 2007), 220, 224
    Bryant, *Himmlers Kinder*, 85–86.
117. Schmitz-Köster, *"Deutsche Mutter, bist du bereit..."*, 252–56.
118. Ibid., 125-26, 238–52.
119. Ibid., 246–47.
120. Ibid., 238–52.
121. Ibid., 226.
122. Bryant, *Himmlers Kinder*, 104, 314.
123. Schmitz-Köster, *"Deutsche Mutter, bist du bereit..."*, 165.
124. Josef Ackermann, *Heinrich Himmler als Ideologue*, quoted in Bryant, *Himmlers Kinder*, 102–3.
125. Schmitz-Köster, *"Deutsche Mutter, bist du bereit..."*, 165–171.
126. Longerich, *Heinrich Himmler*, 289.
127. Schmitz-Köster, *"Deutsche Mutter, bist du bereit..."*, 165–171
    Longerich, *Heinrich Himmler*, 289.
    Bryant, *Himmlers Kinder*, 99–111.

CHAPTER 8

128. Dorothee Schmitz-Köster, *"Deutsche Mutter, bist du bereit..." Der Lebensborn und seine Kinder* (Berlin: Aufbau Verlag GmbH & Co., 2010), 196–98, 203.
129. Ibid., 192–207.
130. Michelle Mouton, *From Nurturing the Nation to Purifying the Volk: Weimar and Nazi Family Policy, 1918–1945* (Cambridge: Cambridge University Press, 2007), 254–71.
131. Thomas Bryant, *Himmlers Kinder: Zur Geschichte der SS-Organisation "Lebensborn e.V." 1935–1945* (Wiesbaden: Marixver lag, 2011), 235.
132. Schmitz-Köster, *"Deutsche Mutter, bist du bereit..."*, 199.
133. Ibid., 253–54.
134. Ibid., 234.

135. Ibid., 239.
136. Ibid., 227–36.
137. Ibid., 234.
138. Ibid., 203.
139. Ibid., 231.
140. Peter Longerich, *Heinrich Himmler* (Oxford: Oxford University Press, 2012), 451.
141. Ibid., 592–95.
142. Marc Hillel and Clarissa Henry, *Of Pure Blood,* (New York: McGraw-Hill, 1976), 159–78.
Longerich, *Heinrich Himmler,* 595–99.
Schmitz-Köster, *"Deutsche Mutter, bist du bereit...",* 279–83.
143. Hillel and Henry, *Of Pure Blood,* 159–78.
Longerich, *Heinrich Himmler,* 595–99.
144. Schmitz-Köster, *"Deutsche Mutter, bist du bereit...",* 218–24.
145. Ibid., 90-95, 131–32.
146. Longerich, *Heinrich Himmler,* 700.
147. Agnes Moosmann, *Die Bagatelle: als Arbeitsmaid im Reichsarbeitsdienst* (Stuttgart: Jan Thorbecke Verlag, 2001), 59.

CHAPTER 9

148. Dorothee Schmitz-Köster, *"Deutsche Mutter, bist du bereit..." Der Lebensborn und seine Kinder* (Berlin: Aufbau Verlag GmbH & Co., 2010), 204.
149. Peter Longerich, *Heinrich Himmler* (Oxford: Oxford University Press, 2012), 654.
150. Ibid., 701.
151. Daniel Jonah Goldhagen, *Hitler's Willing Executioners: Ordinary Germans and the Holocaust* (New York: Alfred A. Knopf, 1996), 387–89.
152. Ibid., 387–92.
153. Ibid., 369–84.

CHAPTER 10

154. Peter Longerich, *Heinrich Himmler* (Oxford: Oxford University Press, 2012), 711–19.
155. Ibid.
156. Ibid., 719.
157. Ibid., 729.
158. Ibid., 733–36.
159. Ibid., 689.
160. Dorothee Schmitz-Köster, *"Deutsche Mutter, bist du bereit..." Der Lebensborn und seine Kinder* (Berlin: Aufbau Verlag GmbH & Co., 2010), 171–74.

161. Ibid., 297–306.
162. Marc Hillel and Clarissa Henry, *Of Pure Blood,* (New York: McGraw-Hill, 1976), 207–14.
163. Ibid.
164. Ibid.
165. Schmitz-Köster, *"Deutsche Mutter, bist du bereit...",* 285.
166. Ibid., 285–309.
167. Ibid.
168. Ibid.

CHAPTER 11

169. Michelle Mouton, *From Nurturing the Nation to Purifying the Volk: Weimar and Nazi Family Policy, 1918–1945* (Cambridge: Cambridge University Press, 2007), 48–68.
170. Ibid.
171. Norman M. Naimark, *The Russians in Germany: A History of the Soviet Zone of Occupation, 1945–1949* (Cambridge: The Belknap Press of Harvard University Press, 1995), 389–90.
172. Ibid., 454–57.
173. Ibid., 170–86, 266, 333.
174. Ibid., 419–29.

CHAPTER 12

175. Norman M. Naimark, *The Russians in Germany: A History of the Soviet Zone of Occupation, 1945–1949* (Cambridge: The Belknap Press of Harvard University Press, 1995), 238–50.
176. Ibid.
177. Peter Demetz, *Prague in Danger* (New York: Farrar, Strauss and Giroux, 2008), 182.
178. Ibid., 231–41.
179. Cornelia Rabitz, "Berlin Exhibition Reveals Role Police Played in Holocaust," *Deutsche Welle, DW-World.de,* April 10, 2011. http://www.dw-world.de/dw/article/0,,14973508,00.html.

CHAPTER 14

180. Heide Fehrenbach, *Race after Hitler: Black Occupation Children in Postwar Germany and America* (Princeton and Oxford: Princeton University Press, 2005), 17–45.
181. Ibid., 74–106.

CHAPTER 18

182. Dorothee Schmitz-Köster, *"Deutsche Mutter, bist du bereit..." Der Lebensborn und seine Kinder* (Berlin: Aufbau Verlag GmbH & Co., 2010), 314-50
183. Ibid.
184. Ibid.
185. Ibid.
186. Ibid.
187. Ibid.
188. Ibid.
189. Ibid.
190. Ibid.
191. Marc Hillel and Clarissa Henry, *Of Pure Blood,* (New York: McGraw-Hill, 1976), 215–35.
192. Schmitz-Köster, *"Deutsche Mutter, bist du bereit...",* 314–50.
193. Ibid.
194. Michelle Mouton, *From Nurturing the Nation to Purifying the Volk: Weimar and Nazi Family Policy, 1918–1945* (Cambridge: Cambridge University Press, 2007), 149–51.
195. Schmitz-Köster, *"Deutsche Mutter, bist du bereit...",* 314–50.
196. Ibid.
197. Ibid., 191.
198. Mouton, *From Nurturing the Nation to Purifying the Volk,* 148.
199. Schmitz-Köster, *"Deutsche Mutter, bist du bereit...",* 314–50.

Jennifer Garrity was born in Seattle, Washington and grew up in Portland, Oregon. She has lived in Belgium and currently resides in southern Germany with her husband, Kim. *Reich Child—A Lebensborn Life* is Jennifer Garrity's first work of nonfiction. She is the author of *The Bushwhacker* (Peachtree Publishers Ltd., 1999), *The Stone Grave* (Danish title: *Et Sted I Hjertet* – Hovedland, 2003), *Calendar Quest* (BrimWood Press, 2006), *Family Fiction* (BrimWood Press, 2006), and a four-novel series that includes *Secret of the Scribe, The Jeweled Astrolabe, Beneath the Cat's Claw*, and *Rebel on the Path* (BrimWood Press, 2008).